7-26-74

BROADCASTING: The Critical Challenges

BROADCASTING:

International Radio and Television Society
Third Annual Faculty/Industry Seminar

The
Critical Challenges

Edited with an introduction and notes

by CHARLES S. STEINBERG, Ph.D.

Professor of Communications, Hunter College,
City University of New York

COMMUNICATION ARTS BOOKS

Hastings House, Publishers   New York 10016

Library of Congress Cataloging in Publication Data

Main entry under title:
Broadcasting: the critical challenges.

(Communication arts books)
Proceedings of the International Radio and Television Society third annual faculty/industry seminar held Feb. 13-16, 1973 at the Tarrytown House Conference Center.

    1. Broadcasting—United States—Congresses.

I. Steinberg, Charles S., ed. II. International Radio and Television Society.

PN1990.6.U5B7   338.4'7'384540973   74-5101
ISBN 0-8038-0748-1
ISBN 0-8038-0757-0 (pbk.)

Published simultaneously in Canada by
Saunders of Toronto, Ltd., Don Mills, Ontario

Printed in the United States of America

Contents

1819384

* Commissioner Wiley has since been designated FCC Chairman.

Preface

THIS VOLUME is based on the proceedings of the Third Annual Faculty/ Industry Seminar of the International Radio and Television Society, Inc. held at the Tarrytown House Conference Center. The Seminar, devoted to the critical challenges which broadcasting faces in the seventies, embraced four days of special addresses, plenary sessions and discussion groups from February 13-16, 1973. A total of eight significant—even vital —challenges were considered by faculty, industry leaders, government representatives and communications experts. The various sessions were summarized by three "rapporteurs" at the final seminar.

These faculty/industry seminars involve, in a very real sense, virtually the entire broadcasting industry and are prepared under the auspices of the International Radio and Television Society (IRTS) and the IRTS Foundation. Bob Boulware serves as Executive Director of IRTS and IRTF, and the Seminar Co-Chairmen for the Conference were Gene Accas, Vice President Leo Burnett USA, and Aaron Cohen, Vice President NBC.

The concept of the IRTS Seminars is an evolving one. Each successive annual meeting is based, to a great extent, on the experiences and findings that accrued from the preceding session. The structure of the Seminars has been generally adapted from the problem-solving techniques of the American Assembly and the research methods of the National Conference Board. In addition, one of the research experiments of the Third Annual Faculty/ Industry Seminar was a project based on the so-called Delphi Technique, a forecasting method developed in large part by the Rand Corporation. The Delphi study is presented as a supplement to this book, including an outline of the technique, the questionnaire used in the opinion survey and a summary of the results. This material provides a wealth of data which should be stimulative of considerable further discussion.

The themes of the Seminar could not conceivably have been more timely. The seventies are a critical period in the constantly evolving development of the American broadcasting system. Indeed, the future of the system itself—its structure and function—will very much depend on the solution of, or the compromises to, many of the challenges that confront those involved in broadcasting—and that includes not only professional broadcasters, but communications teachers and scholars, government officials, and the viewing and listening public. In some of the eight challenges under consideration there were at least tentative conclusions reached—more implicit than explicit to be sure, but nevertheless helpful as direction-finders. In others, there were roadblocks and impasses, but notwithstanding, the problem was aired, and considered, and discussed. This, in itself, is healthy.

A word to the reader as to the architecture of the Seminar is in order. In each Challenge, a panel of industry speakers provided so-called "input," an effort to identify the problems by way of "verbal essays." Each of these sessions was followed by a question-and-answer period. Following the Plenary sessions, the participants divided into three discussion groups under a Discussion Leader and a Rapporteur who summarized all of the sessions at the conclusion of the Conference.

It is important to note that the Conference was transcribed from tapes. With the exception of some of the special addresses, therefore, the participants had no opportunity to prepare their remarks in advance. Although certain editing of the text was inevitable, because of the spontaneous nature of the commentary, the editor has made every effort to preserve the integrity of the speaker's remarks. In addition, each participant was given an opportunity to read the text of his remarks, before the volume went to the publisher, and to make corrections. It was not possible, unfortunately, to include all of the Discussion Group sessions of the Conference, primarily because of the limitations of space in one volume and also because, in some cases, the transcribed tapes simply did not lend themselves to inclusion. It is regrettable that all of the material could not be included.

Each Challenge is preceded by introductory notes, and there is a general introduction to the volume as a whole. Acknowledgment is made of the enormously helpful assistance of Susan Reiner and Carol Tsavaris in the preparation of the manuscript. A note of thanks is due to the participants for their cooperation in reading and correcting their respective contributions. Grateful acknowledgment is also made to the patience and helpful assistance of my wife, Hortense R. Steinberg.

The appendices to this volume include a brief biography of all of the participants in the IRTS Seminars. Omission of anyone was inadvertent and is regretted by the editor.

CHARLES S. STEINBERG

Critical Challenges of the Seventies

THE BROADCASTING INDUSTRY has always revealed a penchant for indulging in a curiously ambivalent posture of self-flagellation and self-glorification. It harbors a built-in anxiety, based on a multiplicity of problems —some real, but many highly imaginary. For example: Despite the fact that broadcasting in this country simply could not function in a viable way without regulation—at least in a technological sense—many broadcasters would rather yield to ill-conceived consumerism than elect to battle on the terrain of the Federal Communications Commission. Again, the industry railed against the imposition of the prime time access rule when it was invoked, and found that it can function just as profitably, if not more so, by living with the rule until the FCC rescinded it in part. At the moment, half the industry is fearful of the dire consequences of cable and subscription television, while the other half sees no problem with either for the next decade. And so it goes.

The simple fact is that broadcasting—and that includes, of course, the reinvigorated voice of radio as well as commercial television—is achieving the highest earnings in its stormy but meteoric history, despite prime time access, despite antitrust action and criticism from government, despite challenges from consumers. Yet, there is little sense of complacency or security. And the reasons are not only apparent, but have more than a semblance of realism.

Broadcasting is a major industry, but friends and foes alike also realize that its potential as an art form is both formidable and largely unrealized. But, even as a business, radio and television brocasting have a different kind of "hardware," a different inventory from other more tangible enterprises. Its assets are not really liquid. Its core is a vague, but significant, entity called ideas. And ideas which are translated into programs are not only hard to come by, particularly in a medium as demanding as broadcasting, but they are also subject to challenge. Indeed, most of the assumptions under which broadcasting operates are open to challenge from a number of sources which are often contradictory to one another— government, advertisers, critics, educators, consumers, pressure groups and other social, political and economic institutions. There is, then, always present a Pandora's box. And every so often some individual or agency opens it a little to loose a few troubles. That is why the broadcaster, however successful, however profitable, strikes a defensive posture. While the sun shines brightest today, tomorrow can always bring the storm clouds of a ban on cigarette advertising. And who knows what will come next? For beyond the entertainment function of broadcasting, there is the vital area of news, documentaries and public affairs—a terrain laden with obstacle courses from Washington D.C. right down to some fringe special-interest group which cries foul when its sensibilities are injured and which demands access for reply.

The palpable truth is that broadcasting, not always for reasons within its control, has always sat on a Pandora's box of potential troubles. There were always implicit storm warnings on the horizon—the imminence of an investigation or restrictive action by a congressional committee or by the FCC; a sudden awakening of social consciousness by the FTC; a challenge from a plethora of minority groups—self-righteously expressed, but not always in the right; a stiffened resistance to network polity by recalcitrant affiliates; or a sudden change in stance by advertisers. And the broadcasting industry has no genuine inventory of hardware—only creative ideas and services. Finally, there are the critics, in the print media as well as on the academic frontier, who question whether the lowest common denominator concept really constitutes cultural democracy, whether the obligation of the broadcaster is to purvey not what the public wants, but what it needs—assuming, of course, that either critics or academicians know what it needs.

Yet, even the most captious of critics continue to speak glowingly of broadcasting's potential. Even after twenty odd years of television service, the medium is still in a state of becoming, but where it will ultimately arrive no one really knows. Conjecture can be a highly provocative exercise. And what is broadcasting's potential? It is to reach the ultimate in reality programming, to use its facilities to bring to the people the phenomena of our times with an impact unequalled by any other medium of communication. To revive, and forge beyond, the dramatic flowering of radio's and television's "golden age" of Corwin and Oboler, of Chayefsky and Serling. To devise viable programs for deprived cultural minorities. To discover its own aesthetic vision and perception, its innate art form.

Down the road a disturbing question arises to nag the originator of this best of all possible worlds. There is a pragmatic consideration. Because of its very nature, is the medium amenable to achieving all of these potentials of greatness? Does the very all-pervasive, heterogeneous nature of the medium, this "extension of our nervous system" preclude the possibility of reaching the rare peak of perfection achieved by the novel, the theatre and, more rarely, the screen? And apart from aesthetic consideration, does not the very size and the unrelenting pressures exerted on broadcasting make it different in degree and kind from theatre, books, newspapers and film? Could a newspaper function responsibly under the regulations that apply to broadcasting?

So there is reason to speak of the critical challenges facing broadcasting. They are highly visible in the seventies, but they were present from the beginning, fifty years ago. As communications history reveals, broadcasting did not begin as a giant industry and, indeed, few pioneers anticipated that it would become the world's most formidable advertising medium. But it did grow rapidly—perhaps too rapidly—and the inventive genius that made it possible was very quickly absorbed by the industrial giants, with results that were both positive and negative. Today we have a media-industrial complex that the radio pioneers never quite anticipated. The evolving pattern of American broadcasting was set partly by the resolution of patent conflicts, partly by healthy competition, partly by government regulation and (to a much lesser degree) by public opinion and the public interest.

Historically, even the most prescient broadcast pioneers could not predict the future of the medium. David Sarnoff, an empire builder, did not suspect the advertising potential of radio. Lee de Forest, whose audion tube made the growth of broadcasting possible, was sorely disappointed that broadcasting developed as it did. The very first advertisers were cautious and circumspect, holding commercialism to a minimum and selling their own product—radio receivers. That caution was short-lived.

Nor was the government any more prescient then than it is now. From 1912 to 1952, when the FCC issued its "final" allocations in the Sixth Report and Order, the history of regulation is one of failure to foresee the technical enormity and range—and yet the severe limitations—of both radio and television. And so, for too many of the fifty years of its history, broadcasting grew in an atmosphere that was, at best, chaotic. The challenges were resolved, but in piecemeal fashion, so that some of them continued to obtrude as the medium developed. From the beginning, certain practical and philosophical problems had to be addressed. How could broadcasting operate under government regulations and yet function in a libertarian, free enterprise economy? Who would pay the freight—the government, by means of tax on receivers, or the advertiser? Who would determine program choice—the broadcaster, the government, the advertiser or the public? What provision would be made for realizing the educational potential of broadcasting? How would broadcasting be subsumed under the law of the press? How would allocation of precious spectrum space be determined? These, and more, were (and many still are) challenges to the medium that quickened in the communications revolution and the introduction of electrical technology. These were challenges that could not wait for answers, because public acceptance of radio and television was unprecedented from the beginning. And today, in the seventies, the United States boasts more television receivers than any other country. Indeed, it uses almost half the total number of receivers extant in the world.

The resolution to the technical challenge came as a result of the haphazard way in which frequencies were allocated—without apparent comprehension of the chaos that would result from interference of signals. There may have been some historical logic in the evolution of modern communication, beginning with print, continuing through the Industrial Revolution and ushering in the age of mass communications with the invention of radio. But there was little logic or foresight in the growth of the first two decades of broadcasting. As Herbert Hoover pointed out in 1924, the fledgling broadcasting industry knew it needed regulation, but at the same time wanted the total freedom of laissez-faire. And the Supreme Court decision in the *Zenith* case not only allowed chaotic proliferation of stations to continue, but successfully aborted any authority which the then Secretary of Commerce had over spectrum space allocation. In 1927, Congress passed a second Radio Act (the first was in 1912) which became the basis of the Communications Act of 1934 under which broadcasting now operates in this country. But even the establishment of the Federal Communications Commission did not resolve the technical problems, and it created new social and legal challenges. The Commission had to put a "freeze" on television channel allocations from 1948 to 1952 when its final allocation plan called for 2,053 assignments in 1,291 communities and 242 reservations exclusively for educational television.

There were other challenges along the way. Radio had to address itself to the quacks, the astrologers and the pitchmen who threatened the integrity of the growing medium with unethical advertising practices. Yet, even in 1959, the world was shocked by the exposure of payola and plugola in the quiz scandals. And today, the industry faces the threat of FTC sponsored counter-advertising proposals, along with demands for eliminating commercials on Saturday morning children's programs, as well as certain drug advertisements. And such formidable voices as Arnold Toynbee and John Kenneth Galbraith challenge the whole idea of mass consumer advertising as instigatory of spurious needs and values.

Monopoly and social control constitute other long-standing challenges. In 1941, the FCC structured its so-called Chain Broadcasting Regulations, the basic purpose being to foster competition and lessen the growing power of the two major networks, CBS and NBC. Yet, as broadcasting enters the seventies, it faces a government antitrust action similar, in a sense, to the action against the major motion picture companies in the 1940's. There are ironic aspects to this action, however. Television networks, which were once criticized for permitting the advertiser to call the tune, are now in a potential situation where all programming would be turned over to advertisers—although the broadcaster would still be held responsible for what was purveyed over the air.

Other challenges ensued from the symbiotic relationship between networks and affiliated stations. Under optimum conditions, networks service affiliates with entertainment and news content which the local stations simply could not program because of economic and creative limitations. Stations furnish an opportunity for network interconnection, as well as audiences for national advertisers. Under the so-called "option time" arrangement, however, the network literally had the option of using or eliminating time made available to it under the contract with its affiliates—depending upon whether it sold the time to advertisers. With the rescinding of the option time agreements, stations now can either accept or refuse clearance of network programs. On the face of it, this was a valid decision. But it did not resolve the challenge. For, today, stations tend to fail to clear excellent public affairs programs because they are not profitable. And the prime time access rule has not helped, even as revised. Under prime time access, the FCC ordered the networks to turn over one-half-hour nightly—in prime evening time—to the stations so that significant local community programming could be developed. The significant programming turned out to be syndicated re-runs of once popular network situation comedies.

Essentially, these problems stem from the nature of broadcasting and the need to regulate it—a procedure that does not apply to any other medium of mass communication. The very physical limitations of the air-waves imposed physical and geographical restrictions on broadcast services which do not apply to print and, therefore, made government regulation a harsh necessity. The air-waves, as a national resource, belong to the people. Spectrum space is scarce. It follows, then, that those who are assigned this precious commodity must use it "in the public interest, convenience and necessity." And this is the greatest challenge of all. For, despite the Blue Book, despite endless philosophical and semantic meandering, the concept of "public interest" is still ambiguous. Having defined broadcasting as "the dissemination of radio communications intended to be received by the public," little has been accomplished in formulating a theorectical or operative definition of "public interest." In the *Red Lion* case, however, when WGCB-AM-FM refused to grant time to Fred J. Cook to reply to an on-air attack by the Rev. Billy James Hargis, the Supreme Court, upholding the FCC decision that time for reply must be granted under the personal attack rider to the Fairness Doctrine, did point out that "it is the right of the viewers, and listeners, not the right of the broadcasters, which is paramount."

Yet, at this time, the Fairness Doctrine is undergoing an agonizing reappraisal by the Commission. And, perhaps by 1976, the Congress will take positive steps to rescind the Section 315 "equal time" rule which, by ordering time for every legally qualified candidate for office, has actually made time for a Nixon-Kennedy style "great debate" available to none.

The Challenges, then, are much in evidence although they vary in intensity. Some, as we have seen, are recurring ones which have never been resolved satisfactorily. Others are new problems, the result of changing and more sophisticated communications technology. Still others are socio-legal.

There is UHF. Little has happened to UHF since the FCC ordered the all-channel receiver in 1962. There is the very important problem of cross-channel affiliation, of one-newspaper towns with the same ownership operating the television station; of group ownership—which may still have distinct advantages. There is the sharp fear that, in the United States, barely 50% of the TV homes have the multiple choice of channels that are available in such areas as New York or Los Angeles. And there is cable. Since the first innocent use of cable to bring signals over the mountainous terrain of Pennsylvania, CATV threatens to become a full-fledged industry and, some think, a genuine challenge to over-the-air commercial broadcasting. But cable's hurdles are multiple—program origination, copyright problems to be resolved, advertising potential to be evaluated and common carrier status to be determined before the concept of a wired nation or broadband communications system can become an operating reality.

In international broadcasting, much work remains to be done before Marshall McLuhan's "global village" evolves. With the launching of the first relay station in space (the Telstar satellite) in 1962, international communications posed a whole new set of challenges, the most formidable of which was the principle of being able to broadcast freely across geographical boundaries without regard to considerations of politics and propaganda. The challenge is a long way from being resolved. At the same time, the television coverage of the Munich Olympics revealed the enormous power and range of the medium for live, immediate, simultaneous coverage of events—a facet too often disregarded in the heavy reliance on video-tape and film.

And, of course, there is public television. With the publication of the Carnegie Report in 1967, there was reason to hope—among many reasons for misgiving—that television would finally achieve the brilliant future predicted for it when, in 1952, the Joint Committee on Educational Television persuaded the FCC to allocate exclusive channels for ETV. But the Public Broadcasting Service, which the Carnegie Commission envisioned as being a brave new world of culture and information to the public, has suffered vigorous challenges from the Administration (Clay T. Whitehead, Office of Telecommunications Policy Director saw no need for PBS to broadcast news and public affairs) and from the Corporation for Public Broadcasting. Its most serious problem arose when it could not get funding—a result, undoubtedly, of the decision to leave annual funding to the caprice of the Congress and the possibility of Presidential opposition.

The list is long. Many of the challenges are, indeed, critical. But some are not beyond resolution, others will occur, while still others will re-occur—perhaps, in itself, a sign of healthy development. Perhaps the overwhelming challenges are apathy and cultural lag. Because business is good is no reason for an apathetic acceptance and perpetuation of the status quo. Furthermore, there *is* a clear challenge to bring our educational and cultural resources into some focus, some viable method of interaction with the tremendous technological growth of modern communications. This, to at least one observer, is the most vigorous and critical challenge of all—to determine that broadcasting, intended for *all* the people, is devoted to serving *all* the people, all of the time. With genuine dedication to the critical challenges, their optimum resolution is distinctly possible.

C.S.S.

Address by Walter Schwartz

President, ABC Television

Introduction: Gene Accas (Leo Burnett USA)
Question and Answer (*in order*): Stanley T. Donner (University of Texas); Philip S. Gelb (Bronx Community College)

ACCAS: There is a myth in our business that nice guys finish last. I can easily refute this myth by presenting our first speaker, Walter Schwartz, President of the ABC Television Group. He is one of the warmest, most pleasant, most agreeable and withal one of the best executives that our business has managed to produce in its short and stormy history. A survey of the problems which constitute broadcasting's critical challenge, Mr. Schwartz's talk highlights the area which our Seminar will explore.

SCHWARTZ: One of the problems facing television today is assessing the extent of the problems facing television. Do we live during the Apocalypse or the Renaissance? Are we facing the twinges of old age or are we feeling the growing pains that afflict the young and dynamic body? Without minimizing the dangers to our system of commercial television broadcasting, I warn you that I do not intend to deliver a Gettysburg Address for the losers. I believe that our industry and our art and our business will survive the transition we are currently experiencing and go on to provide even greater service and enjoy even greater prosperity. We will survive because we deserve to survive, because we are responsible professionals doing a good job and trying to do a better job of service to a vast and very diverse audience.

In looking at the television landscape today I am reminded of a classic situation that one finds in science-fiction films. The protagonists in science-fiction epics face problems of two distinct types. First, there are swirls of invisible energy that you cannot pin down. You know they're there making malevolent noises, but you don't clearly know which is doing what to whom. There is, however, a more comprehensible set of problems. They come when the invisible swirls become visible and crystallize into honest, genuine monsters. Now a well-meaning person can deal with a monster much easier than he can deal with a swirl of undefined energy. You can sit down and you can talk with a monster and you can reach some sensible compromise. The swirls are much more difficult to cope with until they agree to settle down and crystallize as any self-respecting swirl should do.

In television today we have those problems which have crystallized in the atmosphere and dropped on our heads like Alfred Hitchcock's birds. And we have those problems which are swirling around and gathering force and gathering direction. Both are real and both must be faced, and the issue indeed is survival. As people committed to the idea of change, hopefully for the better, the professional television community is open to creative criticism of our medium. We are always questioning our identity, evaluating failures and successes on the scale of daily experience. We are not rigid defenders of a single set of concepts. We are not electronic Puritans, and the very fact that we are not makes us particularly vulnerable to many kinds of attack, assaults that are often unjustified or misdirected. And I might add that the same elasticity that keeps us from turning as rigid as an old rubber band helps us to meet those assaults from the rear and prevail against them.

Many of the problems which arise in broadcasting stem directly from the nature of the television medium, specifically its effectiveness as a mass communicator. Television affects every area of American life and it increasingly affects the life of the entire world. In its mass media aspect television took hold quickly, probably as quickly as any technology in man's history. While still in its infancy, it took on the task of programming for the largest audience in history. Television was so busy growing that it did not find time to pause and assess the direction of its growth, or even the potential of growth. We took aim, pulled the throttle, and went full speed ahead. What we did not know was that we were heading into a time of huge social change, a time when just about every value of our society would come under question. This great change in America's thinking did not limit itself to the realm of intellectual ideas and practical actions. It also included cultural events and entertainment. The problems facing broadcasting are problems that have grown out of this change. If the history of America in the 1970's is the iceberg, the specific problems of our industry are chips off that iceberg. It's important that we keep a sense of perspective and realize that many of our problems stem not only from the nature of the medium itself, but also from the nature of the society that it serves, as well as its ultimate potential within a free society. Television is itself a common denominator in American life. It is interesting to millions and makes news. Because of this, it can be used to make news by specialized groups waving banners of self-interest. Attacking television not only sells magazines, it sells politicians and dissident causes. Therefore, criticism of television has got to be carefully evaluated and filtered through a common sense device that separates the sense from the nonsense.

A further phenomenon of television that must be noted is its ability to create huge impatience among honest and well-meaning critics. There is something about the nature of the TV beast that makes a lot of people feel that they could run it better than those who are in the audio/visual saddle. Now this group tends to opt for controls, always sincerely believing that when controls are imposed the controllers will reflect the viewpoint of the critic who called for controls in the first place. To me, the question of external controls is perhaps the greatest threat and the greatest danger we in television currently face.

Recently, for example, a group known as Action for Children's Television circulated the Melody Report which contained the suggestion of giving over control of the content of children's programs, by funding, to the Federal Government. One must remember that this report had the overall aim of suggesting ways in which to improve the quality and the content of these shows. The ACT group is made up of sincere and concerned citizens who have effected change in both the quality and content of children's programs. The Melody approach is, however, both unrealistic and impractical. Children's programming should not be denied advertising support. My feeling is that the realm of children's programming should be the most defended against government intrusion, especially in content. I believe that certain critics of the medium feel the sense of its unknown, untapped future glories that exist over a future horizon of time. They are so impatient to cross that horizon that they tend to forget that the horizon is reached one step at a time. These people turn to their legislators for miracles and take what is essentially the passive attitude of giving over the power of decision to others, instead of pursuing the more difficult but infinitely more rewarding path of working with those best suited to affect that change, the practitioners of television and the advertisers who support the experiments that result in better programming.

Finally, any programming changes must be sensitive to audience preference. It was Lee Loevinger, discussing counter-commercials, who pointed out that the most well-meaning could turn out to be the very agents who tumble a great and effective broadcasting system if they persist in shouting for more and more government intervention. Better programming is devoutly desired and is developed through constant experiment. But what makes for the better climate for experimentation? Is it control or is it creative freedom within a matrix of responsibility? This responsibility is not to one fragment of the audience alone, but to the entire conglomerate that makes up the mass audience. For the function of the mass media is to serve the mass audience; to find those common denominators of communication that remind us that we are citizens of one nation, of one planet.

With regard to the subject of counter-commercials it is interesting to note that what began as an application of the Fairness Doctrine to cigarette advertising has led to the possibility of a new Tower of Babel, a mass of claim and counter-claim that can only produce cynicism and laughter from the consumer and might produce the end of commercial broadcasting in this country. We believe the idea of counter-commercials to be self-defeating and unmanageable. The same energy that goes into supervising counter-commercials can be better applied to making better commercials that honestly present the virtues of a product. I think that the consumer movement, in its best aspects, is interested in this kind of positive approach as opposed to more and more rhetoric that will add up to a backlash of opposition from consumers themselves. Related to the question of counter-advertising this is the recently discussed problem of the advertising of drug products on television. And, as you may have read, Representative Claude Pepper's House Select Committee on Crime rejected a staff report containing a recommendation that drug advertising on television be banned between 8 a.m. and 9 p.m. *Broadcasting* Magazine noted: "The committee is still concerned with televised drug ads and has instructed the staff to include in the revised report a statement that TV drug ads might be a problem and that they deserve continued attention, and that self-regulation would be sought." Self-regulation is a far cry from a ban on such advertising and a far more sensible policy. We do feel that claims within commercials for drugs or anything else for that matter, should be factually and emotionally valid. Overstatement of effects is as bad as misstatement of ingredients, and we are constantly working through our Broadcast Standards and Practices Department to remove this practice from our airways. Representatives of advertising have called time and again for sensible guidelines from government. Not controls, but guidelines aimed at protecting the consumer and, in fact, the advertising profession itself from fraudulent practitioners. All business, including advertising and television, must have credibility in order to survive. We desire guidelines that will firm up that credibility, not counter-commercials that can only encourage total confusion.

If counter-commercials become a fact of life, rather than an ill-defined fantasy, we will lose the world's most productive broadcasting system and gain absolutely nothing in return.

Lately there has been much discussion concerning the prime time access rule. While other networks have opposed this rule which limited network prime time in an effort to encourage local station responsibility and independent producers to come up with programming of a competitive quality, ABC has taken a different stand. Our feeling is that the experiment is worth the trying and that the results are not yet conclusive. Ending the experiment would be premature. There is simply no way to tell if the idea makes sense unless it's given time to gel.

Recently Clay Whitehead made a series of speeches which involved two distinct themes. One has to do with extending of local station license periods from three to five years, a proposal that we firmly support. This is based, of course, on the individual licensee meeting certain standards of performance in the public interest. Today, a license has got to be justified through proof of public service as never before. Virtually every group—political, theological, racial and even sexual—not only has input into television, but has realized that the potential of such input has always existed by law. By asserting their demands they have required of the local station manager that he evaluate and react to those demands. The local TV and radio station is more a part of the community today than ever before. Longer renewal periods are desirable, not only from the economic viewpoint of the stations but because of the practicality of testing new forms of service. These experiments in communication take time for which there is no substitute. Today's local station manager is not an isolated, insulated reader of the Nielsen Reports. He is involved, out in the community, and he is sensitized to the community needs and his part in meeting those needs. I can give you countless examples from radio and television of superb community service in recent months along with forecasts of even greater service. There is only so much energy, and the less that is tied up in license proceedings, the more that is liberated for accomplishments.

Clay Whitehead's comments seemed to contain another side. His remarks on the "elitist gossip" by newsmen and his call to be wary of bias on the network news triggered alarms across the land. Along with other administration proclamations, the Whitehead talks gave off the perfume of censorship by telling the local station owner that he must be alert to the man from New York and Los Angeles, from Washington, D.C., who carries network news to his home town on threat of losing his franchise to broadcast. Mr. Whitehead said that "elitist gossip" is a term familiar to all housewives and needed no further definition from him. Perhaps he feels that way, but many people feel that his terms need plenty of definition and need it now. Some felt that the Whitehead talks were attempts to drive a wedge between the networks and their affiliates, an attempt to control the content of news. Mr. Whitehead said he was surprised at the interpretation and reaction to his remarks. He should not have been surprised. The subject of mass media news, what is selected, how it's delivered and ultimately how it affects people is a fascinating subject. Electronic journalism is a subject that is now under deep and profound exploration. More people get their news from radio and television than any other way. Glib phrases do not contribute insight into this vital area of communication. They serve only to raise the hackles of those of us who defend the right of freedom of information as a precious and hard-won constitutional guarantee. The carrot of license renewal, dangled in exchange for repressive censorship of news is unthinkable. To sacrifice two-hundred years of freedom of expression for two more years of renewal is indeed a bad bargain. If, as Mr. Whitehead said, he did not mean to imply that kind of a deal, then perhaps his words should be more carefully chosen in the future.

Another problem under consideration is that of the pattern of first-run programs and repeats. As you well know, the pattern has changed in recent years. There are somewhat fewer originals and somewhat more repeats. At ABC the change has been from 69% originals in 1962-63 season to 65% in the 71-72 season. The television industry has been blamed for allowing this to happen, presumably out of a frantic pursuit of the dollar. The truth is otherwise. The economics of television reflect the inflationary economics of the nation as a whole and programming in particular. Costs have risen so quickly and so steeply that the repeat pattern evolved as a viable, necessary economic compromise. No one in our industry wanted that to happen. Original programs were victims of a cost spiral that was largely out of our control. If legislators intend to set the number of originals and repeats, they should first apply themselves to the economic realities of program production. If the pattern is set by law, not by the market place, we will have cheaper programming and less of it, instead of better programming and greater variety of choice. It has been pointed out by CBS's Bob Wood that, aside from the economics involved, the fact of repeats allows huge audience segments to see the programs they might otherwise miss because of time conflicts with other shows or other activities. Even though this is true, the decision to program reruns is, essentially, an economic one. Economic realities cannot be told to go away by legislation, though economic realities can be changed by new policies applied to the society at large. Perhaps in a peace time economy we will find new answers. The answers, however, must not be arbitrary. Moreover, they must be based on sound economic policy.

In closing, I want to remind you that our nation was built on a system of checks and balances. Our television industry and our radio industry, too, were built on the same system. As a licensed media we're accountable to government. Hour after hour we are subject to an accounting by the clients who support our system of broadcasting as we support their system of marketing. Most importantly we are constantly subject to the attitudes and the opinions of our audience which is informed and vocal. They not only let us know what they like and dislike whenever they turn the dial, but they make phone calls and write letters. We listen to what the audience has to say both locally and nationally. Out of these checks and balances we have forged a broadcasting system that has taken us to the moon, to Moscow and

Peking, into Archie Bunker's living room and Marcus Welby's operating room. We've seen the Olympics, the Superbowl and the Dust Bowl. We learn through our newsmen of war, of negotiation, of a tenuous peace, of civil rights, of ecology, of our neighbors' minds and hearts and the return of our prisoners of war. Our signals go to every corner of the planet.

I submit that, of all the services available to our public, the television and radio professions provide a constantly high standard of performance. I feel that we have earned the right to solve our own problems through responsible, responsive action. We have opened ourselves to young ideas, preserved the best of our tradition and reacted to changing times in a positive fashion. We are only at the beginning of our understanding of television's potential, both domestically and globally as a mass communicator. New developments such as cable and cassette will produce uncommon radio and television service. It is our hope that cables and cassettes do not end up simply doing what we already do free. Program syphoning, competitive bidding by cable for events and programs already available could be detrimental to the entire broadcasting industry. If, on the other hand, cable and cassettes supplement our service and find directions of service of their own, everyone will benefit and prosper.

We will continue to use our advertising revenues to explore new terrain and finance programs that are not profitable but which are essential to the cultural health of the nation. We meet our problems one at a time and we regard them not as obstacles, but as stepping stones to a future that is bright and full of promise beyond our limited imagination.

QUESTION & ANSWER SESSION FOLLOWING SCHWARTZ ADDRESS

ACCAS: Our first question is: Why do young people have a selective attitude toward censorship and in their frame of reference see it as appropriate when applied to a part of the medium, but not necessarily to the whole? It is applied to commercials and program balance, but not to news.

SCHWARTZ: I think that part of the problem is that, for whatever reason, we represent the establishment and youngsters today are usually anti-establishment. I think somewhere along the line the news aspect has penetrated their thinking and they recognize that they've got to get a fair shake at the news and what is actually going on. I believe that, as I suggested in my remarks, because they are anti-establishment, they call upon the government to do their bidding. They feel that whatever it is the establishment does can be done better by the government than by the practitioners of the art. They forget that government—be it local, city, state or federal—changes and that politicians come into office and go out of office, and the only common denominator in government is the bureaucratic segment that holds civil service spots and stays on ad infinitum. However, if the public abdicates control of the airwaves to the government, they will never get it back.

DONNER: There is one question that has troubled me, not only tonight but for a long period of years. When you talk about the possibilities of broadcasters, and what broadcasters are doing to assess needs and to do better programming, I agree with you. But at the same time, you can't help but think of the broadcasters who are not doing this. It has always astonished me that in broadcasting there are, I think, an overwhelming percentage of people who are doing the right thing and working very hard at it. Broadcasters tend to protect even the weakest of their own company; this is not a good idea and I believe that this leads to criticism from outside the broadcasting industry.

ACCAS: Broadcasting, one must remember, is externally regulated; for a group which is among the regulatees to join the regulators in any way would, I think, spell the beginnings of an internecine friction and war that would find everyone consumed rather quickly. Also, we feel that the broadcasting industry is being threatened with unjust controls. United there may be a chance of survival. Divided there is none at all.

SCHWARTZ: Also, there is great attrition in our business. The weak have a tendency to fall by the wayside. Broadcasters, in most cases, don't take long term loans.

GELB: In general, I think your speech was very good but it only dealt with three forces: the industry, the government and an unstable public who might sound off and put pressure on you. I think there is a fourth force: people who can afford to take time and be philosophical about the problems of broadcasting. For example, most of us are members of departments of Liberal Arts, the Humanities. Our obligation then is to humanity. It's not to sponsors. It's not to the public. It's not to the industry. It's not to the government. Our obligation is to humanity. Humanity is victimized by *patterns*. You mentioned that a little censorship is a dangerous thing, and I think most of us in communication know that the most powerful censor is "established procedures." What has been is the most powerful censor of what can be. The existing pattern is both the determining factor and the major censor in communication. In other words, when something has been successful, it's going to be repeated. What kinds of possibilities and alternatives do you present against this most powerful censor: the previous pattern?

Accas: The question, I believe, has two parts: One, is there not another force which should be considered in describing either the challenges or in viewing the perspective of broadcasting—the humanities; and secondarily, whether or not we are captives of the deans of broadcasting and whether or not we still tend to produce TV characters in our own image.

Schwartz: I'm not sure that I agree with you that the past is our censor. Programming innovation takes place at least twice a year on television— during the fall season, the second season and many times in the summer. Let me give you an example of things on the horizon that have just cropped up in the last couple of years. Did you know that the 90-minute show, the long-form show, is really only five years old? *The Virginian* was the first 90-minute show; and yet, it seems that we've had 90-minute shows for a great deal longer. Now, there is a seven-part mini series coming up this summer on the Strauss family. These are all brand new things that have not been done before. The Olympics of last summer have never been done as they were done by us. Part of that was necessitated by the way that prime time fell in the States and what time it really was in Munich, Germany. But the fact is that the Olympic presentation was totally innovative. It had not been done in this manner before, so that there was no censorship, no back pattern that we followed. There are other examples of what I'm trying to say, but my point is that in both radio and in television new things are happening every day. We now have sex radio. Not that those of us in the profession are necessarily proud of sex radio, but it's here and a lot of people listen to it. There are many new programs evolving which are completely uncensored and free form, because there is no way to predict whether or not these shows will succeed. For example, there's our *Wide World of Entertainment,* with at least six different ingredients going into this late night program, as compared to the very successful Johnny Carson.

Gelb: Though you answered my question, it was simply in terms of the way the industry looks at the problem of new programming. You emphasized just a change in form or a change in superficial format as being an innovation. To me, an innovation would be a show that dealt with problems without violence or without an authoritarian figure, a change in basic assumptions and values.

Schwartz: Well, did you see *That Certain Summer,* which was the homosexual story?

Gelb: I don't question that there is a show or two like that. But as a pattern, as a series using non-stereotypes, this does not occur on television

SCHWARTZ: With regard to this question, it is important to note that at the present time, 70% of programming that is on the three networks is in anthology form with subject matter changes from week to week. I believe this grew out of the fact that the public as a whole has reached a higher educational status and their tastes have changed accordingly. So that you will run into a program that deals with homosexuality one week, lesbianism the next week and the drug issue another week. I believe that you're thinking of the stereotypes. Though some of them still exist on television, there is a great deal of comedy programming now that reflects the contemporary moralities. Forgetting the length of the program, whether it be 90-minutes or two hours, these programs cover different issues without the myth of the super-hero. Years ago, there was *The Man From UNCLE* and James Arness in *Gunsmoke*. Today, there is an ABC and CBS anthology on Tuesday and anthologies on NBC two nights of the week. We hope to use this format in order to prevent the creation of super-heroes. In this context you're dealing with a different audience each week and that's the way you develop variety.

Challenge I

Public Television: Where Is It and Where Is It Headed?

P UBLIC BROADCASTING is the culmination of many years of struggle on the part of educators to obtain exclusive channels in radio and television for use by cultural and educational institutions. That educational radio did not succeed was almost totally the fault of the educational community. And, while educators did succeed in securing channels for educational television (ETV), they did not—on the whole—use them successfully, owing to a number of factors—inertia in some areas, lack of matching funds for Ford Foundation grants in others, and simple concern by many teachers that educational television was either a threat to jobs, a nuisance, or generally demeaning to the high ideals of the American philosophy of education.

Educational radio (i.e., non-commercial radio) began with a promising bang and ended with a quiet whimper. More than two-hundred stations were allocated to educational institutions, and more than 80% did not survive. The precious station assignments wound up in the domain of commercial radio. As a result, until the formation of the Joint Committee on Educational Television in the forties, broadcasting operated exclusively under commercial auspices. Indeed, the agency established to protect the public interest, the FCC, saw no urgent need for non-commercial radio, for it felt that adequate educational programming was provided by the commercial interests. To be sure, the FCC did eventually set aside FM stations for educational use, but until the 1952 allocation plan went into effect, educational broadcasting—despite high-minded disquisitions on the educational potential of the medium—remained in limbo until the formation of National Educational Television.

As 1950 approached, a forceful movement developed to secure a place for educational television in the broadcasting environment. A pioneer station, WOI-TV at Iowa State University, functioned on a commercial basis but programmed educational content. And in 1950, the ETV movement received powerful and dynamic impetus with the establishment of the Joint Committee on Educational Television (JCET), an organization which received uncompromising support from FCC Commissioner Frieda Hennock, as well as from several members of the Congress. The JCET argued a forceful case before the Commission, including fairly substantial proof of the paucity of genuine commitment to educational television on the part of the commercial networks and stations. The result, this time, was positive. The FCC's final table of allocations, in 1952 (the Sixth Report and Order), set aside 242 channels exclusively for educational broadcasting. Unfortunately, the majority were UHF but there were, at least, eighty VHF educational stations where none had existed prior to 1952.

ETV grew slowly, but it grew with a promise of ultimate fulfillment. Channel 13, after much scrounging for funds and an outlay of about $6 million, secured a foothold in New York City and became the flagship station for what was ultimately to develop into a tentative educational network. However slowly and although few hours were utilized, ETV was in business, thanks largely to the largesse of the Ford Foundation without whose support it is certain that ETV would not survive. In 1962, however, by means of the Educational Television Facilities Act, the government provided matching funds and enabled a fairly substantial number of stations to become activated.

In 1967, a momentous event took place. The Carnegie Commission on Educational Television issued a Report titled Public Television: A Program For Action. Headed by James R. Killian (as Chairman) and a blue ribbon Commission, the Report seemed to provide precisely the impetus needed to forge ahead finally with a successful educational television service. Reacting favorably to the Commission's call for a Corporation for Public Broadcasting, the Congress passed a Public Broadcasting Act. This set up the recommended Corporation and also the Public Broadcasting Service—a kind of logical extension of National Educational Television.

Two immediate problems remained. One was funding. The other was interconnection. Probably the greatest mistake the Commission made was the decision to recommend federal funding and yet to hope that public television (as now distinguished from classroom or educational television) could function free of government control or interference. Events revealed that it could not. Several Congressmen were highly vocal in their criticism of programs that were broadcast over the Public Broadcasting Service. President Nixon refused to concur with the request for $155 million for annual funding, cutting the figure to a non-viable $45 million. And, finally, Clay T. Whitehead, Director of OTP (Office of Telecommunications Policy) saw no need for news and public affairs on public television, because the networks provided sufficient and better services of this kind! In view of the long-standing Administration criticism of network news, this was an irony of ironies.

Thus, the "broadly conceived study of non-commercial television" resulted, during most of 1973, in a furious vendetta between the parent corporation and PBS over program control. It was clear to many who had high hopes for public television that innovative, courageous program experiment was not welcome—not only by the Administration but also, astoundingly enough, by some of the stations. Out of the struggle for control—and from the parallel struggle for funds—some form of public television will survive. But it is highly conjectural whether public broadcasting will reach the laudable level of national cultural service envisioned by the framers of the Carnegie Report.

It is now reasonably clear that an alternative form of funding—perhaps an excise tax on receivers—would have gone far to give public broadcasting needed independence. Again, while the emphasis on local program origination was healthy, sufficient strength was not given to the imperative need for strong, national interconnection. And, finally, while there was considerable thought given to technology, the Commission (perhaps deliberately) did not call upon those in the various arts who might have offered a paradigm of the kind of creative programming that might be accomplished in a dynamic public broadcasting service. Programs—in public *or* commercial television—are *still* the basic resource.

CHALLENGE I

Introduction: Max E. Buck (NBC Television Network)

Producer: Dan McGrath (D'Arcy-MacManus & Masius)

Moderator: J. M. Ripley (University of Kentucky)

Panel: James Day (formerly President, WNET/13); Keith Fischer (Corporation For Public Broadcasting); Alvin Perlmutter (Television Producer)

Question and Answer (in order): Stanley Donner (University of Texas); Charles E. Phillips (Emerson College); Philip S. Gelb (Bronx Community College); K. Sue Cailteux (University of Kentucky); Daniel Viamonte (University of Hartford); James A. Brown (University of Southern California); W. Knox Hagood (University of Alabama)

BUCK: It's not just the size of this year's seminar that delights me, it's also the make-up of this year's group of participants. For the next few days, here in Tarrytown, we will be discussing "The Critical Challenges of Broadcasting." Our experience with previous Faculty/Industry Seminars have taught us that the challenges of the broadcasting industry and the challenges of the academic world are not unlike. Both groups are eager to respond to the social values and demands that are changing rapidly around us; and both groups are determined to preserve their freedom despite pressures to suppress from both government and private sources; and both groups are committed to upgrading their product to meet society's insistence upon excellence. The importance of this Seminar was attested to by the distinguished gentlemen who have accepted our invitation to play a part. Men like FCC Commissioner Richard Wiley, Clay Whitehead, Director of Telecommunications Policy for the White House, and Walter Schwartz, President of the ABC Television Network do not give of their time and talent lightly, nor do the kind of people who represent this panel. Together with these people, you, representing the universities across the country, can open even wider the unique challenge for a meaningful dialogue which this IRTS Seminar provides.

RIPLEY: This is the first Challenge: "Public television: Where is it? Where is it headed?" We are indebted for our panel to our Producer, Dan McGrath. Each member of our panel—James Day, Keith Fischer and Al Perlmutter—will offer presentations relative to their views or information concerning the general objectives of public television, the tasks that are needed to meet these objectives, funding and the powers of funders and, finally, modes of evaluating public television.

DAY: "Where is Public Television headed?" I wish I knew. This is my twentieth year in public television and never have I been more pessimistic about its direction. It is either the end of the beginning of public television or the beginning of the end. I believe that we're probably very close to the end of a course that was begun in 1967 with the Public Broadcasting Act, which grew out of the recommendations of the Carnegie Commission and which, in turn, grew out of the necessity for finding a way of funding public television. The study began when the funding was very largely from the Ford Foundation. At that time it was felt that philanthropy would not support public television forever. This was not the role of philanthropy. Moreover, the system was requiring increasingly larger sums of money that simply couldn't be derived from philanthropic sources. The Carnegie Commission came up with the only answer that it could, which was Federal tax money for the support and growth of public television.

The question, of course, that was raised then and is raised now, perhaps in more dramatic fashion, is: Is it possible for the public television system to be funded with Federal funds without political control? In theory, the answer is yes. We need only look at most of the countries of the Western world to discover that their public systems are funded from government funds. Perhaps it's useful, at least in the context of America, to make some distinction between government funds and the people's funds, because we so frequently understand the term tax funds in this country to mean it's the government's money. In Great Britain, for example, the public television system is supported by a tax or a license upon the television receiving set; this revenue is more often regarded there as support by the people rather than support by the government. At any rate, it was evident rather early on in the history of the Corporation for Public Broadcasting that there were going to be difficulties with the support of public television with Federal funds. These difficulties have their root, I think, in the following interpretation of the Public Broadcasting Act: The Corporation for Public Broadcasting is responsible for the way in which congressionally allocated funds are spent on programs. When this interpretation embraces either the selection of the programs to be broadcast or their approval prior to broadcast, then it seems to me that it oversteps the bounds that would make for a publicly or governmentally supported public television system without political control.

For the twenty years that I have been in public broadcasting, I have been responsible to a station board of directors. This board was responsible for my actions and responsible for what I permitted to broadcast on that station; and yet, in no case, did the board ever approve the programs beforehand. That responsibility was, and is, exercised through control after the fact. This, I have always felt, is the kind of "responsibility" implicit in the Public Broadcasting Act and should not extend beyond this kind of responsibility. However, I believe that today it does, and this is the interpretation that the Corporation has now and has always placed on the Public Broadcasting Act. Secondly, there was the hope when the Public Broadcasting Act was passed that with it would come some kind of financing that would be insulated from political control. You recall the Carnegie Commission Report recommended a tax so that monies could flow from the public into public broadcasting without the annual appropriations or authorization process of Congress. That never came to pass and it is unlikely it ever will come to pass. Understandably, there is an unwillingness on the part of Congress to permit the flow of tax funds into any activity without exercising some kind of control over those funds.

Thirdly, I think that there is evidence today that perhaps a public broadcast system is not even desired. I believe that there is a general philosophy that public funds ought not to be used to compete with private enterprise—in this case, the commercial broadcast enterprise. Or that if it does compete, it ought to be held to a level where, in fact, it can do no damage to the profits of commercial television. Well, if there is some lack of enthusiasm for a strong public broadcasting system, if there are problems about how it can be financed through Federal funds, then why have a public broadcasting system at all? On this, of course, I have very strong feelings and since I am no longer employed in public broadcasting, I cannot be accused of having selfish feelings about it. They're feelings which I suspect would be shared by many, if not all, of you. These are feelings that grow out of the conviction that public broadcasting is absolutely essential to the political and social health of this country.

Commercial television satisfies only a portion of that need. Commercial television is, of course, a business and thus must operate under business principles. This precludes from its purview certain services that public television must render. The nature of commercial television requires that it place popularity at the top of its priorities. The sponsor or the advertiser, rather, wants and deserves the largest possible audience that he can attract. Because this is so, the programs on commercial television must strive for popularity first. Because the people in commercial television are generally of high mind, they hope that in seeking popularity they will also achieve excellence. This, of course, doesn't often happen. On the other hand, I believe that public broadcasting must place excellence at the top of its list of priorities—always in the hope it will sometimes achieve popularity. When I speak of excellence I do not necessarily mean high culture, but excellence in anything public broadcasting undertakes—whether it's sports, rock, jazz, opera or drama. It seems to me that in its efforts to achieve excellence, it carves a path which commercial television can frequently follow. The existence of as much drama as there is on commercial television today is probably the result of the success of drama on non-commercial television. Commercial television people in general, I believe, seek to provide the highest level of programming. The existence of public television helps them in that effort. Public television can, through its non-fiction as well as its fiction programs, provide what I think we most desperately need in this country—an insight into societal as well as individual behavior. I don't believe commercial television can fully satisfy this need; therefore, I believe that a public television system is necessary.

The question thus remains: If public television cannot be supported by Federal tax dollars without bringing with it the kinds of problems that we have experienced, then how can it be supported? I think that the answer to that may lie in efforts that are now under way to increase by a considerable magnitude the support which some public television stations enjoy from their audiences. We haven't fully tested the proposition that the audience will voluntarily support public television, but we are in the process of testing that now. As a matter of fact, a major test is going on in five markets, employing the best professional techniques that we can recruit—in direct mail, in advertising, in the use of telephone phone-outs—to find whether the magnitude of voluntary support can be increased to the point where some, if not all, public television stations might be free of the need for Federal funds. If my assumption is correct that it may be difficult, if not impossible, to take Federal funds without the kinds of controls that are now being imposed, then perhaps we can reach a time when we ought to go back to Congress and seek Federal support. Hopefully, at that point, we will be sufficiently independent of Federal support so that we could take it on our terms, rather than upon the terms which now exist.

RIPLEY: Mr. Day has joined one particular issue here, that of funding. Our next speaker, Keith Fischer, is currently engaged in the funding question, primarily from the Federal standpoint from the Corporation for Public Broadcasting.

FISCHER: Before speaking to the question before you today, I want to spend some of my time talking about the premise that underlies it, because to my view there is a lack of understanding or total inaccuracy of the premise.

There are some who have misunderstood the law and therefore believe that CPB is a Government Agency. There are others who understand the law but who choose to believe that we at the Corporation are agents of an Administration. I'm not sure from the premise which of these is operating, so I want to deal with both the misconception, if you will, on the one hand and the falsehood on the other. Let us first assume that the premise fails to understand the law, Public Broadcasting Act of 1967, which grew out of the Carnegie Commission Report. I'd like to quote certain salient features of that Act:

> 1) There is authorized to be established a non-profit corporation to be known as the Corporation for Public Broadcasting which will not be an Agency or an establishment of the United States Government.
> 2) The members of the Board shall not by reason of such membership be deemed to be employees of the United States.

3) No political tests for qualification shall be used in selecting, appointing, promoting or taking other personnel action with respect to officers, agents and employees of the Corporation.

Now that's pretty clear language, but it isn't to say that this misconception doesn't exist in other quarters. As a matter of fact, we recently received what turned out to be a form letter from the Office of Management and Budget, telling us what the President's budget plans were for 1974, and in effect saying to us, not too politely, that we ought to be appreciative of the budget the President recommended. This premise, that the Corporation, if not by law, at least by action, is an agent of this Administration, simply isn't true.

The policy making level at the Corporation is its Board of Directors. There are fifteen people on that Board, appointed by the President with the advice and consent of the Senate. A Board member's term is six years. By law, not more than eight of the fifteen members of that Board may be of the same political party. Today, seven of those Board members are appointees of the Johnson Administration. I know that people such as Mr. Curtis, Dr. Killian, Dr. Gloria Anderson and other members of the Board, don't question their independence for one moment. They defend it and they relish it. To my knowledge, during the five years of the Corporation's existence, the Board has never voted once on party lines. I'm told that the closest vote ever taken on any one issue was eleven to four; recent actions within the last year, really follow exactly the same pattern. The real irony, I think, of the premise stated today relates to the actions of the Corporation for Public Broadcasting and not the law. Let us look at these actions.

I would like to ask, if anyone sitting here today can think of a series on public television which propagandized for this Administration? I watched a lot of public television on Mr. Day's channel before I went to Washington. I've watched a lot more since, and I cannot think of a program series funded by CPB, which demonstrates any sort of conspiracy. Now if your thoughts, for example, turn to Mr. Buckley's *Firing Line,* I'm afraid that I've got to tell you that the Corporation has not yet refunded Mr. Buckley and *Firing Line* for next year. Now one thing that we can agree on, the Federal Government does fund public broadcasting. How much of it? Well, for better or for worse, not that much. In fact, all of the funds that CPB is responsible for represents about 20% of the funds in the system. I submit that it would be darned difficult for a 20% partner to control anything, even if that partner wanted to. Yet, you can certainly legitimately ask what these limited Federal and other funds we administer are used for. If for the moment we assume the $35 million continuing resolution level, those funds plus other grants, underwriting income, have to pay for such things as: CPB administrative expense, professional training programs, research. We also have to establish a fund for public radio, to establish community service grants for local station use. That's absolutely no-strings-attached money. We have to pay for the technical inter-connection facility, which costs over $9 million today. Finally, we come to the support of national programming, which I think is one of the specific questions that we've been asked to speak about this morning.

Now, of the $35 million total budget level, there's allocated some $13 million for such programming as: *Sesame Street, Electric Company, Mister Rogers*. When we're done with those activities, we have an available fund, some $2.5 million, for National Public Affairs programming. Now if all of that money went into Public Affairs, and I don't know that it will, we're sitting here today discussing an issue, Public Affairs Programs funded with Federal dollars, which represents between one and two per cent of total system income. Again I ask, is that control? The principle, though, is a terribly important one because, along with Jim Day, we've very much hoped for an increased funding for this system. The issue specifically is: Should we fund public affairs programming? Even within our limited funds, I submit, of course, that we should. You may have read that the Corporation has already announced funding for *Black Journal* and *The Advocates* for next year. Neither of these programs or any others under consideration for next year, could be described in any way, as pro-Administration. The Corporation does, however, have certain responsibilities. One point clearly mentioned in the Public Broadcasting Act is that the Corporation makes certain that all programs maintain strict adherence to balance and objectivity. Now, that's a standard that was imposed by the Congress to ensure that this Corporation or the Public Broadcasting, can never realize broadcasters' worst fears—namely, become a propaganda agency. It's a responsibility we take very seriously.

Public television by its very mandate is educational. This is going to influence our thinking in terms of the kinds of specific programs we do fund. What we're talking about is in-depth analysis of what may well be controversial subjects. In no way is CPB opposed to controversy. We welcome it, but we're hopefully talking about programs whose usefulness is not related to one day's events. We would prefer to leave that to Messrs. Cronkite, Chancellor, et al. We think we are talking about programs that have the potential for instructional usage. Importantly, programs with a long life-span. I suggest that today's impoverished system within public broadcasting, about which all of us would agree here on the panel, cannot afford the luxury of one-time usage. While we think it is very much appropriate for CPB to fund the modest levels of public affairs programming we've talked about today, we also recognize, with Jim Day, that the growth of non-Federal funding in all areas of programming, has to be encouraged. While I continue to maintain that CPB funding is appropriate, I clearly join in welcoming the continuation and even the increase of non-Federal funds from the Ford Foundation, corporate under-writers and others.

RIPLEY: As you can see now, the question of funding obviously carries over to specific tasks. We now turn to an individual who has been con-cerned with the traffic of the media, in terms of the task force, Mr. Alvin Perlmutter.

PERLMUTTER: Public television has offered public television producers many, many satisfactions. In public television there are opportunities to do kinds of programming, techniques, innovations, styles that were just not available in commercial programming. Public television also has created a number of frustrations and raised many questions. I'd like to get into a few of those questions here.

I have noted that, after a number of visits to public television stations around the country, there was a seeming lack of strong communication between the station and the community it served. This seemed rather strange to me and I began to wonder where the public was involved in public television. At this time there is a controversy and, indeed, a crisis in public television. We hear about the crisis almost daily in the press as we have today, from Federal Administrators and from broadcasting executives. The third part of this triangle, the part that is most affected— the viewers—are the only ones who are silent. I think this is not only strange, but sad and quite dangerous. Our question in terms of public television production is not only how to produce better shows, but also how to get the viewing audience more involved in the system that they know very little about—to pull the public into public TV. Now we know the public exists. We have had several marvelous experiences in which the public has shown a great, strong desire to be involved in public TV. We have several examples that have come through the last few years, but we must devise new ways of involving them. Several years ago when the drug crisis was on the rise, we started a program called *Speak Out on Drugs* in which we connected by telephone a studio in Boston which con-tained parents, teachers, educators and specialists in the drug area, with viewers all around the country. The results were phenomenal—many thousands of telephone calls, many thousands of letters and most im-portantly, perhaps, the statistics showed that drug agency referrals were in sharp increase for weeks afterwards. I think what we're aiming for here is the fact that public television can offer an opportunity to open channels of communication that did not exist before and are not generally available on commercial networks. Another example occurred about five years ago when Black Americans rightly complained that there was nothing on TV representing their interests. One result of that was NET's *Black Journal* which, as we've just heard, was recently refunded by the Corporation for Public Broadcasting. There are other examples but they are small in comparison to what could be done.

Now along with the satisfactions and awards and rewards that those of us who produce for public TV have received, there is a strong sensation and feeling of frustration and failure based on our inability to find a regular, sustained method of involving the viewer in the television programming process. There's an old saying in show business, that everybody wants to get into the act; yet, who has a better right than the public in public TV? I would like to pose just a couple of basic questions that we might consider today: 1) Who is this public we talk about in public TV? What does it really want from this unique service? 2) How can we establish the lines of communication to learn of the needs and the desires of the viewers?

Now, I would like to conclude with a possible approach to these questions. I think that we should consider, as one possibility, the combining of the power of communication that is unique to television with one of the oldest and truest forms of communication in our country—the town meeting. Public television has the prime time available to it; moreover, the resources required for this kind of programming are not great by any television standards. The objective, as I see it, would be a regular, perhaps even weekly, broadcasting schedule of specially produced television town meetings on local, regional and national scales to discuss issues facing our communities, thereby providing insight into what areas of interest might be served in other station programming.

CHALLENGE 1: QUESTION AND ANSWER SESSION

DONNER: Mr. Fischer, based upon your information, what happened to the programming that was done by the Public Broadcasting Service? Is that taken over by the Public Broadcasting Corporation? If so, why?

FISCHER: The Board of Directors of CPB passed a resolution at its January meeting in which they asked the president of the Corporation to prepare a plan to take over certain functions from PBS. Those functions do include the program acquisition decision-making functions. Since that time, no direct action has been taken. There were certain reservations expressed by some of the licensees about our intentions in taking over these functions from PBS. There was a meeting headed by Ralph Rogers of KERA, which addressed specifically that point. He and his group want to make certain that the licensees have input and participation in the programming decision process, if in fact we do take it over from PBS. We have not taken it over from PBS, and the plan has not been submitted. The Rogers group is meeting in Palm Beach, Florida with representatives of PBS and representatives of the licensees, and we expect out of that will come a unified point of view from their end in terms of how they want us to operate.

DAY: It may be useful to know that, historically speaking, the national programming was, as I'm sure most of you recall, done for a number of years by National Educational Television. NET was supported entirely by the Ford Foundation and was directed by a governing board which was an independent, self-perpetuating group of distinguished people. Over the years, the stations, the licensees, grew increasingly resentful of the fact that NET was independently funded and independently controlled, and not responsive to what they regarded as their needs. Most of all, they were unhappy about what some regarded as left-wing documentaries and naughty language in plays. They vowed that if they ever had the opportunity they would operate the network in their own interest.

They had that opportunity with the Public Broadcasting Act. The Corporation for Public Broadcasting set up what in effect is a station-managed network. The PBS Board, the majority of that Board, are elected station managers. They decide what shall go on the network system from which they will make their selections. The step which was proposed, that CPB assume that function, means we're moving the program decision process from a group of elected station managers to a group of Presidentally-appointed gentlemen on the CPB Board. Mr. Fischer is quite right. Ralph Rogers, as the head of a station group now representing the Board Chairman rather than the management, has stepped in and forcefully brought the CPB to its present position of at least discussing with the station group some kind of joint decision-making process with respect to the programs you will see on the National Distribution System this coming year.

PHILLIPS: There's feeling in Boston that the Corporation is being somewhat subjective in its support of programs on the local educational station. This, I believe, is because the Corporation has supported only two of eleven programs presented last year. But, Mr. Fischer, you indicated that the funding procedure is more objective than we had supposed. Would you expand on that please?

FISCHER: I wish I could say that we are totally objective. We're trying to develop a system that, if not objective, will at least maximize the input from all interested parties. There has been enormous misunderstanding and, I think, probably bad PR on the part of CPB, relating to some pronouncements made late last Fall. At that time we thought we would be operating in fiscal '74 with a $70 million appropriation. On the basis of that, we asked the stations what they wanted for next year in public affairs and in other areas. At that time, then, we made an announcement really only in terms of the first round of program decisions. What we've done now is to recognize the reality of Washington, recognize that we're probably going to be operating at a $35 million appropriation for next year. As a result, we have now gone back and really started the program decision process all over again.

It is true that only two public affairs programs were funded as of last week. One of them, I'm happy to tell you, is out of WGBH in Boston. It was strongly felt that, because of the discussions now going on with the licensees, it would be the worst time in the world for the Corporation to take unilateral action in the most controversial area, which is public affairs, and announce decisions without the input of the Rogers group. So these groups, when they've decided what they want, will come back, meet with us and we will then make the rest of the program decisions.

GELB: In even more specific terms or specific examples, could you tell us why you believe "the strings of Government funds" are or can be strangling.

DAY: There are two ways in which, I think, it has been done. One is by indirection. As a manager of a production center, I am conscious of the fact that funds will be coming from Congressional appropriation. Thus, it becomes prudent for me *not* to broadcast certain kinds of programs. This is a form of self-censorship which I think has been operating for the last two or three years although none of us would admit it. Secondly, as Mr. Fischer has pointed out, there is no effort on the part of CPB or this Administration to propagandize; yet one need only take a look at the programs that they are not broadcasting, the programs that they have turned down. *Black Journal* has been astute enough to build a constituency around this country. They can press a button and that constituency goes to work. The programs which will not be seen next year, I think, represent the kinds of pressures under which we will operate. Even the idea that public affairs ought to be limited to those programs that can be dealt with in-depth and which in a sense are timeless is a peculiar kind of position for men in television to take. The one characteristic that distinguishes television from all other media, is its ability to operate in real time with pictures. To deny television that opportunity is to deny television its greatest power.

PERLMUTTER: Government funding becomes strangling to the producer only when it gets down to him. If the producer ideally operates as, for many years we did at NET, completely independent of the funding operation, there is no problem. The innuendo, the implication starts coming forward when a program such as *The Banks and The Poor* is aired. Then, you begin to hear rumblings from the head office, to the effect: Well, Washington wasn't pleased with it. We named a number of Congressmen, for example, who were on Committees that influence banking legislation but who were also on the boards of directors of various banks. The head office didn't say anything specific but certainly gave the impression that this was not something to be desired. When this feeling starts coming down, there tends to be less freedom in thinking about what the next program will be. After all, public television is not that independent in terms of its funding.

FISCHER: I think that the question raised on the floor is a terribly important one and a very appropriate one to this morning's discussions. Mr. Day may know what programs have been cancelled or will not be funded for next year. I think that if this discussion were held a month from now, maybe we could debate the issue of what it is the Corporation likes and what it is that the Corporation doesn't like. But nothing in terms of our actions to date, can demonstrate that mode of thinking. The second point I'd like to make relates to the only responsibility that we set for ourselves in terms of judging public affairs programming, and that is: balance and objectivity under the Act. Now you can say, well, that's a pretty broad thing and maybe that's why Mr. Perlmutter has been concerned in the past when he sees that looming and hanging over him. I would point out to you that, it's my understanding at least, the responsibility of balance and objectivity has really only been exercised three times in the five-year history of the Corporation for Public Broadcasting.

CAILTEUX: Mr. Fischer, what problems do you see in determining what programming you're going to fund as it relates to objectivity and balance; and is there a difference between objectivity and balance? For example, *Black Journal* might be said to be objective, but not balanced in some aspects.

FISCHER: The responsibility is a big one, and I've just said that we and PBS have at times had to grapple with this issue and have had to come up to the crunch where somebody has said: Hey, this program, or more likely this series of programs, viewed over a long perspective, is just not balanced in perspective—balanced and objective—and we've got to do something about it. Nevertheless, we can't take that responsibility lightly just because we haven't exercised it very often. That happens to be another point of discussion with the Rogers' licensee group. They, in effect, have raised the same question. They have said: Who is going to make this judgment? To your second point, on the semantics of balance and objectivity, I guess I would define balance, again over a period of time and not within any one program, as that which attempts (at least) to represent more than one side of the coin. I think that *The Advocates* attempts very hard and very effectively to be a balanced program. On one show, Senator Muskie spoke against Casper Weinberger on the issue of impoundment, leaving the audience free to come to its own decision. I think that objectivity in a sense is a harder thing to define and that all we can rely on are the talents and the discretion of the producers. I believe that objectivity as much as anything lies in the mind of the producer.

VIAMONTE: Tony Brown, from *Black Journal,* addressed the SCA convention as the main speaker and he seemed to indicate that there really was a lack of definition regarding the role of CPB in programming. Today, *Black Journal* was used as a shining example of public service or public affairs; yet, the first thing that Tony Brown asked was: "Who said we were public affairs? We're not public; we're very specific." Is there some way that we can deal with common definitions of (a) public television—which I gather as I talk to colleagues that broadcasters in CPB have difficulty defining for themselves, and (b) whether or not, specifically, Brown's charge, that it is not public is valid?

PERLMUTTER: I can give you my own view on this matter. I think that public television has the mandate to address the public in this form to as many minorities as possible. I think that public television does not, by its very definition, appeal to the mass audience that commercial television does. Therefore, I see massive minority viewers as its audience. I think, perhaps, that I can speak to this because I was the one who began *Black Journal* which was then in a totally different form from the way Tony Brown now runs it. It was called public affairs at that point because it came under the Public Affairs Department and it dealt with timely, real issues rather than dramatic, fictionalized situations; thus I think we are certainly dealing in semantics there. I believe, however, that there is also a fake separation of public and cultural affairs. I think that they should always be together, because too many times there are overlaps. But we must look upon the public television audience as serving many minorities, many of which overlap; but certainly when I refer to public, that's what I meant.

BROWN: Do you feel that the CPB is in an ambivalent or awkward position with regard to balance and objectivity? I find it curious that, on the one hand, the Executive Branch of Government says: Centralization was the problem with PBS, now with CPB we would like to get away from the centralization. It seems to me that they are centralizing more. Who in the public sector does the Government, the Executive Branch or the people on CPB, independent of that Branch, think is going to make comment and stimulate people to think? If the commercial people are doing public affairs badly and are suspect, and the public broadcasting should not do it, then who is left? I'm interested in your reflection on this problem.

FISCHER: At this juncture, the Corporation is not, in any sense, opposed to controversy. Really, all I can do is to reiterate that comment. I think that if you go back again, as recent as the year we are now in, and look at the programming which the Corporation has funded, it would include: *Washington Week, Bill Moyer's Journal, Black Journal, The Advocates.* Certainly, much of that programming is thought provoking, stimulating and controversial. The Act made it very clear that they didn't want the Corporation to stay out of controversial areas. What they did say was that, in controversial areas, CPB had a responsibility to balance and for objectivity. Concerning your point about "centralization," I think that is an irony in the current discussions. We are not interested in centralization, yet in terms of having to take strong actions against PBS, I think the appearance was given that we were going to take those responsibilities unto ourselves. I've tried to point out today that we really want the input and participation of everybody in the terms of decision making. In that sense, it is not centralized.

HAGOOD: What percentage of national programming is nationally produced as opposed to local?

DAY: In general about one-third of the station output is nationally produced. Needless to say, in the prime-time hours, a much higher percentage is nationally produced.

RIPLEY: I can tell you that Kentucky's network is running eight hours per week during prime time. Thank you ladies and gentlemen for this discussion.

Challenge II

Is A Television Aesthetic Possible?

A TELEVISION aesthetic is possible. It is not—at least in the immediate future—probable, given the criteria under which television programs are selected. But it deserves, indeed demands, discussion if the medium is ever to realize what so many critics have called its cultural potential, its fruition as an art form.

One glaring fact is clear. Until now, at least, television has been derivative. If the motion picture was based on theatre, television derives in symbiotic fashion from books, movies, radio and theatre. It is not, at this point in its development, an indigenous art form. True, there has been much esoteric discussion of "expanded television," of what can be accomplished on the dimensions of the TV screen, but little discussion of how creative energies can fulfill the creative demands of that screen, or what those creative demands are. The reasons for a lack of aesthetic perception and sensibility in the television medium are to be found in the way the medium itself functions. Television entrepreneurs do not publish select novels, or produce art films, or invest in theatre productions that will attract sizeable minority audiences. Television, despite its occasional special programs, is not considered a minority medium. Even with the new cult of demographics, the greatest number of viewers is still the criterion of success. As a consequence, the means to that end are not aesthetic, but pragmatic. A program is not put into a schedule because it is culturally or intellectually stimulating, but because it "works." And by "works," the program, sales and research departments mean that it will attract large and loyal audiences in its time period and garner an "over thirty" share of audience in the Nielsen Television Index. In a medium like broadcasting, all this is understandable. But it does not foster an expansion of television's aesthetic horizons and it does not stimulate the wellsprings of creative endeavor. An artist does not work well with one eye on the Nielsens and the other on the Arbitrons.

True, as the industry points out with pride, television has produced many memorable programs. But most of these, like *Death of a Salesman* are not original and very few are aesthetically significant. At the same time, even under conditions of genuine creativity, a set of aesthetic norms or values are not easy to structure for a medium that cuts across a bewildering cross-section of society—viewers of every age, race, creed, color, economic, political, cultural and social status. Television is, indeed, expected to be all things to all men, and while great art is universal, it was not deliberately created toward the end of popularity.

At this juncture, there have been few—if any—studies of broadcasting in terms of its aesthetic aspects. Certainly, broadcasting has not generated critical inquiry comparable in substance to that of James Agee on film or Robert Brustein on theatre. As for poetry, literature and painting, these art forms have a history of aesthetic analysis that began in Greek civilization. In the *Poetics,* Aristotle spoke of the importance of the kind of audience that would respond to rhetoric, of art as an imitation of nature. And through centuries of Western civilization, criticism of poetry, plays and novels was an important part of literary history. In the twentieth century, it is doubtful that even so sensitive a philosophy of art as George Santayana's *The Sense of Beauty* could be expanded to apply to radio or television programs. But John Dewey's *Art as Experience* is another matter. Professor Dewey's concept of aesthetics as *experience,* as involving an interaction between organism and environment embraces viewing as an act of engagement between medium and subject and as a juxtaposition of art and life.

And currently there is Marshall McLuhan whose *Understanding Media* probably comes closest to developing an aesthetic of the broadcast media. Unfortunately, McLuhan's "probes" are not only misguided, but his concept of medium as message is one of the most mischievous ideas ever perpetrated on an unsuspecting public. For McLuhan's theory, prosecuted to its conclusion, constitutes no genuine aesthetic at all. If the medium is, indeed, the message what does it matter whether networks program Shakespeare or situation comedy? Having emerged from tribalism after the invention of printing, man now returns to that halcyon environment by means of the magic of electric technology. But McLuhan's separation of form from content is spurious (as Aristotle showed originally). And his view of broadcasting as neither moral nor immoral precludes any serious value-judgment of television as a medium of mass communication.

The movement toward an aesthetic of broadcasting has taken an encouraging direction in the so-called "expanded consciousness" experimentation—the "underground video" movement—by some of the younger writers and directors, many of them working in both TV and film on college campuses. While some of these theories are tentative and some are incoherent, there is—as Neil Hickey indicates—a healthy ferment and a genuine interest in the possibilities of the medium that go beyond traditional and conventional formats.

But there are other practical considerations that make an aesthetic of television difficult. Bosley Crowther points out that broadcasting operates primarily toward the goal of commercial success, not aesthetic achievement. And John O'Connor comes close to the central problem when he indicates that the aesthetic function of the television critic is secondary to his obligation to write color stories, features and personality interviews. And so, in short, a combination of the limitations of the medium itself, the interest of the public and the coverage of broadcasting in the print media all tends to make a genuine aesthetic difficult—but not, one hopes, ultimately impossible.

CHALLENGE II

Producer: Charles S. Steinberg (Hunter College; formerly Vice-President, CBS-TV)

Moderator: Robert H. Stanley (Hunter College, CUNY)

Panel: Neil Hickey (*TV Guide*), Bosley Crowther (formerly motion picture critic, *The New York Times*); John O'Connor (*The New York Times*)

Question and Answer (*in order*): K. Sue Cailteux (University of Kentucky); Charles W. Shipley (Southern Illinois University)

STANLEY: I want to welcome you all to this discussion. Our topic is the potential of television as an art form. Is a television aesthetic possible? Our distinguished panel includes Mr. John O'Connor, television critic of *the New York Times,* who, in his columns, has done a great deal to generate discussion and concern about television's potentials as an art form. Next to Mr. O'Connor is Mr. Neil Hickey, Bureau Chief of *TV Guide,* which in addition to program schedules, also contains many insightful articles on the character and structure of American television. Mr. Hickey has contributed many articles to *TV Guide.* On my right is Mr. Bosley

Crowther, who, for many years, was the film critic of *the New York Times,* and is presently consultant to Columbia Pictures. Mr. Crowther has written several books concerning the communications media. We will begin with Mr. Hickey.

HICKEY: The premise of this session is to discuss whether television aesthetics are possible. We ought to posit immediately the truism that television is not movies, even though they are both visual events. There is no lack of scholarly scrutiny of the work of Hitchcock, Truffaut, Bergman, Fellini, Bertolucci, John Ford, Howard Hawkes and any number of others, and even Andy Warhol. The fact is there is far more film criticism being retailed in this country than is required by the circumstances. Film critics are eternally reviewing each other's reviews in a scramble to establish dominance. One man's ten-best list may coincide exactly with another man's ten-worst list, and I think the posturing, attitudinizing, eye-scratching and back-biting that goes on among the John Simons, the Rex Reeds, the Vincent Canbys and the Andrew Sarrises is frequently more entertaining than the films they are considering. They are, in short, film buffs.

Well, have you ever heard the term television buff? I don't think I have. I don't think it is a term in common usage. Now, the reason for that must grow out of the discrete nature of the two forms. Movies are fiction; they are either drama, comedy or they are music, or they are some mix of these three, but they are almost always fiction. Television is fiction too, but only sometimes. It's also at least half a dozen other things that we could think of—it's journalism, live sports, vaudeville, games, talk and certainly advertising. Any aesthetic in television would have to consider all of those. Of course, there are hundreds of books that do consider all of those; those that speculate about the effect of television on children, about the conspiracy of Eastern Egg Heads that does or does not distort the news we receive, about the banality and cynicism of television network managers, about the ephemera of the television programs themselves. These books do not add up to an aesthetic and they never will. They are popular sociology or "pop sock" as I like to think of them. There is no Edmund Wilson to sort out the development of television fiction, no Bernard Berenson to put television's archive in order. No Alfred Kazin or Brooks Atkinson or Mark Van Doren. I happen to know that Edmund Wilson liked puppet shows. I would see him occasionally at the Bill Baird Puppet Theatre on Barrow Street in Greenwich Village. And he wrote thoughtful essays on puppet shows, essays which truly constitute an aesthetic of the puppeteer's art. As far as I know, he never wrote anything about television, which gives puppet shows an edge in the artistic hierarchy, and pulls poor television even further down into the middle-brow mire.

There is a line in the prospectus for this particular panel which states that "many thoughtful critics believe that the central problem stems from the aloofness and disdain of the intellectual community" towards television as a subject for extended exegesis. Well, I think that's really nonsense. There is nothing the intellectual community won't stoop to if there is a chance for its members to improve their positions in that rocky and precarious cliffside to which they cling, and from which they view from the tentative safety of their own narrow ledges the relative positions of their peers. After all, the intellectual community has not been monolithic in its disdain and aloofness towards the allegorical content, if any, of *Jonathan Livingston Seagull* or the poetry of Yoko Ono or the finger paintings of orangutans. Someday I expect to find reviewed in *The New York Review* a book of long essays, steamy with the sweat of its author, titled *Edgar Guest, A Re-appraisal*.

But, in brief, what I would like to say is that great armies of academicians are lying in the wings out there in America, waiting to ambush any stray or outlaw intellectual concept that hasn't already been riddled with bullets by the sheriff. To put it another way, the object of the exercise is to induce the heavy breathing and the deep intellectual nods of one's peers. But television, as we discovered, has never really been a vehicle for that kind of ambition. Its needs have gone largely unconsidered by scholars, although demonstrably, they watch about the same amount as anybody else. They treat it as if it were a kind of compliant prostitute, somebody they don't really respect, but who somehow fills a need. Nobody seems sufficiently concerned about the poor girl's well-being or her soul to help her move to the suburbs and become a virgin.

You are not aware of it, but there exists in this general subject area a theorem which is called: THE FIRST RULE OF AESTHETICS. You're not aware of it, because I just made it up. And I certainly hope it makes a big splash in the academic world. The rule is that critical efforts can only be proportionate to creative effort. For example, in the few dozen lines of the poem *Fern Hill* by Dylan Thomas, there is a greater expenditure of creative energy than in six episodes of *All In the Family*. I know, because I have made that measurement. In three pages of *Finnegans Wake* there is evident a greater creative urge than in four seasons of the *Doris Day Show*. *Finnegans Wake* is like one of these pineapple bombs that we were so fond of dropping on Viet Nam. When it explodes, it sends thousands of tiny little bomblets out into the surrounding atmosphere. Of course, I'd have to admit that the *Doris Day Show* is also a bomb. What this proves is that while *Fern Hill* and *Finnegans Wake* are susceptible to an almost infinite amount of mastication, massaging and dissection by critics, both perceptive and merely ambitious, Archie Bunker and Doris Day are not. Those two TV entertainments were created on a five-day shooting schedule by teams of engineers, writers and "hangers on." *Fern Hill* and *Finnegans Wake* are the work of painstaking and uncompromising artists working in a terrible solitude.

Thus the first rule of aesthetics precludes the birth and growth of any corpus of scholarly scrutiny with regard to television, or I should say, television as it is constituted at this moment, in this country. And what is it, here and now? Well, it's a commercial enterprise involving visual home entertainment and information of various sorts. It is a closely held tripoly of giant competitive corporations whose goal is to pyramid their profits by selling advertising. You'll notice that there is no mention of the word "art" in that tentative definition. Of course, movies are, or can be, an art form. The irony is that television will still be here when movies are a thing of the distant past. I really believe that. The time is not far off when extra-large screen, cable-fed color television in the home will obviate any need to drive to the movie house and sit there immobilized in a miasma of buttered popcorn. Television is destined to drive the movies out of business, and I spend a great deal of time worrying about what's going to happen to Rex Reed. Well, there are many other aspects to the subject, but I just want to say that if television has not had, nor deserved, an aesthetic in the past, I think it will most surely have one in the years to come.

I think we are at this moment teetering on the brink of an enormous change in our television service in this country. The phasing out of TV networking is being predicted, and many more TV channels will come into the home. The public will have a far wider choice available and greater access to television channels. Of course, all such predictions about the greening of television could be wrong. I recall reading Prof. Charles Reich's book *The Greening of America* and being suffused with hope and tingling anticipation that the younger generation was indeed going to usher in a new era of cultural sanity, initiative and love. Well, somewhere along the way, as the song "Miss American Pie" puts it, the music died. There wasn't any green revolution and there isn't going to be. In fact, if one is to believe the results of certain recent national elections, a lot of those blue-jeaned, bearded and slightly stoned love children out there were really latent, crypto-middle Americans.

But I really do believe that the greening of television is going to happen. All over the country, young people are working with inexpensive video equipment making their own programs, getting them shown on cable television and in video theaters. Serious articles about their work are appearing in publications such as *Art in America, The Village Voice, Harpers,* and *TV Guide.* Last year, the Whitney Museum presented a two-week exhibit of new video works by some talented artists. Theoretical and practical work on television is going on in places that some of you are familiar with: the National Center for Experiments in Television in San Francisco, the Television Laboratory in New York, connected with WNET, and station WGBH in Boston. Serious examination of those efforts by perceptive critics is now beginning to find its way into print.

I'd like you to consider this. The movie industry in this country is roughly sixty years old. James Agee wrote his first film criticism for *The New York Times* in the year 1941, roughly twenty-five years after the industry's birth. Television in America is now twenty-five years old, and I think, right on schedule, we are starting to see it taken seriously by some pretty good minds, minds that can help it realize itself and lead it to a destiny which I believe is exorbitantly more promising than anything that the film industry ever dreamed of.

STANLEY: Thank you very much. We hear next from Mr. Bosley Crowther.

CROWTHER: Ladies and gentlemen, I think I had better apologize for being here in the first place because, as I explained very carefully to Charles Steinberg when he asked me if I would be on this panel, I do not do a great deal of television viewing. I have looked at a great many motion pictures and certainly have looked at a lot of television, but I am not a consistant television viewer as are the other two distinguished gentlemen on this panel. However, Charles told me that perhaps that qualified me better than anything else for being a member of this panel. Ignorance usually is a most distinct qualification for expertise. I am familiar with the theatrical motion picture in all of its many manifestations, I could discuss with you some of my experiences and knowledge of the aesthetics in that area and perhaps bring some application to this meeting.

The essential question here that we will probably have to clarify and try to define is what do we mean by an art form for television. Indeed, why do we have to have a so-called art form for television? The matter of defining an art form is something that has gone on in motion pictures ever since the beginning of the motion pictures. It began before Jim Agee wrote anything about motion pictures, even before Jim Agee began seeing motion pictures. Some of the very finest discussion and clarification of what the motion picture does psychologically and emotionally, in stimulating people, is conveying to them something more than just the excitement of watching movement on a small screen. Much of that was written before, in fact a great deal of it was written even before sound films. Perhaps one of the very best, concise pieces on the motion picture as an art form was written and delivered by Erwin Panofsky in a very fine essay called, "Style and Medium in Motion Pictures" which was delivered in 1954 at the time the Museum of Modern Art film department was about to be formed. He was actually trying to do something in the way of convincing art lovers that it would also be justifiable to have a motion picture archive department in the Museum of Modern Art. It was delivered at Princeton University, which has the reputation for being a little more liberal than some other academic areas in the country. I say it because I am a Princetonian.

But we cannot assume that motion pictures, the theatrical motion picture, have ever really lived up to what we assumed are the total and complete possibilities of an art form. Indeed I think that practically everybody in movies during the time I was a critic, was fighting constantly to find out what was art. Many film producers, film makers, directors and writers, of course, were perfectly satisfied that if you gave their picture a very good review and said it was art, you were right. But if you gave them a poor review, then art was not a question at all. I think that on this subject of what is art in these popular media of communication, we are concerned about using that particular term. People who are creative in that field, are anxious to have you use the term primarily because they want something that will satisfy their pride, or their vanity, or elevate their status to a little higher level than they feel they have or possess. Therefore, to be called artistic, or to be told that you are creating something artful is very important to them. I dare say this is the case with many of your people who are producing television shows of one sort or another. But, of course, in television, as well as in motion pictures, the important matter is what is commercially successful, and what is going to gratify not only the eggheads, the intellectuals and so forth, who are constantly viewing your medium, but what is going to draw a lot of people. This is the case certainly in motion pictures.

There is a famous story, and a delightful one, of the time one of the executives at Metro-Goldwyn-Mayer went over to talk with George Bernard Shaw to find out if he would let them make films of some of his plays. The executive went to great lengths to explain how magnificently a film would be done, what fine actors they would use, what superb directors they would employ and so forth, and when he was all through, Shaw said to him, "I'm afraid there is a distinct difference of aim and purpose here. You happen to be interested in art and I'm interested in money." And I think that frequently that is the case with some of the people who considered themselves to be the great artists. Insofar as television is concerned, I think in my observations of this medium, we have to do here what we long ago did with respect to theatrical motion pictures. And that is to categorize areas in which you recognize that some artistry can be applied above and beyond expert craftsmanship. I think that occurs quite frequently in television production, in various areas.

What areas of television can we really use or expect to profit by a kind of artistry? I would say that in television you are not going to get a great deal of artistry in the area of just straight news reporting. You may get some very clever craft skills in editing the live footage or film footage, and you may get some interesting combination of voice and image that you can consider as first class craftsmanship. But you are not going to get art. Nor are you likely to get it in children's programs, quick little cartoon performances, though some cartoons we know have some artistic qualifications (certainly in the theatrical motion picture area). I don't think you are going to get it in the sports area, which, of course, takes up so much of your television time. Certainly that isn't artistry; that is pure straight journalistic reportage. I don't think you are going to get it to any large extent even in some of the better documentary films. And by documentaries I mean programs that go as far as Cousteau's very fine underwater scenes, oceanography and so forth. Now the *Snow Goose,* which I happened to see the other night, I thought was quite an artistic job of documentary coverage. I will have to qualify that, because I don't think that reaches the level of artistic quality of which I am speaking.

Therefore, I think you have to limit the areas in which you can expect a development of a kind of artistry. I think you have to limit that to the kind of communication by television that really is the kind of communication that we get from theatrical motion pictures. That is to say, the development of an illusion, fantasy, a kind of communication of feeling, of thought and spirit, that takes you out of yourself and generates within you, the viewer, a sense of an experience, that is quite above and beyond an ordinary commonplace experience. In other words, it makes you feel and sense very strongly and with inspiration, what you have not realized before. Of course, this depends a great deal on your recognition and your empathy, so that you can feel that somehow this is exactly what life is and yet it has carried you beyond life, or beyond the life you have experienced.

This is very elaborate and somewhat philosophical, but we have to be philosophical when discussing an art form. I think that an art form and accomplishing something artistic in other media—in painting, in literature, in the novel—artistry in portrait, artistry in music, these things that the television medium is capable of doing (other than simply being a medium of transmission of some other art form), are very different and limited. I hate to say that I am thinking of shows such as the Tom Jones series, which I did watch with great interest on television the past few weeks. The Jones series is not really artistry and yet it did use the medium very effectively to convey a story and create an area of recognition or an area of expansion of new experience. It took us out of our own environment and for a while absorbed us in other areas.

As we all know, the real effectiveness of the narrative communication or the dramatic communication in television (which includes anything from delightful comedy—and believe me it is quite possible to be artistic with comedy), is the real accomplishment of the artist. There is the ability first to prevail upon the viewer to suspend his disbelief. That old phrase is used many times, but the suspension of disbelief is a most essential thing. Here we are sitting in a room looking at a picture on a box about people on a screen that's in a box, and about people we may never have known, about a world we may never have experienced. And yet, naturally, we would be inclined to disbelieve what we are seeing right away. But the artist, the creative person there, is making us suspend our disbelief, so that we are actually involved in it. Then of course, he has to do all sorts of things with craft that will inspire us and excite us to feel a great deal more identification with it and a great deal more excitement and inspiration from it.

That is where you've got to begin looking for and asking this question: Is an aesthetic possible? I think that an aesthetic is possible in this area if we will recognize two or three very basic things about the television medium which distinguish it from the theatrical motion picture. The first is mainly the physical aspects of the size of the box and its location. Most people are right in their homes and are not removing themselves from their familiar environment. This box is almost a piece of furniture in the room. There is a great difference there, and that is one that aestheticians are going to have to understand very thoroughly. There are aestheticians in the field, and to say there has been no writing about the aesthetics of television is incorrect. Gilbert Seldes wrote a great deal about the aesthetic of television and how it reaches the audience. Certainly, we have to acknowlege Marshall McLuhan's writing about television has definitely been in the area of aesthetics, even though he is involved with the psychological impact. But even psychological impact is part of aesthetics. The very fact that we are looking at it in a familiar environment is important. The opportunity to get this thing to generate the kind of mood that you get if you are reading a story in front of a fireplace in an old house where it's dark and the excitement that the area itself generates, becomes very important.

A second important factor in the consideration of an aesthetic potential here is how the actual cutting, editing, construction of the image and so forth on the screen are accomplished? Now in that area, I think you are following the theatrical motion picture aesthetic, because cutting is a very important factor in motion picture creation, and the shift and the mood from one shot to another is tremendously important. But to me the most important factor that you have to realize in the aesthetic is the continuity, the flow, the consistency of the stimulation. And as long as you have even your best dramatic shows interrupted by the commercials, I think you have got something that is completely opposed to and obstructive to the development of genuine aesthetic. You cannot expect the creation of the things that artistry does achieve, and you can't expect that flow to be consistent, as long as you interrupt for commercials. *Much Ado About Nothing* was effective mainly because it did not have the interruption of commercials, except at the regular specified ends of acts. The pauses at the end of the acts made it consistent, to a certain extent, with the form of a live stage play aesthetic. At least it was logical, it was reasonable to have that break.

I realize that commercials have to be somewhere in your medium and slipping them in and out in a hurry, is a very definite challenge to your aestheticians. The best way possible is avoiding commercials altogether, or even placing them at the beginning or at the end of the program. Then the consistent flow of communication continues. I think that we are all likely, when talking about artistry, to make one slight mistake. If we see something that is an enthusiastic support for one of our own prejudices or biases (such as some of the coverage of the political events), we develop a kind of appreciation of them, and we are very likely to call those things artistic. Yet we would not call something done with as much craftsmanship which does not appeal to one of our biases, artistic. There again, that is just a matter of finding your terms and trying to define them. As a last observation, I don't think that you are going to get artistry in everything that happens in your medium. Don't expect artistry to occur in so much of your medium that is strictly reportage by means of the picture. One of your problems in artistry is again to use the image, to use the action, to use what Panofsky calls the dynamization of space— the visual things you are looking at. You should use that much more frequently than you are using words. It is my observation that you use many more words in television than you really are justified in using, because of the pictorial nature of this medium. Therefore, you are going to have a situation where talk can become as damaging to your medium as it was to the early sound motion pictures. And speaking of talking, I am doing a great deal more than I should and I'm going to stop. I am going to remark only that what is very likely to happen to Rex Reed when the motion picture becomes extinct, is that he is going to move over to television, and start knocking you, just as hard as he has been knocking movie people. Don't let that worry you in the least!

STANLEY: Thank you very much, Mr. Crowther. Our last speaker addressing himself to the question of television's aesthetic potential is Mr. John O'Connor.

O'CONNOR: Both speakers have already touched on many of the points I wanted to cover. And what I would like to do now is give a scatter-shot approach to some of these various problems. I don't know about you, but the word "aesthetic" alone gives me a kind of dull headache. Certainly it's a problem, it's something that is hardly touched upon in television. Speaking as a daily critic, it's very closely aligned with quality on television. What I'm appalled at is that most television criticism tends to take a personality approach. There is a reason for this. Many television critics are also reporters, and they are forced to fill up space every day in their newspapers. They interview stars and starlets, they are impressed by certain life-styles or not impressed, and they get various reactions. But the attitude in that type of work tends to carry over into the criticism itself. The basic content, the aesthetic approach, of the program is generally ignored.

The word "aesthetic" immediately conjurs up the image of Joe Papp's *Much Ado About Nothing.* It is the type of programming that they do on public television (or import from BBC), that we hear so much about in terms of quality. I feel that American television is lacking in so many areas. I don't know why. I'm still trying to find out (after two years of reviewing), why certain types of programs, such as Mary Tyler Moore, for instance, which is a very good, well put together, well produced, well acted, well directed program, succeed week after week. It's the type of program that's putting the Broadway theatre out of business. It's that basic format that was the situation-type comedy on Broadway when Broadway was producing 55 to 110 plays a season in the twenties and thirties. Well, that was a staple, the situation comedy. Television is able to do that now and does it well, as in the case of Mary Tyler Moore, and even *All in the Family,* which is —regardless of what you think of the basic program—very well done.

On the other hand, television does have it's own form. Obviously, television is just a conduit for other forms, for movies. When you put a movie on television you are not seeing the original. They showed *Diary of a Mad Housewife.* I didn't see it, but I had several telephone calls telling me that all the key scenes were cut and censored. The movie itself was only making two or three minor points about contemporary life in the big city, and they managed to cut all those points out of the movie. Now what that meant to the average viewer, I have no idea. We are going to get *Who's Afraid of Virginia Woolf.* I don't know what is going to happen to that, but I am sure it's not going to be the movie that people saw in a movie theatre. But also as a conduit simply for the theatre, I think of two productions. One was *Young, Gifted and Black* that was done on television. I happened to review it as a play in *The Wall Street Journal* and the movie was consciously adapted for the television screen. There was a television aesthetic working, it was made more intimate. The use of time was jumbled, the short commercial techniques were used to great effect and as a result, I thought the television production was much better than the stage production. The *Much Ado* that was on, in many ways was better than the stage production. It had greater fluidity, it wasn't as messy as the stage production, and it had live quality. Of course, nothing is ever going to replace the live quality of theatre, but obviously a great deal of care was taken, and a great deal of attention to detail was given. The cost of the production was over $800,000, and Joe Papp is frantic because he is out $50,000. Is this possible for commercial television to put that kind of money in that type of production, often?

The question of young film makers was brought up. So far, the things I have seen in video are all very interesting experimental centers and what have you. They are especially trying to put together and define a grammar of television, a grammar of electronics. What does constitute a type of image, what types of shapes mean certain things to certain people, what does color mean, what does one color next to another mean? These questions have hardly been studied. But as far as the young video film makers themselves, (I was discussing this with Mike Wallace and Morley Safer.) and occasionally in *60 Minutes,* they buy material from outside. They either buy it from Europeans or they contract somebody to do a piece for them. And one of the big sources, when they started this program, they thought would be young film makers. And it's turned out to be very disappointing. They have gotten hardly anything at all. As Morley Safer puts it, "They are all alike, everyone, everybody seems to be discovering his penis and that's the approach to it."

As for areas for artistry, that Mr. Crowther went into, I disagree with one thing. I think children's television, certainly, has proven it's an area with artistry with regard to *Sesame Street* and *The Electric Company.* In the area of the documentary, we get a situation where two weeks ago, two documentaries were done on Red China. One was by Antonioni, the Italian film maker, which was on ABC for two hours, and the other was done by Lucy Jarvis on NBC. Now there was nothing wrong with either one, but I was struck by the contrast. I don't happen to be an Antonioni freak at all, and I was accused of this after writing about it. I did admire his early films, but his last few films I thought were dreadful. However, I did go to the screening at ABC, and I watched for over ninety minutes and was very impressed by the fact that he was not spoon-feeding the audience. He took his camera, he was very slow, he took his time. There was very little narration, there were shots that were held for an awfully long time, and it was difficult. You had to sit down and make an effort to follow what he was doing; you had to contribute something of your own to it; you had to interpret an awful lot of it yourself.

The Jarvis program was very different. There was absolutely nothing wrong with it, on one level, but it was a typical news documentary. That type of news documentary has fallen into a pattern, and it *is* spoon-feeding.

It starts with a teaser, and it goes into short clips, and it shows you an art object, and it gives you facts on Chinese history. The whole of Chinese history was covered up to present, including Mongol hordes and the invaders. In thinking about it later, I found that I learned more about China from the Antonioni film than I did from the Jarvis piece. I forgot all of the facts a half hour after the program was over. Unless I was actually going to sit down and take notes, it was useless. It's a problem in all of television and most documentary makers admit this. Craig Gilbert, who just did *An American Family* for public television, did it in twelve episodes. He could afford the luxury because it was public television. Obviously, this type of program would never be done on commercial television. He did it because he had done several documentaries that were in the traditional style, and he felt that when he had worked on something for six months, it went on the air, it was over an hour and ten minutes later, and everybody forgot about it. Is there any way of devising a form, perhaps not even getting rid of the old form, but at least trying to expand, and experiment? Maybe there is a different way of doing things, a more effective way. I happen to think that with *American Family,* he hit on the right way, and people are talking about it. Evidently it is hitting home for an awful lot of people, whether they identify with the family or not.

The whole business of television has usurped a lot of Broadway's function, and I do think that it will usurp the function of the movie house eventually. John Schlesinger, one director who came from British television and settled into American films with *Midnight Cowboy,* says that at this point, he is interested in the movie because there is a commitment made by the movie goer. He goes to this house, he makes the effort to go, he pays money, he goes in, he sits, he concentrates on the screen. Well, of course, you don't get that with television viewers, or at least most television viewers. You get constant interruptions, not only from the commercials, but from the telephone, family problems and so forth. And one other objection he had was simply the scale. There are certain things you can do on a movie screen that you can't do with the small scale of the television screen. We know now that next month Sony is introducing a video projection system that will give you a 50-inch diagonal. I've seen a projection system developed by three artists on their own that produces a 90-inch diagonal. It's a device that you put on the television screen, and it projects the picture without distortion to a 90-inch diagonal.

With all of these things developing, I think we can at least start concentrating on what it means. The Ford Foundation recently did a study of television just simply from the point of ecology. What does it mean for the viewer to see Lucy turn on the water and then walk away from the sink and have a five- or ten-minute conversation. That's a sociological approach. But what does it mean in a program called *Tenafly* with a black detective.

If you shut your eyes, you wouldn't know that the detective was black in a white situation. What are we willing to show? What are we intent upon hiding in the contents of this, and how well is it done technically?

CHALLENGE II: QUESTION AND ANSWER SESSION

STANLEY: I'll open the panel now to questions from the floor.

CAILTEUX: I was glad to hear about Rex Reed and Edmund Wilson and Van Doren. But, I was wondering why there seems to be a conspiracy of people in media in general, and perhaps among us, to ignore that? If you go back to Eliot, to Shaw, to Aristotle, you really can find standards that overlap every single art form. They do exist. Forget craftsmanship. There is something called human interest, and it applies to people (not stereotypes) and places that are universal. It goes beyond ethnic and national boundaries in time. I can only seek the truth, I can only relate it, survive and enjoy it. I can't really alleviate pain. I can only present alternative values. I didn't discover those values. They've been here for three thousand years. Why doesn't that come out in your presentation? Why didn't that come out as something to go back to in looking for aesthetic standards?

STANLEY: Is this statement addressed to any particular member of the panel?

CROWTHER: I'd like to remark that accomplishing any of these excite-ments, these stimuli that you speak of, is dependent in each medium upon the tools of the medium itself, upon the craftsmanship of the medium. Now, I think that when the craftsmanship has been used in television, just as is true of the motion picture, it was used very skillfully and effectively. It is the same when the craftsmanship of words has been used effectively, or the craftsmanship of paint. I think what we have been trying to explain and discuss here is the limitation upon the use of the craftsmanship freely and fluidly, so that these things can occur. That's what I think this panel has addressed itself to, and I think fairly well in the brief time we've had.

QUESTION: Mr. O'Connor, could you explain just briefly under what conditions you preview television programs; describe the rooms to us, how it's presented?

O'CONNOR: Generally, it's a medium-sized room and there is a television monitor that's on closed circuit. Occasionally, I might have to watch it on a screen, a projection screen, which I don't like and which I discourage. That happened with *An American Family*. They had shown the first two episodes at the Museum of Modern Art, and I walked out after the first one because I felt it was too distorted. I must say that when I do go to see something in those very controlled kinds of circumstances, I wonder how my experience may differ from the average viewer. But I have gone home many times and watched the same program, and found very little difference as far as my own reaction was concerned.

STANLEY: Mr. Shipley?

SHIPLEY: I am just wondering where the audience comes in? When you think of films that were popular in their era and two decades later are forgotten, the aesthetics developed over a period of years and are determined more by the audience than by the critics. How will that effect television?

CROWTHER: Well, I think that I remarked that our prejudices or our biases as viewers often excite us to say something is artistic, when we are gratified. We say it's artistic and therefore, is part of our temporal limitation, our temporal environment. I think that many things that we are seeing now and find most exciting on television, won't look that exciting if we see them many years from now. This will be in all of the areas, documentary or *Much Ado*. Certainly the immediate conditioning of the audience for any medium is a factor in the critic's remarking whether it's art. If it's stimulating to that audience, and gets from that audience a kind of response that is to be expected, then I think it is art in this day and age. Lasting art, permanent, undying art is something else, and I doubt very much if we are going to find it in any of the ephemeral media that are operating in our day and age, including music.

HICKEY: Could I just say that it's the nature of the product more so than the audience that determines whether or not we use the word aesthetic. I find it as burdensome as everybody else. But we are talking about television, and the difficulty is that the television programs are produced on a very tight schedule. As television is constituted in the United States at this time, the programs are interrupted by advertisements. That, as Mr. Crowther says, is the absolute death of any kind of flow. I think it is really impossible to do it under those circumstances. We can now envision a time when the economic base for television will be somewhat different than it is today. We will pay a charge per program for the things that come into our home, or we will (perhaps for some interim period) buy them on cassettes, and subsequently get them on cable television. The body of American television as it stands militates against any potentially serious corpus of scholarly work growing up around it. As I said before, I think there is an excellent chance for that happening in the future, and the occasional successes such as the BBC and the network specials that transcend the ordinary, are not things that we ought to be judging television by. Television is a commercial venture which is in business to sell advertising and to increase the profits of the companies that surround it. We have to remember that ratings are what count in television as opposed to the box office success of films, or the number of copies a novel can sell. You can't compare them and I think for such reasons, a serious body of study has not developed.

Challenge III

Broadcast News—Is It Biased?

IF WE ARE to believe the analysis of the semanticists, dictionary definitions are useless, because they simply use words—verbal symbols—to
describe other words. In this way, as Korzybski and Hayakawa explain it,
we run ad infinitum into a circular argument. Yet, such terms as "bias"
are difficult to define operationally. One cannot point to an extensional
"thing" called "bias" in the external world. Bias is an intentional or
connotative term, and what is biased to one may be objective analysis to
another—depending upon his orientation and his own degree of "bias." In
general, however, it is not unreasonable to suggest that bias is manifested
by a disinclination to view an individual, institution or idea from a
number of possible viewpoints, to shut out a spirit of free inquiry in
favor of a priori judgment, to accept stereotypes uncritically and to shut
out from one's conscious perception a pluralism of ideas.

Some—fortunately relatively few—have revealed their own two-
dimensional thinking by accusing broadcast news of bias. Former Vice-
President Agnew's vitriolic criticism of the media in 1969 accused broadcast journalism of concentration of power in a few who distorted the news
to propagate their own prejudices. But implicit in the former Vice-President's presentation is its own refutation, for the very media which were
accused took pains—foolishly it now may seem in retrospect—to broadcast Mr. Agnew's remarks over coast-to-coast television and radio and to
give his remarks widespread coverage in the print media.

More recently, Edith Efron published a book purporting to show that
network neutrality in reporting the news is a myth. But Miss Efron's bias is
revealed by a careful analysis of her own methodology. Using methods
which were largely quantitative, Miss Efron accused the network news
divisions of bias by counting the number of words used on air for and

against various policies and people and then concluding that quantity of words was equated with bias—without regard, it appears, to meaning. Not even the Fairness Doctrine calls for a perfect equating of the number of words employed by the protagonists on a controversial issue.

And subsequently, no less an official spokesman than Clay T. Whitehead, Director of the White House Office of Telecommunications Policy, accused network news of dispensing "elitist gossip" and "ideological plugola" while assuring the broadcasters that his ultimate aim was to render unto them more, not less, freedom to communicate. To many observers, however, Mr. Whitehead's thrust and parry seemed more a contrivance to create dissension between networks and affiliates by convincing the latter that the former aired biased news which the stations really ought to view with jaundiced eye. Significantly, Mr. Whitehead steadfastly refused to cite a single example to document his accusations.

The history of journalism in this country has not been, of course, without instances of bias. One need only cite the partisan press that followed the Revolution, or some of the more lurid excursions into yellow journalism by the Hearst papers at the period of the Spanish-American War and, again, during the Nazi regime in Germany. But these stand out as exceptions so blatant and so glaring that they merely tend to affirm that the press in America has produced the most fearless and most honorable journalism of any country in the world. Even those officials most critical of press performance had not a scintilla of doubt as to its essential integrity. And so, Madison and Monroe and Jefferson, rejecting "print by authority" clearly saw the press as essential to liberty and Franklin declared that "if print offended nobody, nothing would be printed." Thus began a healthy adversarial relationship between the media and the government—a system of free communication that encouraged a foreign observer, De Tocqueville, to note that the media flourished in this country because they enjoy "utmost national freedom combined with local freedom of every kind."

These remarks were made long before the advent of electric technology. But there is no doubt that the power and reach of the broadcast media raise special problems and impose special responsibilities. Television is immediate, visual, all-pervasive. The effects are not easy to evaluate. Sociologists and psychologists differ in their opinion regarding the impact of broadcast news. Did coverage of the Chicago convention in 1968 instigate violence by the very presence of the media? Did the depiction of the killing in Vietnam reduce the viewer to a state of apathetic acceptance of violence as a way of life? There are many opinions—and considerable bias either way—but no definitive answers.

One aspect must not be overlooked. Television is protected by the First Amendment, but in a different way from print. It is regulated. Print is not. Stations are licensed. Newspapers are not. The over-all programming performance of stations is evaluated at intervals by the FCC. No government agency requires newspapers to keep logs of what they print. The law of the press, therefore, does not apply in the same way to print as it does to broadcasting. And the FCC provides for the balancing of controversial issues by invoking the Fairness Doctrine.

Nevertheless, broadcasting still operates, to a large extent, under a combined philosophy of libertarianism and social responsibility. Like the Canons of Journalism of the newspaper publishers, the broadcasting industry has its own Code of the National Association of Broadcasters, along with its individual network departments of program practices and standards. Evidently, some news executives thought this was not sufficient, in view of increasing criticism, and a group of print and broadcast news executives have organized a National Press Council, sponsored by the Twentieth Century Fund. The idea is not new. It has been suggested before. But there is little reason to believe that such a council will solve the problems, and good reason to conjecture that it will only create a host of new problems. Indeed, there is some basis to the conviction that any negative findings by the Council (and who, incidentally, would assure that the Council members were free of "bias"?) would merely add grist to the propaganda mill of both the Administration and of special interest groups. It is possible that a Press Council would—implicitly if not explicitly—involve regulation by the Council instead of by government.

In any event, the public does not seem concerned over the issue of bias. The study under Professor Robert T. Bowen, *Television and the Public,* prepared by the Bureau of Social Science Research in 1972-73 indicates that most people believe that television "gives the fairest most unbiased news." An encouraging finding, but not the ultimate answer to what will undoubtedly remain—given the nature of the medium—a constant critical challenge.

CHALLENGE III

Producer: Charles Tower (Corinthian Broadcasting)

Moderator: Thomas McCain (Illinois State Broadcasting)

Panel: Eugene Methvin (Reader's Digest); Thomas Wolf (ABC News)

Question and Answer (in order): Jon T. Powell (Northern Illinois University); Peter K. Pringle (University of Florida);

William H. Cianci (Rider College); Stanley T. Donner
(University of Texas); Charles W. Shipley (Southern Illinois
University); William Hawes (University of Houston)

McCAIN: Is there now or has there been a significant amount of bias in
Broadcast News and in Public Affairs Programming. Further, if there is,
what can or should be done with it? Will the establishment of a review
board of distinguished citizens be a helpful mechanism? And what is the
application of the First Amendment to broadcasting? Our distinguished
panelists are: Eugene Methvin who is a senior editor of *Reader's Digest*
magazine, working out of Washington, D.C. and Thomas Wolf who is Vice
President and the Director of the Television Documentary Programs for
ABC News. First of all, we'll be hearing from Mr. Methvin.

METHVIN: Thank you. As the lawyers say it: Let me qualify the witness.
I guess I am somewhat like a skunk at the lawn party in that I'm out of
the print media here talking about my fellow gentlemen of the Fourth
Estate of the broadcast media. And I'm not quite sure what mystical
process got me here, except perhaps there is a masochistic urge among the
broadcasters—they are enjoying being plagued so much, they'd like a little
more of it. But qualifying the witness, I can say that I'm about as complete a pedigreed news-hound as I think you'll ever lay eyes upon. I was
born into a newspaper family. I'm the fourth generation in my family
afflicted with this genetic disease. Like the Romanov's, I'm a hemophiliac
of the news media. Cut me and I bleed printer's ink instead of the normal
stuff. One of my first cribs was a bale of newsprint, and I never had any
dream of winding up in the magazine business until I got a job offer
when I was a young reporter on the *Washington Daily News,* and this
particular experience of moving from the news media into the magazine
media, particularly a monthly magazine like the *Digest,* has given me an
opportunity to see my profession of journalism and the news media business from a little different perspective. And in this process, I've had to
make some rather jolting psychological adjustments of my own, and also I
have come to see some of the professional practices to which we are
conditioned in our journalism schools and our daily practice, or on-the-job
training, in a little different light. And I've come to question some of the
basic canons we have been taught all along about what is news—the
number one question of Journalism 101 in every journalism school in the
country, the question whether or not there is such thing as objectivity,
what is objectivity, what is subjectivity? I'm sure that we'll never wind up
with a completely satisfactory answer, except to say that somewhere between

high noon and midnight, there is a difference. The fact that there is a twilight zone, doesn't eliminate the difference between objectivity and subjectivity. Now, bias, our topic for today, is defined in the dictionary: a mental tendency, preference or prejudice, a leaning, an inclination, a partiality. We all have those. We're all biased. "I have convictions, you're opinionated and he is a stubborn damn fool." It's the viewpoint. One of the finest definitions of news that I have ever heard was David Brinkley's, "News is what I say it is." It's news because I say so. There is a great deal of truth in that, but on the other hand, that can be carried too far. I'd just like to read to you a comment that I happened to pick up a couple of days ago, on Lincoln's Birthday. My fellow Georgian, Alexander Stevens, who was Vice President of the Confederacy, in 1878 was asked to unveil a portrait of Lincoln signing the Emancipation Proclamation. I think it is important for us as journalists to remember what he said: "Prejudice! What wrongs, what injuries, what mischief, what lamentable consequences have resulted at all times from this perversity of the intellect. Of all the obstacles to the advancement of news and human progress and in every department of knowledge, in science, art, government and religion, in all times and ages, not one on the list is more formidable, more difficult to overcome and subdue, than this horrible distortion of the moral as well as the intellectual faculties."

Now, what is the nature of prejudice, or bias? Just let me give you a little catalog of the biases as I have seen them and analyze them. I am trying to judge my role as an editor and as a journlist, as well as from the standpoint of a consumer of the news media. I am probably one of the most voracious consumers of the print media, to say the least, print news media, you'll ever find, I spend more hours of my day than I like to say, reading newspapers. I'm not an expert, though, on broadcast journalism, but I do think that it is impossible to separate print media and broadcast media when we're talking about this question of bias. I think that you'll find some foibles and failings in both in approximately equal proportions.

But let's talk first about a bias that I think is quite common to journalism, or journalists. It is the *abstraction bias,* the bias toward glittering generalities. This bias is innate in the journalist's own personality, as an individual who is attracted to the profession by virtue of his skill with words, with abstractions. I've made it a practice, as I've gone around the country, to find out how somebody else can excuse his affliction, and I ask young people how they decided that they wanted to be journalists, and invariably it was because they were good in English, good in words, they liked writing, they got on the school newspaper, and there they are, ten years later, twenty years later, they're major journalists. It was NOT because they liked reporting that they got into the trade. It was NOT because they liked going out and using their legs. It was because they liked using words.

And this creates an inclination toward a second major bias—the *bias of shallowness,* the bias to fail to look behind glittering labels. We're right now engaged in a great fight in Washington over Mr. Nixon's efforts to cut some programs out, and one of my major jobs in Washington has always been to get behind the press releases of Government programs, to get behind the speeches in the *Congressional Record* of Congressional sponsors of bills and see NOT what the program is intended to do, not what the press releases say that the program does, but to find out what really happens out there. And when a shoe-leather reporter takes some of those press releases out and compares them to the reality, you find an astonishing disparity. For example, specifically in current context in Washington: Mr. Nixon is trying to cut out a program called REAP, Rural Environmental Assistance Program. Well, that little label got pinned on it two years ago by some bureaucrats who decided that this program was in trouble, and so if we had the word "environmental" in the title the public would be behind us. And it is working. It was originally called the Agricultural Conservation Program. And here again, if you go out into the field and look at some of the things that are happening under this title, you'll find out that it is *anti*-conservation, because in fact, much of the money is spent for draining natural wetlands. And, of course, over in the Department of the Interior in the Game and Fish Division they have another vast program to spend money to try to conserve these wetlands. All the revenue from duck stamp sales to hunters goes to buying up wet-lands and conserving them. So here you've got two different programs doing a hundred-and-eighty-degrees opposite things, and the environmental program is actually an anti-environmental program in some respects. Nobody goes out and examines this. They take the press releases and the speeches on the House floor and say that Mr. Nixon is cutting out funds for the environment. Well, that's an example of the 'shallowness bias.'

Now, the other two areas of bias are most controversial; you hear them talked about all the time—Liberals versus Conservatives. Now I should probably state my own bias in this area. I detest labels. The Chief Justice, in the current issue of the *Reader's Digest* when we asked him if he was an Activist or strict Constructionist or what his label is said that he thinks "labels are sophomoric over-simplifications." Well, certainly, when you put a label on a person you're pigeon-holing him, and pigeon holes should be for pigeons, not people. But I suppose I would come out a moderate-conservative, and I think Edith Efron is correct when she says most of the media, the news media, tend to be moderate-liberals or liberal-leftists, as she calls them. And this goes right back to that fascination and penchant for abstractions that I talked about, but what are the baises?

Well, let's take first the *conservative biases*. First of all, I think that conservatives tend to be in favor of authority. They tend to think that the police are right—if the police say so, then the police will have a good case, and they get at least a fair hearing, if not an overly sympathetic hearing, from conservatives. The social programs that are a large part of government function these days, tend to get a long hard look by conservatives. The problems that the social programs are designed to solve don't get much conservative attention. Take the Pentagon, for example, the national defense. The cause of defense gets a sympathetic hearing and the Pentagon tends to come out always right. Whatever the Generals say we need, we need. And on a deeper level, the conservative tends to think that man is flawed by original sin. His view of man is that man is open to folly, and he's a fallible creature. Incidentally, George Washington had this view and so did the framers of the Constitution. Washington said in a letter in 1786: "We must take human nature as we find it. Perfection falls not to the share of mortals."

On the other hand, the *liberal biases* tend to come out *against* authority: against the use of authority in any policing action, or any upholding of the norms or any coercive action on the part of government. Yet, for social programs, the liberals have an extreme tolerance. They don't look behind the labels. If a program is labeled as "housing for the poor," then liberals do not go up to Detroit and see that the Federal housing program up there has degenerated into a subsidy for the middle class, real estate exploiters. In effect, an out-and-out corrupt program is being exploited by modern day robber-barons. They don't look behind those labels; instead, they enjoy Herblock cartoons which show Mr. Nixon when he cuts off these housing programs and suspends them, throwing little old ladies out into the snow. The liberal viewpoint, on the other hand, goes a little further. They're for peace (which is a glittering label); they're against the war machine. They have a Rousseauist view of humanity: "Man is a noble savage, but he is corrupted by institutions." And yet, you get a dissonance here, because the liberal tends to think Government social programs are above criticism, that they do work, and that the Government can solve things. We saw a marvelous illustration of how the liberals get impaled on their prejudices in the case before the Supreme Court over whether Wisconsin had the right to force the Amish to send their children to public schools.

Now, what I think is really an area of concern, particularly for journalism-educators and for groups such as this one, is the *professional journalistic biases*. The biases that are built into our profession by our habitual norms and canons. One, of course, is that conflict is news. Violence is news. Freaks are news. But concord and consensus are not news. Normal human life is not news. If you cannot put a "today" lead on it, it's not news; it doesn't exist. The TV medium, I think, has an innate tendency to magnify these canons of journalism. The TV medium has to have action. Talking heads are death on the screen, and thus, the peace makers, the consensus makers, do not tend to come out as well on television in the news area.

What are the solutions? Well, I'm not sure that we can solve this problem because I think it is innate in human beings to have biases. As the poet, Robert Burns, said: "Would some power the gift to give us, to see ourselves as others see us." This is in the nature of the human being. But there are certain things that we need to do to try to counteract our own biases. And particularly in the television medium, I think that we need to try to work toward depth and against the problem of superficiality. Jack Lyle at U.C.L.A., a researcher, has done some research that finds, for example, that an hour of television news is equal only to about a page of news print in terms of the transmissibility of information. The net result is that there is an innate tendency toward superficiality which magnifies these professional biases that I have talked about. What is the antidote for this? I'm not sure that there is any simple solution. I am sure that it has to come from an open dialogue, not only among the journalists at professional workshops, such as this one, but between journalists and others outside the profession. Between journalists and politicians. Yes, between the broadcast media and Mr. Agnew, for example. Between broadcast media and print media. And, of course, a continuous dialogue between the producers and the consumers of news. Because truly, in the era of megaton bombs, if war is too important to be left to generals (as Clemençeau said) then news is too important to be left to the journalist alone.

Now, some journalists decry the rising public concern. They say we're in a repressive era and then denounce Mr. Agnew, and they seem to think that it all began with him. And yet, if you look at some of the things Hubert Humphrey was saying in 1968; if you look at President Johnson's speech to the broadcast journalists in Chicago the day after he announced his retirement from office, you'll see that what Agnew was saying was not new at all and it is a perennial complaint. And we should not take an overly defensive attitude which I think the journalists have taken. You know, somebody could stand on the street corner and say that the *Reader's Digest* was a lousy publication all day, and they would not interfere with my First Amendment right a bit. Agnew has not interfered with anybody's First Amendment rights, and I don't think the problem of coercion, the threat of coercion, has really been used too heavily here so far, but it is something to guard against, naturally. But let us not forget that basic truth, stated by Alexander Hamilton in his *Federalist Essay Number 84*. He was answering those who were opposed to the Constitution on the grounds that it didn't have a Bill of Rights, and he said (talking particularly about the need for a First Amendment): "What signifies a declaration that liberty of the press shall be inviolably preserved? What is the liberty of the press? Who can give it any definition that would not leave the utmost latitude for evasion? I hold it to be impracticable, and from this I infer that its security, what ever fine declarations may be inserted in any Constitution respecting it, must altogether depend on public opinion, and on the general spirit of the people and of the Government. And here, after all, must we seek for the only solid basis of all our rights."

I think this is where we have to end it. We have to leave it open for all of us to participate—not only the professionals, but also the consuming public in defining what is news and what is news bias. Thank you.

MCCAIN: We'll hear now from Thomas Wolf, of ABC News.

WOLF: I suppose that my bias is conservative. I'd like to get back to the Constitution. I do think there is a difference between the *Reader's Digest* and television news and I'll get to it in a minute. Obviously, it doesn't matter what Mr. Agnew or anybody in the Federal Government says about any print medium, because the print medium is not licensed and obviously it becomes a totally different ball game if the man criticizing the medium is also in a position to influence, or if the medium thinks he can influence, the issuance of licenses.

Several years ago, when Dr. Barnard first came to this country, he was doing a CBS show, and he was invited to a cocktail party up in Westport and he told the story of coming home late after months of not being home very much, working at the almost breakthrough point on the first heart operation, and his wife met him, and it was at eleven o'clock at night, and she said: "You've got to do something about that bathroom upstairs that you've been promising to get fixed." He said: "What do you want me to do?" She said: "Get the plumber." He said: "It's eleven o'clock at night." She said: "I know, but if his kid was sick, you'd go over and see them." So eventually he agrees, and he calls the plumber and the plumber says it's eleven o'clock at night, and he goes through the same thing. So the plumber eventually turns up, but he's got his satchel, and he says: "Okay, Where is it?" And the Doctor points to the top of the stairs, and he takes the bag and goes up; lifts up the seat, opens his bag, takes out a couple of aspirin, throws them in and says: "If it isn't better in the morning, call me."

The reason that I think professional journalists are more capable of curbing what bias they have than bankers or politicians is that we're the only group that really does not have an axe to grind. We have nothing to prove, and it's going to be my contention that, since the question of what is fair is a subjective question, it's better to have those people determining what is fair, than any other group. What is news, for that matter? It is indeed what is not the rule. Several years ago in Pittsburgh, we sent a camera crew out to see a huge new crane that had come into town. They were starting a project, and the crew came back without any pictures. And we said: "What happened?" And they said: "Well, there wasn't a story. The crane fell over."

This brings me to the question of what is bias. We recently did a show on the Rockefeller Commission Report on population in the American future, and Rockefeller was at a North Carolina University and a student asked him whether something he had just proposed wasn't, in fact, propaganda. And Rockefeller said: "Well, that depends, of course, on whether you believe it. If you believe, it was the truth, if you didn't, it was propaganda." And the same thing can be said for bias. Of course, there is bias in television programming. But the thrust of what I want to say is that I think there is less bias among top newsmen, than there is among any other group. The three television networks have so few jobs, and there are so many, many people seeking them, that I have a feeling that you are getting the most trained, the most professional people in those jobs.

After Vice President Agnew made his famous Des Moines speech in 1969, we were concerned as to whether or not network news was, indeed, unfair to the Administration which he had charged it was. And Elmer Lower, as President of ABC News, decided to have a content analysis each year. The analysis was undertaken by three journalism school professors, and they analyzed every single newscast. And they used a pro-or-con Administration yardstick simply because that was the way the charge had been placed. They surveyed more than ten thousand separate judgments on stories. In the 1972 election year, taking from the first of the year through the election, they found that 27% of the news that we aired would be pleasing to an Administration supporter, 31% would be displeasing and 40% would be neutral. So that's pretty close. And it should be remembered that these measurements take in all the news, not just political news. We have a commentary segment and in 1971, which is the last year that I have figures for, 33% would have been thought pleasing to the Administration, 17½% displeasing and 50% neutral.

Now, let's look at the area of documentary and public service, which is my particular responsibility. You all know that the FCC's Fairness Doctrine doesn't call for equal time. Equal time applies only to the case of a candidate for political office. What the Fairness Doctrine says is that, if on a controversial issue of public importance, there are several viewpoints, viewers should be made aware of those viewpoints and have the right to know the substance of them and the reasons for them. The FCC doesn't require balance within a single program. We, as a matter of just making it practical, do insist on balance within the four walls. It's too difficult to say:

"Well, this program doesn't need to be balanced, because two weeks ago the evening news spent three days with the spokesman for the other side." So we do insist on balance in the four walls.

Obviously, fairness and balance are a matter of judgment. But the people making these decisions (as far as ABC goes) have been journalists for a good number of years. I've been in full-time editorial journalism for over thirty-five years, and my boss, who sees all the programs before they are broadcast, is in his fortieth year. But, quite candidly, I always ask myself twice when I look at a program: Is it fair? For example, we had a program on population and the American future, which I mentioned earlier. The producer was Marlene Sanders, and Marlene personally is a strong advocate of legalized abortion. So, at the outset of the program, I reminded her of the special need, in view of her own predilection, to get the views of the Catholic Church and other anti-abortion groups, effectively and prominently presented. When I saw the first cut of the film, I thought she had carried out the mandate, but I still wanted to be sure that we were totally fair and I asked her to stick in a couple of minutes of a statement by a representative of the Catholic Church which she'd filmed but hadn't used. And I guarantee you that the program, as aired, was fair and balanced. But even before the program was broadcast, we had a flood of letters asking for time to reply. And it isn't unusual, because as soon as a release goes out, all interested groups—whatever their areas of interest— write in. Parenthetically, it's usually easy to tell when you have this kind of a pressure campaign. In this case, a great deal of our mail came from within a hundred miles of Chicago. It was all addressed to James F. Duffy, President of ABC Television. His middle initial is "E" and it isn't hard to suspect that it wasn't all an accident.

From time to time, sloppy research occurs and we've run into it. The most recent example that I can think of was on a show we did called *Arms and Security: How Much is Enough?* And there were several stupid, sloppy and mostly unimportant factual errors: we called the B-52 a supersonic aircraft (it isn't), we mis-identified a sponsor of a film, calling it the parent organization of the sponsoring group rather than the subsidiary, and there were a couple of errors of substance. One was the question of the percentage of the Federal budget going to defense. One was the position of the American Security Council which is a very strong "we-want-and-need-more arms" group on major Pentagon evaluation. Within a few days we were being flooded with letters, pointing out our errors and demanding that the stations which had carried our program, carry a program which had been produced either by the American Security Council or a subsidiary now. It was a "We're losing the arms race to Russia" campaign. It wasn't long before we discovered that a publication called *Accuracy in Media* had taken aim on our show and torn it apart from the position of the advocates of greater defense expenditures. Well, what should we do? We reviewed the program and decided that we had been fair and balanced, giving the pro-arms advocates sufficient time to state their case clearly and cogently. But we had indeed, made errors of fact. Since the question of "arms and security: how much is enough," is a continuing and a valid question, we decided that what we'd do was to take the next week's *Issues and Answers* program and devote it to a continuing discussion of arms and security, to which we invited the American Security Council to appoint a representative. At the opening of the show, we said: "We did a documentary on this ten days ago. We had some factual errors, and we corrected them."

To come back to the question that I was asked, I don't believe there has been a significant amount of bias in television news and public affairs programming. All of you know that you can appeal to the FCC if you feel that you have a grievance, and if they disagree, they can direct the broadcaster to make amends. A number of Congressmen and Senators are concerned about this. One, of course, is Senator Pastore, who's Chairman of the Senate's Commerce Committee, Sub-Committee on Communications. He most recently has been watching violence and also the question of the projection in national elections of Eastern winners on the over-all outcome, because the Western polls haven't closed. Then, of course, there is Representative Staggers, who is Chairman of the House Interstate and Foreign Commerce Committee's Special Sub-Committee on Investigation. He's been looking into, among other things, alleged staging. Then, there are the private groups like "Accuracy in Media" which I mentioned, and various individuals and other groups who watch what we do like a hawk.

The question was raised whether a group like the British Press Council would help. I recently attended a seminar in Santa Barbara, The Center for the Study for the Democratic Institutions, on the First Amendment and broadcasting, and one of the participants was Lord Richie Calder, who is Britain's top science writer. He was very familiar with the British Press Council, and he said that in the beginning the entire British press was totally opposed to it, but at the moment, he thought it was pretty well supported by the press. He also stated that before you can appeal to the Press Council, you must have asked the publication for redress and have been denied, and secondly (and this is the important part here), you must agree in advance not to go to Court if you lose your case before the Council. Well, when you come over to the possibility of an organization like that in America—and the Twentieth Century Fund, as you undoubtedly know, is setting up such a group or in the process of trying to—the question arises that, even if we insisted that the Twentieth Century Fund or a similar group, insisted that a complainant sign away his post decision right to sue, could the FCC agree in advance that it would not consider this case when license renewal came up? I think it was the group feeling out in Santa Barbara, and I certainly feel strongly, that the FCC couldn't and wouldn't.

And now, you get to the guts of it. The FCC position would be of no concern if we'd clearly established that the First Amendment covered the broadcast press. We, of course, believe that it does, and that logic dictates that it does. But no case yet has reached the Supreme Court to test this belief. And until there is a clear indication that the threat—real or implied—that a broadcaster can lose his license, if the news he broadcasts isn't fair, then the gut question is: fair by whose standard. That of the broadcaster or that of the Government? Clay Whitehead, Director of the White House Office of Telecommunications Policy, recently raised this question to a broadcaster where he wrote: "The core of the issue is who shall be responsible for assuring that the people's right to know is served? And where should the initiative come from? The Government or the Broadcaster?" And Mr. Whitehead, as he has so effectively done in all of his speeches, comes down squarely on the side of the broadcaster. That's splendid if the First Amendment does, in fact, cover broadcast news. But so long as a possible shadow of doubt remains, the broadcaster isn't really all that free to make his decisions purely on the basis of his journalistic training and his integrity. You all know that licenses come up for renewal every three years. You know that the seven members of the FCC vote on these renewals, and you know that the President of the United States appoints these members, and while it's true that no more than four of the seven can be from any one party, it's always seemed to me that the President has considerable influence over the broadcaster. And until the First Amendment issue is decided once and for all, no broadcaster fails to see an implied threat (where, of course, there may not be one).

But take the case of the *Washington Post's* stations in Miami and Jacksonville. The *Post* has been considered by the Administration a very antagonistic organization. Right now, there are four license applications, one in Miami for Channel 10 which is W. Phillip L. Graham, and three in Jacksonville, fighting for the *Washington Post-Newsweek* stations and (by coincidence) most of those license applicants are close friends of the Administration. Now, maybe that is purely coincidence. Station licenses are valuable products—properties. It seems to me that it is somewhat naive to say that the determination of what's fair, really rests solely with the broadcaster. He's got to consider what the Government might think is fair. And therefore, it isn't a broadcaster's sole determination, unless the First Amendment applies.

Well, why does it matter? Why does it matter whether the First Amendment covers broadcasting? Why did the framers of the Constitution want a First Amendment, specifically that part which covers the press, in the first place? This morning in the Op-Ed page of the *New York Times,* Senator Ervin said: "The founding fathers state the existence of America as a free society, on its faith that it has nothing to fear from exercise of the First Amendment freedoms, no matter how much they may be abused, as long as truth is free to combat error." The First Amendment was adopted to help guard against an all-powerful national Government, which is why every national Administration since George Washington has had problems with the press. I submit that that's just what the framers wanted. It is my personal view that the tensions resulting from this planned "adversary relationship" have never been greater than with the present Administration, and for the reason the Founding Fathers could not have foreseen. Television has an impact on the public unequaled by the print press, yet I personally feel certain that the very power of the television press, would have warmed the hearts of the framers, strengthening, as it does, the hand that they wanted strengthened—the people's right to know —and by knowing to throw out the rascals when they need throwing out.

I'd like to take one second to quote Julian Goodman, the President of NBC, when he said:

> The news media whatever their faults, are not the danger. The danger is two-fold. It is the Government that would try to re-shape the news in a fashion more to its liking, and it is public apathy that attacks the freedom of the press. The campaign to undermine the public trust in the news media is perhaps the media's most serious problem. But it's a much more serious public problem, because the public will be injured if the Government interferes with the free flow of news and information to the public itself. Press freedom belongs not so much to the press, as it belongs to you.

This is the message I would leave with you, and I hope you believe as I do, that the preservation of that freedom is worth every ounce of energy which we can give it.

CHALLENGE III: QUESTION AND ANSWER SESSION

McCAIN: Thank you. Chuck Tower has produced this program and brought our distinguished panelists here so that you may use them as resource people for the small group discussions.

POWELL: Mr. Wolf, could you tell us if there is any sign on the horizon of this problem being settled as far as the First Amendment goes?

WOLF: Well, there are cases. The only case on broadcasting yet to reach the Supreme Court, I think, was the *Red Lion* case and that was a five to four decision. As you know, based on availability of channels, there are twice as many television, and probably seven times as many radio stations on the air as there are daily newspapers. What we were advised, in Santa Barbara by a couple of the FCC's lawyers, is to get the case before the court. How quickly it will be heard, I don't know.

PRINGLE: I have two questions for Mr. Wolf. The first one is that I think we're all fairly familiar with the bias charges that were leveled by Edith Efron and the American Institute for Political Communication. The things that don't make news are the letters that come to your office every day. I would like to know what kind of people, except pressure groups, level charges of bias against you? And what kind of news coverage are they concerned with, or what do they believe they see bias in?

WOLF: That's a terribly hard question to answer. Just before I left the office I saw a wire sent in by an individual from the Middle West complaining, bitterly, that Harry Reasoner, on the special we did on the returning prisoners, had said, "tonight we celebrate life." The question had come up, why all this celebration for two or three hundred guys when fifty thousand were killed? And Reasoner said: "Because we always celebrate life." And this guy called him a Communist and said he was never going to watch him again. One of the things I would hope is that one of the journalism schools in this country would make a very long range project on how television communicates. Nobody knows how it communicates. The second is: Why people see television much more subjectively than the print media? The answer, obviously, is that if you see something you don't want to read, you flip the page. If you're looking at a news report, and you want to hear what's left you're forced to hear what comes in between. But, several years ago, the People's Republic government of China used to put out (they still may) newsreels on a quarterly basis. They got hold of some footage in which black Americans were burning their draft cards, and they put it out with a script saying: "The third world unites against . . . and so on." What the people in the theatre saw was that black Americans have wrist watches and Zippo lighters, and all they saw was how good life must be in the United States. And this had to be pulled back. I don't know if that helps to answer.

METHVIN: You know the old poem: "Pussy cat, pussy cat, where have you been. I've been to London to see the Queen. Pussycat, pussycat, did you see her beautiful crown? No. Did you see her beautiful ermine gown? No. Did you see her beautiful jeweled throne? No. But what did you see, pussycat? I saw the mouse beneath her chair." Sometimes bias is in the eye of the beholder.

CIANCI: I do agree with Mr. Wolf about this tremendous threat to freedom of the press by the government, and I'm concerned about it. What bothers me is this idea that we've tossed around about the First Amendment protection of broadcasting. I just don't know whether I can agree totally with you, because the history of broadcasting has shown that broadcasters are not always the most concerned with the public interest, because of the amount of money being put into broadcasting. If broadcasters were under no governmental compulsion at all, in any way, like the print media, there are other social and economic pressures that can be put on them. But if there were no government compulsion, would these people have the right of access? In other words, the First Amendment has two prongs: the ability to have access to the microphone, so that we may have the opportunity to hear diversity of viewpoint. But would the people have that diversity of viewpoint if there were no compulsion hanging over the broadcasters? The idea of the First Amendment, in the beginning, was freedom from the government, protection from the government. But in the last several hundred years, we can see that the government isn't always the major threat to our freedoms, it also comes from private concerns—and in many cases the government is the ally of freedom. My bias is extremely on your side Mr. Wolf, but I just don't know if you can really have the government totally out of the broadcasting picture, because of this limited amount of access.

WOLF: The whole problem of access is not what the people requesting access think it is. People don't want access, per se, they want access to audiences, and there is a huge difference. I was in Brazil, and in Brazil the Government owns all broadcasting between six and seven at night. All radio and television stations must carry government programs. Well, down there they call it either the second hour of siesta or the hour of silence. Access, per se, is more complicated than it seems, and quite honestly, at the moment the Fairness Doctrine helps the broadcasters in a funny way, since obviously the people with the money to present programming tend to be the rich and tend to be the conservative. Ninety-five per cent of the requests that we have to put on a program which comes in non-fiction I turn down, because they do not meet the requirements of the Fairness Doctrine. They will be, in a loose term, right wing. So in point of fact, from the broadcaster's point of view, what there is on a fight about access is a very conservative thing. So it does help the broadcaster. But if you believe that the broadcast journalists do, indeed, value fairness (and I believe they do) I think access is a mythical question.

DUNNER: In your main discourse, Mr. Wolf, you mentioned the adversary function of the newsman, but I wish you'd enlarge on that, because it strikes me that that's at the heart of a lot of the objection that the Government seems to be having against television news.

WOLF: Well, there's no question that that's absolutely what they're complaining about. If we simply took the releases, as Mr. Methvin said so many people do . . . First of all, obviously, television network news, the daily news program, is a headline service. And as a member of television news, I would be the first person to say that anybody who is relying on television for its information, is ignorant. You have to read, and you have to read a lot.

METHVIN: Thank you.

WOLF: And I don't think any serious person in television would dispute that. But the role that the press—historically, I believe was meant to play, and I believe the reason for the First Amendment—was to say: "President Washington says this. But, you know, the reason that he says that, fellows, is this this this . . . and this." And, you see, one of the reasons (and this is a totally personal point of view and doesn't represent anybody in the company for which I work, or the company), that this Administration is so violently anti-television is that we are the last national organization with clout. If you'll look at the "New Federalism," it means the break up of national groups; decentralize out to the states and regions. But it also means breaking up power, and it means the destruction of anything, anywhere else on the horizon that can oppose the central authority. And the one thing left, with any clout, is television news. I believe that this adversary position is the crux of our lasting democratic process.

METHVIN: May I make a comment on that? I think that there is a tradition here, and I believe you put your finger on it when you ask about the complaints which arise as a result of this adversary relationship. We have in Washington an intellectual, incestuous, inbred bunch of reporters—the White House Press Corps (a pampered bunch)—and also many immature young journalists who think it's their duty—and they haven't read deeply historically, they've just been taught a little bit—to get that guy in public office whoever he may be. And my own comments earlier about taking the press releases, and looking behind them, indicated how easy it is to slip into the role position that you've got to find something wrong in them. You've got to find that they're guilty of fraud, that somebody is trying to pull the wool over your eyes. And quite frequently, this leads into the false adversary position where the journalist becomes a partisan, very unfairly impugning motives and so forth, in a judgmental area where you have no objective tests. And you go to some of those press briefings at the White House, and you find really a puerile kind of adversary relationship, a looking-for-a-fight relationship. And this is one of the biggest professional bias factors I know. The idea that the press and the government have got to fight always is an immature, adolescent attitude. The fact is, in this country, the government and the media have a congruence of interests. The interests are serving the purposes of the Constitution and the Preamble of the Constitution. I think that we need, in our journalism education, to build in a governing device to warn young journalists: Don't get caught in this tradition trap.

WOLF: The only reason that I'm not quite as concerned about that, is that the Administration can be heard any day, every day, and there is no possibility of its viewpoint not being thoroughly heard. So if there is going to be an error, one side or the other, I think it better to have it on "I wonder" than on "You bet."

METHVIN: I may be overly idealistic, purist here, but I don't think that any error is too good, and the purpose is to try to locate and reduce that perpetual biasing factor. The President may have access anytime he wants it, but he's not the whole government. There are different agencies, different individuals and so forth. One of the most tragic cases I know of, is the character assassination of Senator Tom Dodd. There was a case where the man had no real opportunity to come back at Pearson and Anderson. We've recently seen, in the Eagleton affair, what Mr. Anderson's standards of fairness are, and if the truth ever came out about the whole Tom Dodd story, it would show the news media lynching him, and it was terribly unfair. I happened to be very close to that office over a long period of time, and I knew in intimate detail what happened there and how the truth was terribly miscarried. Many of our fellow reporters joined in; "Oh, boy. We've got to get that guy." They weren't interested in truth, they were interested in getting that guy. And they got him.

SHIPLEY: The real heart of the First Amendment feud right now, is the identification of sources, of course, which in itself, does not abridge the reporter's rights to make a statement. It is the interpretation of the secrecy or the protection of his source. And the question that many people raise, then, is: How is the reporter's news to be evaluated for accuracy? If the sources can be protected, what do you propose would be the manner, aside from journalistic integrity, to guarantee that there would not be character assassination.

METHVIN: I don't believe in a shield law of the absolute kind that is being proposed. I don't believe that it's constitutional. The Sixth Amendment gives the defendant the right to compulsory process. The legislature has no power, since *Marbury v. Madison,* to repeal the Sixth Amendment and I could elaborate on that at great length, but I won't. I was just reminded of what Ben McKelway said about Dave Lawrence, who died a couple of days ago, and this was in his obituary: The job of the journalist really is to be different, to be questioning. He said that Dave Lawrence's attitude was to go against the tide because he'd be likely to say, "I doubt it," when everybody else would say, "It's a sure thing." Well, in this one case, I'm far apart from the general Fourth Estate. I think we're demanding an extraordinary privilege and I hope we don't get it. There is a First Amendment interest at stake here. We ought to define it carefully, but we ought to be careful in emphasizing to young reporters not to fall into the tradition trap that a guy like Bill Farr fell into. I think he was wrong in that instance. He himself admits that the story he got had nothing to do with any real interest in protecting the public interest in exposing corruption or anything to do with the function of our institutions. It was purely a sensational story, which happened to raise some minor threat to Charles Manson's right to a fair trial, even though the jury was sequestered. But Farr seemed to think that he had to have that story, and he seemed to think that he had to go to jail to protect his sources. I don't know if journalists want to be in a position of protecting a lawyer or two lawyers, who'll take the stand and perjure themselves, and from all we know, two of them have done so in this case. I don't know that journalists want to protect lawyers who will perjure themselves in their function as officers of the court. In fact, it seems to me, that we journalists ought to be after those lawyers more than anybody else.

HAWES: I understood Mr. Wolf to say that top newsmen are not biased, because they have nothing to sell. Sir, do they not attempt to sell themselves, through the intensity of their material?

WOLF: Perhaps you are right. I didn't say that they weren't biased. I said that they have fewer axes to grind as a group that didn't have much of an axe. Yes, everybody is competing with everybody, and a good story makes you look better than the other guys.

METHVIN: May I just add very quickly that that is the biggest factor in all of journalism, print and broadcast. You can't come out with a newspaper that says: Nothing happened today. But you have to pretend sometimes that something's bigger than what it is, because you've got to have a lead story on the front page. I've done that. We've all done that.

WOLF: Good news programs have been tried and have failed as recently as a year ago. There was a station on the West Coast that had only good news and it went out of business. So the theory that good news sells, or that we should be doing good news, is not necessarily unassailable.

METHVIN: Coming from the *Reader's Digest,* which has been condemned for too much sweetness and light, yet has the world's largest circulation, I'd say 'taint necessarily so!

Challenge IV

Is There Counter-Advertising in Broadcasting's Future?

T HAT THERE should be a critical need to weigh the advantages, or disadvantages, of counter-advertising on television might well be subsumed under the general explanatory heading, "What Banzhaf hath wrought."

But first a word about advertising as an integral part of the American system of mass communications, and its singular role in the business of broadcasting. Even before the invention of printing, the posting of informational and persuasive messages and bulletins of one kind or another probably constituted advertising—or promotion—of a rather naive kind. With the development and growth of the print media, and particularly with the revolutionary appearance of the penny press in 1833, it was inevitable that some instrumentality would have to pay a good part of the cost of newspapers and magazines if the public were to receive these media at a minimum cost. And, if the press were to develop into a free and responsible medium of communication, it was equally clear that one source of support could not be the government. Thus, advertising became the substantial support for our communications media.

With the growth of advertising, however, came challenges of institutional power and social control. And so, the question of how great an influence the advertiser would exercise, at least implicitly, in terms of control over media content became one which has involved sociologists, communications students, journalists and advertisers in endless hours of fascinating debate. The conclusions, for the most part, have been that, for the most part and with occasional exceptions, advertisers actually wield relatively little control over the media which their dollars go a long way to support. Under our system of media responsibility, that is as it should be. Broadcasters, for example, bravely presented documentary programs on the perils of cigarette smoking even while the tobacco industry was a major advertising source. And the late lamented *Life* magazine could refer critics to the celebrated case of the major movie company which withdrew its advertising from *Life* after a poor review—only to capitulate and make a chastened return.

But the nagging questions remain. How little is precious little advertiser influence, and is even that too much? How is the consumer to be adequately protected from the motivation research technicians? Critics, for example, can always dredge up the classic case of the *Playhouse 90* drama about the Nazi gas chambers and the pressure brought to bear by the sponsor which happened, curiously enough, to be a major gas association.

In any event, the role of advertising in our communications spectrum is ubiquitous and powerful, and it is more significant than ever, since the spectacularly steady growth of radio and television. Mass audiences are the ideal target for national advertisers, and the new wrinkle of demographic analysis makes the target audiences even more direct. The advertising business itself has grown, over the last century, from the modest broker who bought up space in the press and sold it to merchants, to a multi-billion dollar industry employing highly trained analytical and creative talents who use enormously sophisticated and ingenious techniques. This mode of persuasive communication, advocates of advertising insist, makes a significant contribution to the American system, moving goods from producer to consumer and exerting a healthy influence on the economy.

But prestigious critics differ. Arnold Toynbee laments the waste and frivolous character of the media and suggests that our society has more goods than it needs without the artificial stimulus created by advertising. And John Kenneth Galbraith declares that, not only does advertising create unnecessary and spurious needs, but also siphons money away from the public sector where it could be employed to better social ends. Where, in the scheme of things, does the consumer find his voice—or is he forever to remain a passive recipient of the message?

At this point, enter John Banzhaf III. Mr. Banzhaf, in 1967, exploded a bombshell. He cited the Fairness Doctrine before the FCC to show that WCBS-TV in New York City had been in violation of the doctrine in refusing time to make counter-advertising claims about the effect of cigarettes. In a surprising interpretation of fairness, the FCC agreed, and the courts upheld the Commission decision. Communications and legal experts will debate endlessly whether this was a fair application of the doctrine. In 1949, when the FCC reversed its Mayflower Decision of

1941 and permitted stations to editorialize, the Commission declared that licensees had an over-all responsibility to provide "a reasonable amount of time" for discussion of public issues and must "operate on a basis of over-all fairness," to "afford reasonable opportunity for the discussion of conflicting views on issues of public importance."

There is a philosophical case to be made for such an extension of fairness to counter-advertising. But in terms of pragmatism, the issue can only result in consequences that are pernicious. As former FCC Commissioner Lee Loevinger has indicated, to open the broadcast stations literally to the babble of counter-advertisers who will demand use would set a climate for unwarranted government intrusion and control. It would open the door to an infinity of claims by special pleaders and manipulators. And, finally, is there an advertiser in his right mind who will buy time, knowing that his presentation will be challenged by counter-claims—whether justified or not? Surely, there must be a better way to give the consumer a needed voice. To find that way is the critical challenge. But counter-advertising is not the answer.

CHALLENGE IV

Producer: Robert Kasmire (National Broadcasting Company)

Moderator: K. Sue Cailteux (University of Kentucky)

Panel: Judge Lee Loevinger (Hogan and Hartson; formerly Commissioner FCC); Robert Pitofsky (New York University; former Director, Bureau of Consumer Protection, FTC)

Question and Answer (in order): J. M. Ripley (University of Kentucky); Roderick Rightmire (Ohio University); Robert Schlater (Michigan State University); James A. Brown (University of Southern California); Eleanor Applewhaite (Columbia Broadcasting System); C. A. Kellner (Marshall University)

CAILTEUX: The Challenge is a very interesting one for us this afternoon, and probably the one that will provide for quite a lively session. The question is, "Is There Counter-Advertising in Broadcasting's Future?" There are several aspects that we need to address concerning consumerism and the right to know. What systems should there be governing the content of counter-commercials? Should there be counter-advertising, counter-commercials at all? This afternoon we have two distinguished gentlemen to present statements on the question of counter-advertising. First, Judge Lee Loevinger.

LOEVINGER: I'm not quite sure how formal this is supposed to be. I guess I'm supposed to give you a report from Washington. The latest report I have is from a survey that was made by the Commerce Department that women spend 85% of the consumer dollar, teenagers spend 15% and the rest is spent by adult males. I told them that I didn't know anything about counter-advertising and they said, that's all right, we made a survey of everybody in Washington and you're the best informed. They didn't however, deny my statement. And having read the FTC statement on the subject, I think that they're correct.

As you probably know, at the request of the IRTS some weeks ago I did write a paper on this subject. I managed to compress my thoughts into 42 pages. Then they told me, when I was to address the IRTS, that I could have fifteen or twenty minutes, so I cut it down to twenty, and I understand for this I'm supposed to give you a 3- or 4-page precis of those 20 pages. So this is a condensation of a condensation and will probably sound like it.

I think that, if you're going to talk about counter-advertising, you've got to distinguish it from a few other things. There has been a lot of activity in the FTC lately and they have engaged in some new frontiersmanship. They have come up with a doctrine of implication which Mr. Pitofsky claims isn't new, but takes on a new luster in the hands of the new, new, new FTC. Which means that advertising says not only what it explicates, but also whatever the FTC or its staff reads into it, of which perhaps the most shining example is the implied claim of uniqueness when Wonder Breads says it "Builds Healthy Bodies 10 Ways," or whatever the number it is. You can't say this unless you say that all other bread does the same thing, because otherwise people might think that you were claiming that other breads did not. The doctrine really is much broader than that. As I say, it means that any implication they care to read into the statements are also statements that must be defended by the advertiser, based on whatever evidence he has. They have created a new doctrine of substantiation, that states that you must have evidence for claims made in advertising before the claims are made. And then there is the new remedy of corrective advertising which you have probably read about, that, if there have been misrepresentations, the FTC claims the right to require advertisers to run disclaiming or self-incriminating ads saying that they have erred in the past and will sin no more than 25% of the time for the next year.

Counter-advertising is none of these, and it is something quite different. When you're talking about the doctrine of implication, substantiation, corrective advertising, the FTC is dealing with the advertiser. It has jurisdiction over the advertiser. It controls within reasonable degrees what the advertiser says or does. When you're talking about counter-advertising, you're talking about somebody other than the advertiser, somebody other than the government, somebody other than the FTC. In effect what you're saying is, well, we're so sick and tired of all this advertising, we're going to open the door and we're going to invite whoever is walking by on the street to come in and have his say, and any acid comment he has to make about the product or the advertising we will welcome, because this is a great thing.

Now, I'll give you the points that I have in reaction to that in a moment, but I suggest that this is a wonderful example of a bureaucratic product. Bureaucracy, I would define as a system for shifting the benefits of noble or altruistic projects from the intended recipients to the administrators. I think in the most literal sense this is true. If you will examine the field of welfare—I'm getting far afield here—I believe the facts are that we spend more on social work than we do on welfare recipients. I remember in my old university I used to fight with the Dean of Student Affairs. Six of them up in that office: a Dean of Men, a Dean of Women and a couple of assistants and a secretary or two and, there were fifteen thousand students enrolled in the University of Minnesota at that time. A few years ago, I was back and the enrollment had tripled from fifteen to something over forty-five thousand. The Dean of Student Affairs had a hundred and seventy-five people working there. A perfect example of bureaucracy. If the students were any better behaved, it wasn't at all noticeable. Now, I think that counter-advertising is a bureaucratic project in this sense. Unfortunately, I'm pitted against Professor Pitofsky who is not only intelligent but quite reasonable. In fact, I've been reviewing a speech he made last October at Northwestern University, and it is a very persuasive and plausible statement of what the FTC has done in the advertising field. On the whole, he presents a very reasonable case for the various things that the FTC has done. However, I think it is not without significance that he does not mention counter-advertising. First, the function that is assigned by statute and court decision, is that of policing and preventing false, deceptive or misleading advertising. This is the traditional function, the function it has performed and the function it was not intended by Congress to perform, because Congress didn't have advertising in mind at all, but a function that has been ratified since then by Congress, once the FTC assumed it. And it is unquestionably its appropriate legal function today. The second function is that of requiring disclosure of data needed or desired by some unnamed people, presumably consumers, but actually, I suppose, the FTC, in order to permit what the FTC or Professor

Pitofsky regards as intelligent consumer decision. Now, if counter-advertising relates to anything at all, it relates to this second function and it is clearly wholly unrelated to the first. If anything, it detracts from the first to some degree. Well, let me tell you some of the reasons why, and as I say, all I can do is to give you a précis of the condensation of my paper. Incidentally, if any of you want the paper, I think that the Television Information Office is going to print it, and it should be available.

The reasons urged for counter-advertising are quite logically fallacious if you attempt to analyze them. In the first place the FTC, in its statement on counter-advertising that has already been put out, says that its proposal applies only to some kinds of advertising, and then they go on to say that one of the kinds of advertising is any advertising that omits mention of negative aspects of a product. Of course, we all know that this includes all advertising. So it's inherently self-contradictory. Second, the advertising faults alleged by the FTC to require counter-advertising are not confined to broadcasting. They are not only as obvious but they are even more obnoxious than various other forms of advertising, and yet they insist that it applies only to broadcasting. The reason, obviously, is that they've got a lever here in the Fairness Doctrine. They think that they can somehow or other get the FCC to do their work for them by ordering counter-advertising. In the third place, the FTC proposal isn't really relevant to the Fairness Doctrine. The Fairness Doctrine requires specification of a controversial issue on which opposing viewpoints shall be heard. This is the very fundamental intellectual foundation of it. The FTC urges counter-advertising to permit the expression of general views without the specification of any issue, without there necessarily being an issue on which opposing views can be heard. It's quite clear that the FTC is urging counter-advertising because they're getting a little tired of the unglamourous job of policing and they're just promoting the general educational or informative function Mr. Pitofsky mentioned. Finally the FTC urges, as one of the reasons for counter-advertising, that it doesn't have adequate resources to do its job, which is about like saying that I don't have enough money so I'm privileged to hold up the next guy that comes along and lift his wallet. The FTC has exactly the amount of resources that the public, through its representatives in Congress, has allocated to its functions, and if it thinks it needs more it goes to Congress and asks for more. And the idea of saying that they are going to lift some of the resources from broadcasting or advertising in order to perform their function is just about as legitimate as saying that, since I don't have enough money, I'm privileged to borrow or steal somebody else's.

Second, counter-advertising clearly will destroy the economic foundation of broadcasting, and I can analyze for you the sources of income and the impact it would have but I don't have time. Anybody that wants it will just have to get the figures out or get hold of my paper.

Third, counter-advertising would clearly cause a deterioration of broadcasting programming and journalism. The biggest expense in broadcasting by all odds is programming, and the biggest element of expense in programming is news reporting and journalism. And by decreasing the revenue, as well as increasing the costs of broadcasting, counter-advertising is clearly going to impair the ability of broadcasting to be informative through its journalism.

Fourth, counter-advertising is unreasonably discriminatory against broadcasting. That's almost self-evident. However, one of the points that I like to make and that I haven't heard anybody respond to yet is this: if the government really thinks that counter-advertising is something great as a reply to objectionable advertising, why doesn't it do it with its own medium? Now, the government does have one medium and, in fact, there is so much objectionable advertising through its medium, Congress has found it necessary to pass a law saying that you can turn off certain kinds of direct mail advertising if you don't like it. Why don't they offer free counter-advertising through the Postal Service?

Fifth, counter-advertising would not be informative, would result in diatribe rather than dialogue. And, in order to prove this, I guess you have to look at the kind of people who are going to do it. I have had some experience with counter-advertising, and it's perfectly clear that the notion of impartial and public-spirited scientists devoting their time in laboratories to making tests which they then meander down to the local broadcasting station and report to the public is sheer idealistic. It's no such thing at all. It's frustrated law students that can't make *Law Review* and want a chance to get out and practice and get a little publicity, and aspiring politicians and other frustrated and unhappy people who are going to demand time for counter-advertising. They're down at the FCC right now. You can go down and take a poll if you don't believe me.

Sixth, counter-advertising proposals are based on the false premise that the consumer doesn't have diverse information sources now. In fact, statements about advertising products are prolific, all around us. You can subscribe to *Consumer Reports*. You can just tune into your local radio station and get all kinds of reports if you want to. But it certainly is not the case that we do not have diversity of information. The problem really is sorting out the mass of information that's available to the consumer today.

Seventh, counter-advertising would diminish the amount of useful information now available to the consumer. This is not so self-evident, but there are several reasons why it is true. Among other things, it would increase the clutter on broadcasting. It would decrease the audience's tolerance for listening to the kind of junk that you get. How many people sit and listen to long, educational lectures about the technical qualities of products? It's pretty easy to find out that you don't have much tolerance for this kind of thing.

However, even more important than this, the bullseye of counter-advertising is factual advertising. This is not a hypothetical or theoretical thing. The way to get yourself attacked is to make factual claims in advertising, and you are certain to draw attack. This is inevitable, as any intelligent lawyer or advertising agent working in the field now knows. The way to avoid it is to eliminate factual statements in advertising. So it's going to diminish the amount of information available in advertising.

Eighth, counter-advertising is unfair to the honest advertiser. If it can be assumed that there are any, they're the ones who are going to get it in the neck. We already know what this kind of thing does. We've got this wide open-door policy with respect to license oppositions and license renewals. So now what you have are license oppositions and oppositions to license renewals being filed by people who say, "Well, you people really don't have touch with the pulse of the community. In order to get in touch with the pulse of the community, you've got to have advisors who are in touch with the pulse of the community and we are obviously the pulse of the community and for $1,000 a month we will keep you in touch. Pay us, and we will withdraw our opposition."

And it's happening today. What do you think is going to happen with counter-advertising? Blackmail. Sheer blackmail. Read the history. This is what the governments used to do when they needed money a couple of hundred years ago.

Nine, counter-advertising would create new bars to innovation and improvement and the entry of improved products into the market. How do you get new products on to the market except by advertising? What kind of new products are we going to bar from the market? I'll tell you what kind of new products: ecologically good products. Advertisers who have invented or developed a way to make their product less polluting are the ones that are going to draw the first fire. The FTC has already indicated this. We've got cases in court right now. Suppose you've got a gasoline that cuts down pollution in automobiles by 50% How do you think you're going to introduce it with counter-advertising? You're not.

Ten, the purpose and effect of counter-advertising clearly is to increase government power. The government is the one that is going to control the opening and shutting of the door. They are going to control the attacks that are being made on business, that are being made on advertising without having any responsibility for what is said.

Eleven, counter-advertising will increase the power of small militant groups. I can show you the organized groups. They're all around the country. They all have their own special interests to serve, their own special axes to grind. And I mean axes. The professors who are interested in research aren't going to be there writing counter-advertising. The people who are interested in getting their faces on TV, their voices on radio, are going to be down pounding on the doors demanding it, and these militant groups are going to become the semi-official voices insofar as they are recognized by the FCC or the FTC.

Twelve, counter-advertising meets no real needs and solves no important problems. I have looked at the summary of community problems that the FCC forces broadcasters to make. I've seen whole volumes on surveys of community problems. I've read Harris, I've read Gallup, I've read all the rest of them. You can get all kinds of lists of problems starting with the Viet Nam War, inflation, race relations. You name it. I think I once made a list of a hundred of these things. I haven't seen advertising on one of them, anywhere. This is a synthetic problem.

Thirteen, on the other hand, we will have problems that are not synthetic. When you have counter-advertising it is going to create a host of new problems, including a test of free speech under the First Amendment. Clearly, the counter-advertising advocates are going to raise all kinds of controversial political and social issues. Broadcasting today is overwhelmed with demands for honest time under the Fairness Doctrine. What are they going to do with the demands that arise out of the demands for counter-advertising? How is the broadcaster going to maintain some balance? How is the advertiser who is attacked going to respond? Are we going to have counter counter-advertising? How are you going to keep these things balanced? These are just a few of the problems. It is not a response to a real problem, it's going to create real problems.

Fourteen, and this I think is quite important, counter-advertising is urged as though this were an expansion of the right of free speech. And if there is any proposal that has done violence to these sacred and revered old principles, and believe me I am not speaking ironically, this is it. The free speech advocates in this country are beginning to be like some of the Russian revolutionaries who, in the name of the proletariat, say that you can have free speech as long as you speak the truth and we will tell you what the truth is. It's just a complete misapplication of the principle.

Now let me suggest this to you. Suppose that the FCC did adopt a requirement for counter-advertising. Suppose some public-spirited engineer demanded time to show consumers that Chrysler cars really are better engineered than others. Can you imagine that he'd get time on the counter-advertising hour? Or suppose that a labor leader demanded time to urge the consumers to buy domestic rather than imported products—automobiles, textiles, cameras, whatever? Obviously, this is something labor favors. And suppose he advised people what brands in this country are manufactured by union labor under good conditions, and are well manufactured. Do you imagine that such a plea would get any time on the counter-advertising

hour? Of course not. But what about the opposite viewpoints, that automobiles are not well engineered, or that domestic products are produced
under sweatshop conditions. Certainly this is the very kind of thing that
would be welcomed by the counter-advertising sponsors. This is what
counter-advertising is.

Now suppose that some advertising advocate quarrels with this particular delineation of issues. I don't think it makes any difference. The
significant point is that, inherent in the very concept of counter-advertising,
is the idea that certain viewpoints are entitled to a government mandate
compelling their broadcast. So that the demand for counter-advertising is
not a demand for free speech at all. It's a demand that the government
sanction and mandate a particular kind of speech. This step is wrong in
principle and dangerous as a precedent. If the government can prescribe
the expression of a specific viewpoint in the economic realm, it can do so
with equal logic and perhaps greater force in the political realm.

At this point all pretense of free speech in an open society and political democracy vanishes. The whole scheme becomes apparent for what
it is, an effort to use the power of government to promote the expression
of a particular viewpoint held by a favored group. Such an effort is not
redeemed by the fact that this group today marches under the banner of
consumerism. Tomorrow that same group may march under the banner of
National Socialism, or Communism, or free love, or some other ideology
and make the same demands.

The proposal that the government mandate the broadcast of any
special viewpoint, no matter how defined, is a basically subversive one that
is inconsistent with, and dangerous to, the principles of government neutrality and the protection of free speech.

Thus, fifteen, I believe that you can understand the counter-advertising
proposal only as a political power play. When you fully examine the
counter-advertising proposal it simply makes no sense from the logical, the
economic or the sociological viewpoint, and it can be understood only in
terms of politics. The most obvious effect of counter-advertising will be to
impose substantial additional costs on broadcasting and to diminish its
revenue. This will diminish the power of broadcasting in general. It will
drive the broadcasters to a dependence on government either by way of
subsidy or support, and thus to greater subjection to government control.

The big fight today is between those advocates of a more powerful
government who see in this some vindication of their vision of individual
rights and those who believe that government today is already powerful
enough and that, if we are to preserve an open society and a democratic
political system, and a system in which an individual does in fact have the
rights that we have assumed, or have fought for, that we must have a
balance of power. And we are not going to have balanced power by

diminishing the second most powerful force in our society—that is, our organized economic groups—at the expense of the single pervasive, enduring monopoly—the government—which is a single unchallenged monopoly of power. And I suppose that basically I believe that the power of government is so great it should not be increased, except to deal with clear, demonstrated abuses. And no abuses have been charged which would warrant the dangers to the political and social system that are implicit, and explicit, in the counter-advertising proposal.

Thank you.

CAILTEUX: And now, Mr. Pitofsky.

PITOFSKY: I should start by saying that I disagree with, or would qualify, many of the things that Judge Loevinger has said. But none more than his claim that the counter-advertising proposal represents the high-water mark of bureaucracy. I've just left the Federal Trade Commission, after two-and-one-half years, and I would like to read to you a document that came across my desk during one of the first months I was there as a sample of what I regard as the high-water mark of bureaucracy.

This is a memo that I received!

> Recommendation: Lost file be closed. The subject file was opened in 1969 and involved alleged misuse of the word free. By today's standards the file would never have been opened in the first place. Apparently, shortly after opening the file was misplaced, as we can find no evidence of the proposed respondents having been contacted. In fact, the physical file itself seems to have disappeared into thin air. We have had a temporary file established to afford a physical file in which this closing memorandum and Commission action may be placed.
>
> Recommendation: For obvious reasons it is recommended that this file be closed without closing letters to the respondent.

I didn't know what to do with the memo, so I put a buck slip on it and sent it over to our Office of Policy Planning and Evaluation. Between my office and that office, it was lost, and it was only months later that I even remembered the whole incident. Now, that's bureaucracy.

Well, my time is limited, and I am sorely tempted to pick Judge Loevinger up on his fifteen points. But I'm afraid if I do that, one of the things that I'm anxious to accomplish today will be lost. I fear that what's happening with this debate over counter-advertising is that the proposal has been distorted—not necessarily by Judge Loevinger, incidentally. He disagrees with it, but does not distort it. But others in the industry have distorted it to the point where I wonder if informed people in this industry have any idea what the proposal was in the first place.

Let me state a few premises. If you don't go along with them, you probably cannot agree with the counter-advertising proposal, and that's not unreasonable, because I do regard it as a very controversial proposal about which reasonable people can differ. These are the premises:

First, that broadcasting on radio and TV is not a business like that of selling soap or gasoline. It is a business that must operate in the public interest. It's licensed to operate in the public interest, and in that respect is different—even from other forms of publication like newspapers and magazines. Now, that's the position taken by Congress in the Communications Act, and it has repeatedly been ratified by the courts in review of those Communications Acts. This special obligation to operate in the public interest arises, of course, in return for the right to use a public asset—the airwaves. Second, it would not be justifiable, in the name of the public interest, to impose any program on radio and TV that would undermine its economic viability in any substantial way. If counter-advertising is a threat to the economic base of radio and TV, it ought not to be adopted. Of course, my argument is going to be that it is not nearly so costly as to threaten in any way this economic base. Third, and this is crucial, much advertising today touches on some of the most controversial matters in the area of public debate. Thus, tobacco companies are back on the air selling little brown cigarettes and calling them cigars, as if smoking were a fun-filled, pleasant, adult thing to do. These advertisers do not mention, however, that smoking is a road to early death. Phosphate detergents are being sold with the argument that it's very important to get clothes "whiter than white" and to eliminate "ring around the collar." I have nothing against that. But, many people feel that there is a direct connection between phosphates in detergents and the so-called "death" of Lake Erie. Leaded gasolines are sold with all sorts of claims about how efficient they are, but with few remarks about the contribution of leaded gasoline, if any, to air pollution. Drugs are sold constantly with appeals that they will pep you up or calm you down, wake you up, put you to sleep, help you gain weight, or lose weight. Many feel that there is a connection between these kinds of appeals to mood enhancement and drug abuse problems in this country. Some foods are sold which are devoid of any nutritional value. Jean Mayer, one of the most respected nutritionists in the country, has suggested that there is a direct inverse correction between the amount of money spent on advertising and nutritional value—for example citing candy, snack foods and soda pop which are highly advertised, but lack nutritional benefit, as opposed to fresh vegetables, fresh fruits, etc., which are hardly ever advertised on TV or radio.

I would urge that these are important questions of public policy. Right now, people who sell these products have a monopoly in discussing these issues. These marketers are in sixty million homes every night, selling their products, and yet they are understandably silent about the adverse effects, about the hidden costs, of their products. Finally, commercial advertising on TV presents a distorted, one-sided view of the public questions that are implicit in commercial advertising. Judge Loevinger talked about balance of power, and talked about the government favoring one view or another. I would suggest that, because the government does not make any sort of counter-advertising opportunities available, what you have now is a one-sided view. What you have now on these public questions is the view of people who sell products. I do not oppose advertising on TV. I think it must remain on TV. But to urge that counter-advertising would unbalance the process seems to me to be ludicrous.

Now, what was the Commission's proposal? First of all, it urged that those who can afford to pay for counter-advertising be allowed access to the medium on a non-discriminatory basis. In short, that the networks not discriminate against advertising on the basis of its content. Now, I don't know what Judge Loevinger would say about paid counter-advertising. Many of those who oppose free counter-advertising also oppose paid counter-advertising for reasons that are beyond me. It seems to me what they are saying is that, if you are selling soap and gasoline, you are the backbone of the American economy, but if you want to buy some time on TV in the public interest to point out the hazards of certain kinds of soaps and gasoline, you must be some sort of fanatic. It says something about how we define "fanatics" in this country. The Commission went on, however, to say that, to be practical about it, we must recognize that there is not a great deal of money available for paid counter-advertising and therefore some amount of advertising ought to be made available free. It came out against back-to-back commercials and against a ratio response —for example against a one-to-six proportion—but instead suggested that a block of time be made available—and at one point the statement suggested fifteen minutes a week. The Chairman and I, before various groups, have talked about a half hour a week. I mention that because I'm going to grant one of Judge Loevinger's points, and that is that much commercial advertising—not all, but much—has public questions implicit in it. But I don't see that as a threat to the economic viability of broadcasting, because only fifteen minutes a week will be made available for counter-advertising opportunities. Even fifteen minutes a week is not costless, and therefore could threaten the economic viability of some small affiliates in some towns in this country. In that instance, I would suggest the FCC make an exception for counter-advertising for those affiliates which, in three of the last five years, made a profit that averages, say, less than 1% or 2%. In other words, put out of the picture the possibility that any network or affiliate will be driven to the wall by counter-advertising opportunities.

Now, what are the arguments against free counter-advertising on a "block-of-time" basis? I will try to touch on a few of the principal ones. First, it is suggested that counter-advertising will undermine the economic base of broadcasting. Well, I say again, we're talking about fifteen minutes. It could come out of spot-announcement time. It could come out of special events programming. I think it's really impossible that fifteen minutes are going to drive the networks to the wall. The argument occasionally is made that, if counter-advertising were to appear, all the companies in a particular product group would desert television, rather than allow themselves to be exposed to messages that undermine the validity of their sales pitch. If that were true, I think that would be a powerful and telling argument against counter-advertising. But it is almost certainly not true. Who would leave television, even in the face of counter-advertising, if his competitor stayed on selling the product? Would any one cigarette company leave if the others stayed? Would any one soap company leave if the others stayed? So the possibility of companies deserting only arises if they all leave together. Well, they can't agree to leave together, because that's a violation of the antitrust laws. And if you have no faith in the current Department of Justice bringing a suit like that, you need not depend on it, because there is a private antitrust right of action for boycott. It's conceivable, I suppose, that the message the counter-advertisers were going to introduce would be so devastating that every company, independently, would abandon TV. Now, nothing like that has ever happened before, and I suppose that I would take the position that if the counter-advertising message really is that dreadful, people are entitled to hear it.

Judge Loevinger says that, if we have counter-advertising, all sorts of nuts, fanatics, kooks, and unhappy people will have an opportunity to be on TV. I would grant that. If there are widespread counter-advertising opportunities, some careless and foolish people will misuse the privilege. Now, that's not what happened with respect to cigarettes. Judge Loevinger kept referring to the fact that we've had experience with counter-advertising, but in fact the only commercial counter-advertising that we have had on a broad scale was the American Cancer Society's campaign against smoking. And except for people in the tobacco business, I know of no one who thinks that they said things about smoking that were unfair, deceptive or misleading. The truth about counter-advertising with respect to cigarettes is that it was the only time in this century in which per capita cigarette consumption declined, and for good reason, because the same techniques used to sell the product were used to unsell the product. That's what advertisers are really worried about, that counter-advertising is effective, not that it will be in the hands of fanatics and kooks. But more important than that, as I've said in response to Judge Loevinger's points before, I think his argument is not really with counter-advertising but with the First Amendment. What he is saying in many different ways in his fifteen points is that it's dangerous to let those irresponsible types get on the air. If he were back in New England in the Seventeenth century and someone proposed a New England town meeting, he would say: You mean everybody is going to get up and talk? Everybody? You mean the speaker doesn't have to own a factory? He doesn't have to be the banker, or the butcher or the candlestick maker? Don't you understand what irresponsible people will get up and say things if that happens? Of course I understand that, but that situation accords with my view of the First Amendment. To talk about commercial TV now as being a fair and impartial and balanced contribution to a sensible discussion of these issues is unrealistic.

The argument is often made; what do you need counter-advertising for? People know all of this information already. First of all, I would think those that make that argument would be a little uncomfortable saying on the one hand that it will drive all these advertisers off the air, but on the other hand everybody knows these facts already. If they knew it already, I would assume it wouldn't have that kind of dramatic impact. In any event, that argument has been made and rejected before. It was made with respect to cigarettes by the tobacco industry and the courts found, quite simply, that massive pro-cigarette advertising more than outweighed the occasional news notice that the Surgeon General had made another study and found that cigarettes contributed to health problems. When was the last time that you saw a news special that really stepped on some major advertiser's toes with respect to phosphates in soap, or the lead in gasoline, or empty calories? Now I don't mean to say it never happens, because I think the networks are quite responsible, and do a marvelous job of reporting the news and covering special events. But the fact is that eight minutes an hour, every night in sixty million American homes, products are being sold, and possible arguments against the use of those products are infrequently made.

Let me pick up another few points. Judge Loevinger said that counter-advertising will drive factual advertising off the air and all we will get are jingles and ditties. Well, that was the same argument that was made two-and-a-half years ago when the FTC embarked on its campaign to require substantiation of ads and corrective advertising and came up with more stringent limitations on the definition of truth and relevance. Every study indicates that contrary to those dire predictions, there is more straight-up, factual advertising on TV now than there was two-and-a-half years ago. That's not because of the FTC or its progress, it's because advertisers understand where their interests are and must respond to the consumers' demands not to be treated like children; as a result they are responding with more sensible advertising data.

Judge Loevinger says that counter-advertising will bar new products. I don't understand that. First of all, I wonder what new products he has in mind: little cigars, vaginal sprays, chocolate marshmallow cereals—these are some of the new products that I see on TV. More importantly, the FTC's statement pointed out that rarely would counter-advertising be available against particular brands, but only against categories of products. And if, in fact, there is a plausible case that some new product category has hidden health hazards or environmental hazards—for example, if there is a plausible case, as I think there is, that this new little cigar is just as dangerous to health as cigarettes—it seems to me that people ought to have an opportunity to hear that.

Finally Judge Loevinger points out that there will be difficult administrative problems in handling counter-advertising. I agree. I think that's where the strongest case can be made against it. You will have many applicants seeking fifteen minutes of time and, even conceding a good deal of discretion to the affiliates on whom they will allow on the air and what kind of substitution they will require, there will be difficulties. But that's the price that you pay for a multiplicity of voices in a society. The *New York Times* has that problem. Every time Albert Shanker places a column in the Sunday *Times,* challenging all sorts of individuals and doctrines with respect to education, the *Times* reviews letters from people asking for an opportunity to reply. And they've got to select among the people who ask for that opportunity, either giving them response time or access to the Letters to the Editor column. Right now the networks are doing very little of that sort of thing.

I don't believe that if we have no counter-advertising, the free speech traditions of this country are in any serious danger. I also doubt that if we do have counter-advertising, the networks and the economic viability of communications are in any serious danger. What you really have here is a proposal which you will go along with or not depending on how you feel about free and open debate. Most important, how concerned you are as a citizen about a growing problem in this country—and that is that access to the means of communication and opportunity to argue effectively is frequently in the hands of only those people who can pay for it. And I believe that is a problem.

CAILTEUX: Thank you, Mr. Pitofsky.

CHALLENGE IV: QUESTION AND ANSWER SESSION

CAILTEUX: Now please, questions for the panel.

RIPLEY: Mr. Pitofsky, in the past when controversial issues have arisen about advertising, we have taken care of them by such things as the Flammable Products Act, the Wool Labeling Act and so on. At this point, I'm in some confusion as to what your view is about counter-advertising with respect to the normal treatment of legislative and adjudicative treatment? Would you tell me how this fits in with that pattern?

PITOFSKY: I don't see counter-advertising as a substitute, either for the FTC's jurisdiction to challenge advertising as misleading or unfair, or of any agency's jurisdiction to protect the public from dangerous products such as flammable fabrics. I think the problem is that a good deal of advertising talks about the virtues of products but, of course, does not talk about their adverse consequences or costs. The failure to disclose adverse aspects is, in most situations, not unfair or deceptive. I can't see the Commission bringing a case against all of the cereal and snack food companies, challenging them for failure to disclose a lack of calories or nutritional value in a product. What I'm getting at, and this is partly in answer to Judge Loevinger's point, is that I think counter-advertising has been misunderstood as an effort by the Commission to pass the buck to another agency to do its job. I don't think that's the case at all. It's an effort to get another agency to deal with problems that do not fall within the jurisdiction of any present agency.

RIGHTMIRE: Mr. Pitofsky, who will make the decisions? You alluded to the stations making the decisions. This kind of thing obviously has caused lots of problems in the past, in the appeal to the Commission and into the courts and what not. Do you see it strictly as a station problem, where each station makes a decision on whether to allow a counter-ad?

PITOFSKY: Yes, that is to my mind the key question. Most commentators, and I agree with this, would have the decision made by the local stations and would accord them a very generous degree of discretion, so that it would be rare that their decisions would be overturned on appeal. You would have a system where the FCC, as part of the licensing process, made affiliates aware that part of their responsibility was to make some time available. I think fifteen minutes a week is reasonable. I can imagine a program in which that responsibility could be discharged through spot announcements time, such as the "Smokey the Bear" time that we see now, enhanced public interest broadcasting and so on. The decision would be made by the affiliates.

RIGHTMIRE: You mentioned the public service announcements. Let me ask you just one other thing. Would public service announcements be subject to counter-advertising, or just commercials?

PITOFSKY: Let me put it this way. Neither one would have to trigger reply time. That was the decision of the court in *Banzhaf,* where the Court rejected the tobacco industry request for reply time to answer the Cancer Society.

RIGHTMIRE: Savings Bonds don't strike me as being a particularly good investment, you know, if you're to look at the real interest return. We have been led to believe by advertising that they are. There is some deception in those public service spots.

PITOFSKY: Let me finish my prior answer. I think that it ought to be in the discretion, but not required, of the affiliates to make that block of time available to companies who claim that they were ill-treated or maligned in a counter-advertising spot. But I do not believe that advertisers have a *right* to reply time. If that point is vague, and it probably is vague under FCC law, then I would urge the FCC to suspend the Fairness Doctrine as it applies to counter-advertising, or to assert, in connection with counter-advertising, that it will not trigger reply time.

SCHLATER: I would like to ask Judge Loevinger to ask himself the question that he would most like to have asked in reply to Mr. Pitofsky.

LOEVINGER: Thank you. You will make a good counter-advertiser. The single point that I am most concerned about is stuff about free speech. And Mr. Pitofsky, who I said is not only intelligent but reasonable and eminently fair, and highly plausible and persuasive, said that I am the one who is against free speech for everyone—I'd get up in the Town Hall and have people silenced because they are irresponsible. Nonsense. Actually this implies what is factually a wholly false premise, that broadcasting has limited the rights of free speech. Now, I happen to have investigated this subject. There has never been a time in the history of this or any other nation on the face of the earth—and we have more people clamoring to be heard today than ever before—when so many people have had so much access to so much communication. There is scarcely a large city in the world without an open mike program on radio. I've seen TV stations pull this sort of thing. Every kook and nut in the country today can, and half of them do, get on broadcasting. There is no lack of free speech. I am not opposed to it. I have argued in the FCC that this sort of thing was good. My colleagues were the ones who were arguing for more responsibility. I am all in favor of it, but don't ever lose sight of this when people start talking about counter-advertising or you've lost 50% or more of the fight. This is not free speech. This is not just anybody who can say anything. That I am in favor of, and will defend to the last gasp of the last kook. This is government-mandated and selected speech. The questions that have been asked, and Mr. Pitofsky's difficulty in dealing with them shows we are going to have very calm, very nice, very reasonable people, at least until we get an unfriendly Administration, sitting there and deciding who shall be heard and what shall be said. This is government-mandated expression of a specified viewpoint. That's what I am objecting to, and anybody who says you can do fifteen minutes a week is out of his cotton-picking mind. Mr. Pitofsky obviously hasn't read the cases. The FCC suspend the Fairness Doctrine? The court has told them they can't. They tried to confine it. They said it applies only to cigarettes. The court says you can't do it. And fifteen minutes a week is going to be like telling an alcoholic that he can have a half a pint a week. It can't be done. This is just sheer insanity, and once you open it up the courts won't let you. It's going to be wide open, and you're going to be inundated with some of the worst hogwash you ever heard. But it's going to be government-certified hogwash. It isn't going to be free speech. We've got free speech now. Believe me, this is going to drive free speech off the air, because they aren't going to have time, they aren't going to have the money, they aren't going to have the facilities to sustain the kind of free open kind of broadcasting we now have. They aren't going to have open mike programs. They're going to have their hands full coping with the kind of counter-advertising that is going to result once you get this started on the basis that the FTC and Mr. Pitofsky are talking about. This is going to kill free speech.

PITOFSKY: Two quick points, if I may. One, Judge Loevinger says there is completely open access now. Let me point out what happened when a public interest group in Washington made a 30-second witty and amusing spot commercial with Burt Lancaster. In effect, it said what FDA panels have been saying for some time, and that is that combination analgesics are irrational and that aspirin is aspirin. I take it you've all seen analgesic advertising more than once or twice on TV. When was the last time you saw anywhere—news, special events, spot announcement—someone making the point that combination analgesics are irrational? When the public interest group went around and tried to get that commercial on TV, they placed a few spots on the West Coast and placed a few in New York, but by and large they were refused an opportunity to get on TV. Now, you may call that free speech, but I say that's a one-sided street in which all of the information is coming from those who have an economic axe to grind. The second point—that you will never stop at fifteen minutes—I don't know how to answer. Obviously if the pendulum swings too far, a counter-advertising program will be unwise. But right now the pendulum doesn't swing at all. It's at zero. And what Mr. Loevinger is saying is that, if you give them fifteen minutes a week, it will go all the way to the top of the meter. I don't see how he can predict that.

BROWN: I'm very sympathetic with the problems of freedom of people and the media, and the two views that you have expressed on this, and yet I'm tangled, as I was with prime time access, with the regulatory quagmire that immediately comes rushing in. I think there should be local and live programming and creative innovation, but the prime time access is the regulatory route to disaster. And here is fifteen minutes a week, if you can hold it, which I question. Will it be prime time, fringe time, sign-off time? What about those several stations that make 1% to 3% margin? Ok, they get waived. What about 5% to 20%? What about the 0-and-0 with 35%? They get thirty minutes, and you end up with all this nit-picking and, like prime time access, it's a disaster. And then again, how do you select those that want the time and those that feel they should also have time? I think it's just a maze of problems, but I would like your reaction to it.

PITOFSKY: I agree with you. There will be a maze of problems and I suppose there is a maze of problems when a municipality has to decide which of ten applicants is going to hold a parade down Main Street on the Fourth of July. Now, there is one way of solving that problem— nobody holds a parade. And, there's another way of solving the problem. The only one who parades is the fellow who pays the most. That's our present system with respect to access to TV. I am suggesting that it is worthwhile to have these administrative problems in order to allow some dissenters to get a word in edgewise.

On your first point about prime time, the Commission proposal was that it would have to be some form of prime time. You couldn't put a counter-advertiser on at three o'clock in the morning, because the counter-advertisers want access to what the advertisers want, which is an audience, and the audience is there at certain hours. Which time it is, whether it comes out of special events programming or whether it comes out of news or whether it's 6:45 or 7:15, I think the answer there must be left to the discretion of the affiliates. The program is not government mandating a specific program, it would be the FCC telling these affiliates that part of their responsibility to hold these licenses is to make some sort of counter-advertising available, with a good deal of discretion in their hands.

APPLEWHAITE: Mr. Pitofsky, I hesitate to say before I get your answer, I'm with CBS. I have my main problem with the limit to fifteen minutes and a number of other things that arise in the context that this proposal was made by the FTC in the FCC's Fairness inquiry. I'm not altogether clear from what you've said today whether you feel that it is a purely public interest concept or it is a function of the Fairness Doctrine. And I ask the question because to me, if it is a function of the Fairness Doctrine, then leaving aside the administrative quagmire, I just don't see how you can say fifteen minutes. How can you say it doesn't go to specific brands? Now, I would like to clarify what you think the theoretical basis of counter-advertising is?

PITOFSKY: That's a very discerning and perceptive question, if I may say so. The Commission's statement was very careful, if you read it closely, not to go off on Fairness Doctrine grounds, but rather on a general public interest standard—the responsibility of the networks and the industry to continue to use the public airwaves. Therefore, it is not a Fairness Doctrine program in my opinion. Of course, it is a program that has First Amendment overtones to it, but it was not intended to fall squarely within the Fairness Doctrine.

QUESTION: As the term "advertising" implies urging the public to buy, do you see counter-advertising as not only informing, but actually urging the public *not* to buy?

PITOFSKY: Well, I would not attempt to tell the counter-advertisers what to say within the limits of the laws of libel and slander. I suspect that counter-advertising frequently has a combined function. For example, what did the American Cancer Society do with respect to cigarettes? They were telling people not to buy cigarettes, but they may be interpreted as telling people to buy low tar and nicotine cigarettes—in which case they're really coming out in favor of one brand as opposed to another. I would think that both of those functions could occur, and I find it hard to predict whether you will have most of your counter-advertising urging people to do without a product as opposed, for example, to telling them to buy soap with low phosphate instead of high phosphate, or gasoline with low lead instead of high lead?

KELLNER: Mr. Pitofsky, in line with what you said just a moment before your last response, it seems to me that, inherent in the proposals of the Commission is basically a distrust of those who can advertise because they have the money to advertise. There is a distrust in the claims of advertising. Does it make you uncomfortable that you are only tackling the problem of advertising on radio-television? What about other media, and if it is valid for one medium why not the other medium?

PITOFSKY: Let me deal with your premise first, because I would not subscribe to that. I think if the problem is lack of truth in advertising, the way to deal with that is for the Federal Trade Commission to exercise its jurisdiction under Section 5. I think the problem arises because advertisers, quite understandably, trumpet the virtues of their products and no one ought to expect them to talk also about the hidden costs. I don't expect the tobacco companies to talk about cancer in their advertising. It would be absurd for them to do so. On the other hand, it seems to me that people are entitled to a warning in that respect. So it's not really a lack of trust. It's endemic in the system that hidden adverse attributes will be submerged in advertising, and I think those ought to be brought to the surface.

On the question of discrimination against radio and TV as against print. Remember, I started off by citing a premise here, which is that radio and TV are different. That's a decision made by Congress and ratified by the Courts repeatedly. I can go through the theories here. Judge Loevinger, believe me, can offer some good arguments challenging those theories. My answer to you is that I am a little uncomfortable with radio and TV being singled out, but I think the case for doing it is valid. There is limited spectrum, which means that only a limited number of people have access, as opposed to the newspapers and magazines where the opportunities are more varied. There is an enormous difference in audience and impact; sixty million people every night in their homes being sold on products. And the licensing system which is there and has been confirmed by Congress. The courts have said radio and TV are ubiquitous. It's in the air. You can't avoid it. It's not like turning your head away from a page of advertising copy in a magazine. That's the case. I don't think it's beyond challenge, but I think it's adequate to justify regulating in the public interest. And I repeat that the Congress and the courts have repeatedly made a judgment that this is not discrimination, it's a distinction based on a difference.

LOEVINGER: I don't think that's quite true. I don't know of any case that holds this. The courts have done a lot of talking about the necessity of licensing, and to deny a license to one and grant it to another is not to deny First Amendment rights to the man who doesn't have a license. In the *Red Lion* case, the Supreme Court validated the Fairness Doctrine in quite different circumstances in respect to quite a different situation. The United States Court of Appeals hasn't squarely faced it. The case that it considered was the *Banzhaf* case where Judge Bazelon, the Chief Judge of the U.S. Court of Appeals and one of those who would by any standard be regarded as the most liberal, has been the leader of the so-called liberal wing of the Court. Judge Bazelon, in a recent case, has written a very long, strong dissenting opinion saying that he has been sitting on the Court for these many years and he has now just begun to see some of these Fairness Doctrine cases come to the courts, and he has concluded from his viewpoint that the Fairness Doctrine is an abridgement of the right of free speech. He now thinks that perhaps it is misconceived and perhaps we should reconsider whether we have a Fairness Doctrine altogether. I believe that Mr. Pitofsky is such an eminently reasonable guy, I haven't the slightest doubt that if he were in charge it would be a fairly, reasonably administered program, no matter how bad it was in conception. And I've had so many arguments of this kind. I used to argue with Commissioner Cox all the time, and the basic argument that he is urging is this: we have so much speech in broadcasting and it is so influential we can't really permit it to be wholly free. Newspapers aren't that influential, print isn't that influential, mail isn't that influential. But broadcasting is influential, because sixty million people watch TV every night, just think of it. Now really, what these people are asking for is not access. There is access. Don't kid yourself. I could prove mathematically and quantitatively there is more access for more people to express more divergent viewpoints about more things, including all the counter-advertising points that he mentioned. There is more on broadcasting mathematically than there has ever been anywhere on any medium at any time in world history or anywhere on the face of the earth. What they want is audience. What they want is prime time, a VHF-TV network audience. Now the real irony of the whole business is they can't get it. No way. They can get government mandated, government certified speech. But can you imagine what your fifteen-minute Pitofsky-sponsored quarter hour is going to be? The real objection is that it's going to create the worst water shortage you ever heard of.

Address by Clay T. Whitehead

Director, Office of Telecommunications Policy, The White House

Introduction: Aaron Cohen (National Broadcasting Company)
Question and Answer (in order): Peter K. Pringle (University of Florida); Richard B. Barnhill (Syracuse University); Robert D. Kasmire (National Broadcasting Company); Charles S. Steinberg (Hunter College); Stephen Labunski (Chuck Blore Creative Services); Richard Pinkham (Ted Bates & Company)

WHITEHEAD: Let me talk first about broadcasting. If you go back and read the debates in the Congress, and throughout the United States about broadcasting, you'll find that it started off as something the telephone company was playing with. It later became the broadcasting service we know today. Originally, it was viewed as an entertainment medium, hardly anything to which freedom of speech applied or hardly anything to which freedom of the press applied. There was actually quite a divided debate in the Congress about whether freedom of speech and freedom of the press were even relevant to a discussion of broadcasting. We have, in effect, nationalized the airways and said that the Congress of the United States, through the FCC, is the custodian of those airways on behalf of the public. As a result of this position, the following question arises: How do we apply the First Amendment to somebody who is using a public resource and using it on the behalf of the public? Now "freedom of speech," as I understand it, means that you're free to say whatever you damn well please, and "freedom of the press" means you're free to print whatever you damn well please (with some exceptions as in reference to obscenity and libel and incitement to riot). But generally, you have the freedom, and we (the government) have the vexing problem of being the custodian over the channels. People come to the Government and say: "I'm unhappy with the way that channel is being used. You don't have enough liberal programming on . . . that broadcaster is a "red neck" . . . conservative . . . or under the guise of a religion, he is promoting some far-out liberal cause and I don't like it . . . and I don't think he's serving the public's interest, and the Congress said he was supposed to serve the public interest and the Congress said that the FCC is supposed to decide if he is, and I'm here to tell you that I don't like it."

Now, what does the Congress—the FCC—do? Well, the first thing they do is to start abridging the free speech rights and the free press rights of the broadcaster. Now, within reason, I think that we all accept that that's the way things have to work. The trouble is that, from time to time, you find processes where things are carried to some kind of logical or emotional political extreme, and it gets very hard to be reasonable. Precedents are built up. Courts act on the basis of precedents, and we have found ourselves in a situation where the FCC simply interprets what the public interest means in each case. Remember, this is not particularly evil. It is citizens coming to their Government asking to be heard, and wanting to know how their airways are being used. We end up with a situation where the FCC, through an accumulation of case law (which nobody understands, much less the FCC), dictates the kind of television programming we're going to have in this country.

When you get into the Fairness Doctrine, which after all is derived simply from the idea that a broadcaster ought to be reasonably fair, the problems begin. How many sides are there to the fluoride toothpaste controversy? There are the toothpaste forces; there are the fluoride forces; there are the anti-fluoride forces. Now, are those three sides to a controversy? Or do we merge the fluoride forces with the toothpaste forces? It may sound silly, but the problem is that these issues are brought by the people to their Government. The FCC makes decisions. The Courts follow the precedents they have established. When the Courts start making decisions, they start establishing new precedents. What I'm trying to sketch for you is a situation where, with fairly liberal backing (I use that with a little "l," not a capital "L") from the Supreme Court, the FCC has taken unto itself a tremendous amount of power over broadcasting, programming and the day-to-day activities. The people who come to the FCC are unhappy with big, powerful, rich broadcasters. The only way that they can be effectively heard on our electronic mass media, is at the dispensation of the broadcaster, or by getting the FCC to give them some access. And everyone likes to think that his cause is a good cause. Some people are interested in the problems of the black community and feel that they have been misrepresented. To most reasonable people, it would seem like a fairly good idea to schedule more black programming. The trouble is that when the Government begins to establish that kind of procedure, it also *has* to handle it in a fairly equitable manner. Obviously, the "red neck" who thinks that blacks are an inferior people, is entitled to his point of view even though most of society disagrees with him. After all, the purpose of Government is to protect minority points of view, and suddenly we have the "red neck" being viewed as the minority, and the Government protecting him. And then, suddenly, people don't like that either. What I'm trying to sketch is the difficulty the government has in making these decisions. The Government can try to make them in a very even-handed way, in a way that reflects the political dispositions of the Administration in power. There are a lot of people around who would like to suggest that this Administration would like to do precisely that. I suppose in his heart-of-hearts every politician dreams of a media structure of press and broadcasting which tells him how wonderful he is. But I think that most reasonable people would conclude that most administrations simply would not want to do that. Most administrations believe in the principles of free flow of information, believe in the idea of free speech, and believe that the Government should not be arbiter of these freedoms. Government should not be the place where it's decided who says what, who gets to say what, or what issues are important. When my office was established some two-and-a-half years ago, we identified this as one of the most significant, long-range problems facing broadcasting. We *continue* to think that it is one of the most significant, long-range problems facing broadcasting. We think that, to the maximum extent possible, Government should get *out* of some of the things it's doing and we are perfectly prepared to advance legislative proposals and recommendations to the FCC that will lessen the Government's power over the broadcasting media. I know that seems very hard to reconcile with what you read in the press these days. They say that what we really want to do is to *control* the media, and we are soundly criticized for offering informal criticism. The dark hand of Government is licensing and regulating the media and somehow, Spiro Agnew and Clay Whitehead are going to go talk to Dean Burch (in the dark of the night) and tell him to do bad, illegal things to reflect our political philosophy.

Now, let's suppose that's true, for the moment. It's not, but let's suppose it were. Then, it seems to me, that Clay Whitehead would be arguing that the FCC should continue to have the kinds of powers that it has. An FCC that has the power to require of all broadcast stations in the country to program so many hours of news, so many hours of religious programs, so many hours of public service announcements (for the public interest), is also an FCC that is perfectly capable of requiring two hours of local news for every hour of national network news. An FCC that is capable of passing a Prime-Time Access rule is an FCC that also has the power (and the Courts are going to uphold it) to *expand* that Prime-Time rule, thereby taking more time away from the networks. It is an FCC that is going to have the power to decide what programming to put into that access period. Why, I ask you, did the FCC decide that *Wild Kingdom* deserved a waiver, and the Olympics did not? What about some other series that were not granted waivers? In fact, the Government is making value judgments on the kind of programming that is good for the people in this country.

If we wanted to use our political position to appoint men to the FCC who are willing to violate the law, who are willing to manipulate all this confusion in our behalf, I suppose we could do it. But I know this President well enough to know that that's not what he wants to do. I know that he sincerely wants to make a distinction between the Government and the media as absolute as possible. He believes very firmly that there is no role in this country for a blurred distinction between the Government and the media. When the two become intermingled (as they are in so many other countries), the result is blandness. We also find that the Government attempts to use the media to put out messages that it thinks are good. The industry begins to cozy up to the Government that is regulating it. The President has stated to me, and to broadcasters, that the ultimate result of positive censorship is the legal power for negative censorship. The fact that we don't care to use that kind of censorship, doesn't mean that the precedents aren't going to grow. We're not going to move in a direction that will let another President do that kind of thing. We feel very strongly that the question of censorship, the question of the freedom of the media, should not be addressed from the standpoint of the political philosophy of the Administration in power. The discussion should be about the tools of the censorship, about the tools that the government uses to control the media. The fact is that we have been moving for a very long time (under the FCC and the Courts), toward a situation where the tools of censorship—both positive and negative—are taking shape. We think that we've got to reverse that. I've given a number of speeches that I suppose you have read, and we've sketched some directions that we think make sense in an effort to minimize the Government's intrusion into the broadcast media's operation. That means reducing the number of controls that the Federal Government has over broadcasting. They have to be reduced if we want free speech and free press to mean anything. They have to be reduced if we want the political process and the editorial process to be kept separate. We can't do that over night and we can't do it ourselves. There are a lot of people who believe that the Government should have firm controls over the broadcasting industry. A lot of people believe that those controls work to their political benefits, and they are going to be opposing some of the steps we're taking.

About a year-and-a-half ago, I proposed that the Fairness Doctrine be done away with. At the same time, I proposed a new license renewal legislation to extend the term and to provide more stability to broadcasters. I suggested that we move in the direction of less detailed government control over broadcast programming, and in particular, begin to de-regulate radio. The FCC is beginning to review its regulations in radio. They are finding that they can repeal some regulations because they are unnecessary, and the broadcasting industry might do a better job without them. A number of Congressmen and Senators (some of whom we've worked with and encouraged) are submitting resolutions and bills into the Congress urging the FCC to pursue this radio de-regulation process further. The FCC is discovering that they can get some pats on the back and some positive press by moving away from controls of the media. Progress is slow, but the trend is in the right direction. Since I have spent some time working with other regulatory agencies in Washington, I can safely say that this is the only regulatory agency where you see that kind of trend.

I don't see any place for the Fairness Doctrine in the kind of media structure or the kind of society we have. But it's there, and it's upheld by the Supreme Court. Legislation to do away with the Fairness Doctrine, I think, would be doomed to failure. The FCC should conduct a thorough inquiry into the Fairness Doctrine, clarify it, limit its scope, and minimize its opportunities for capricious or simply arbitrary application. Under Commissioner Wiley, that inquiry is going on, and I understand that they will be making some proposals in the not-too-distant future.

The Government really has the power of life and death over the broadcast industry where license renewals are concerned. We have proposed legislation that would extend the license terms to five years. It would give the broadcaster more time and he would come up for government review less often. In that legislation, there is a prohibition against the FCC adopting any preconceived program standards. It would mean that the FCC could not set minimum percentages or minimum standards in certain categories for favorite programming. An intrusion into the editorial process is a power that the Federal Government should not have, and we propose to take it away from the Federal Government. There are some other aspects of that bill. I think the most important is in judging a licensee who is coming up to have his license renewed. The burden of proof, if he is doing a bad job, should fall on the person who is trying to prove it. Most broadcasters are good businessmen, they are members of their community, and they try to do a good job. Anybody who want to use the power of the Government to take away that man's vehicle for doing business (namely his frequency), should have to prove that the Government should take that drastic step. Now, many people are upset about that; they say that it is heartless, that it means that the community doesn't have any effective recourse against the broadcaster. I think that's nonsense, because if a broadcaster is doing a really bad job then you should be able to make a case. If he's just doing a mediocre job, then we shouldn't use this tremendous, heavy hand of the Federal Government in dealing with freedom of speech and freedom of press. Finally, most importantly, we're taking two things into consideration here. The public should have the right to come to their Government and get recourse from a bad broadcaster, but the Government should not use these tools in a capricious way, and *that's* the situation that we're trying to avoid. So, the picture that I'd like to paint for you is this: progress in the direction of a broadcast media structure that, from a First Amendment standpoint, is just as free as the print press and the print media. The First Amendment ought to apply fully and completely to the broadcasting media. As a result of the license renewal process, and the nationalization of the airways, we can't change the structure over night. We may not even be able to move completely to the ideal, but we should recognize that we've gone too far the other way. The proposals that we've made, the progress that we are making, is a very constructive first step.

Let me now stop, and talk about cable television for a minute. I'm in an awkward position when talking about cable, because I'm on the verge of sending my report to the President, and I'm perpetually having to say that I can't divulge what is recommended until I've talked to the President. I can tell you some of the principles that guide us and, hopefully, when you see what we've proposed, you can evaluate it fairly.

The basic consideration of the Cabinet Committee making the recommendations to the President on cable television was the First Amendment: that the dilemma, the dichotomy, the mess that we've gotten ourselves into in regulating broadcasting, should be avoided if at all possible, with cable. We look at the potential of cable television (technically and economically) and we see that it can become a tremendous new medium in this country. We see the opportunity for many, many channels—not the few channels that are in the communities now—but twenty, fifty or a hundred channels. And again, properly structured, the number of channels in use should be basically a supply-and-demand situation, not a matter of Government fiat.

Cable television does not use the airways. It can supply a multitude of channels. So, we come down to the basic concept that the use of cable television channels ought to be basically like the use of printing presses. Some regulations are necessary, but no questions of governmental licenses should be used on those channels. There should be no need to come to the Federal Government and ask for dispensation to speak, no need to come to the Federal Government and ask for dispensation to run a crazy, left-biased news show (or a nutty religious right-wing show), just go and pay your money and do your thing. Now in that kind of a structure, there is no legal rationale for the extension of the Fairness Doctrine, or license renewals. And if we do things right, we can have a situation where the First Amendment *does* apply to the electronic media as fully and completely as it does to the print media, and that is our primary policy consideration.

Now, I wish I could tell you that it is that simple. In fact, the Committee has been working for nineteen months. It's an exceedingly vexing problem. There are many political realities. We have a Congress that is not likely to give up Federal regulation over anything that resembles broadcasting. There is the realization that we cannot have unfair competition with the broadcasting industry. We can't tear down something that provides such valuable service to this country. But, nevertheless, we see an opportunity for cable to provide good service, and avoid the kinds of problems that we find in broadcasting today. In conclusion, I hope that I've sketched out a general theme, a general trend for what we are doing in these areas. We need to begin moving in the right direction as solidly as we can. Now, if we still have some time, I'd like to answer any questions.

QUESTIONS AND ANSWERS FOLLOWING WHITEHEAD ADDRESS

COHEN: Will you please make the questions as succinct as possible and let's begin as quickly as we can.

PRINGLE: I'd like to ask if your aim to get the Government out of broadcasting applies equally to public broadcasting as it does to commercial broadcasting? Some of us have interpreted quite the opposite: that the Government wants to get more heavily involved in the activities of both commercial and public broadcast worlds.

WHITEHEAD: The Government . . . this Administration doesn't want to. But we were very upset with the trend that public broadcasting was taking. We're upset with two aspects of it: One was the growing trend to make the Corporation for Public Broadcasting, and the Public Broadcasting System that it funds, work as a cohesive network. That was not our understanding of the conception of the Public Broadcasting Act of 1967. We saw it with the air connection as being a low-cost way of the stations interchanging programs. And we saw an explicit prohibition in the Act against the establishment of a fixed schedule network. Feeling very strongly that there is no place in our society for a Government funded television network, we felt that a way had to be found to allow the local stations more of a say in what was going on. We found very little willingness on the part of the people at the Corporation to move in that direction, and (a corresponding necessity we thought) to insist that any financing arrangements that were adopted reflect the intent of the Congress that some of the money was to go to the local stations. We felt that long-range funding could possibly be done by the Congress *only* if limitations were set.

The other thing that upset us was the very heavy emphasis on public affairs programming dealing with current politically controversial items. The networks and local commercial stations, do quite a bit of that, and argue whether they could do more. Public broadcasting was intended to do programs (educational and cultural) not generally economically feasible on commercial television. We are very concerned about the use of Federal interventions in the editorial process, and recognize that the Congress and any reasonable President is not going to let Federal funds be used unless they're convinced they are used in a responsible way. And if you're doing this very current topical political programming, there is tremendous temptation for politicians to debate what the programming is, and to try to affect it. Those were our concerns, and we think that public broadcasting has an important role in our society. We think that its character needs to be a little bit better defined before we go to long-range financing, and we think that perhaps there are priorities that ought to be shifted a bit. They were using, at one point, almost 40% of their program money for news and public affairs shows. *Sesame Street* and *The Electric Company* were funded by the Office of Education and by the Ford Foundation. That situation, we thought, was unwise from a policy standpoint. So we think that the Corporation is now beginning to be more responsive. The Corporation *has* to tell the Congress, *has* to tell the President, *has* to tell the country, that they have ultimate responsibility for how Federal funds are used. But they should use that responsibility (and I think they are trying to do that) in a way that is responsive to the local stations. In that way the local stations will be more influential in what programming actually gets done.

BARNHILL: Is there an inconsistency between what you are going to propose on cable television and the rules recently issued by the FCC?

WHITEHEAD: I think it is safe to say, that there will be some difference. The FCC dealt with a fairly narrow range of subjects on cable. Their main concern was to get cable going at the end of the freeze and the top hundred markets (an action that we supported). I really can't go much beyond that. The FCC is constrained to deal with cable television as an adjunct to broadcasting. The Communications Act only creates two classes of regulations: Common Carriers and Broadcasting. Any authority that the FCC has over cable is derived from their authority over broadcasting, and so you find them regulating cable as basically adjunct to the broadcasting business. This is not the healthiest way of approaching it. We think that sooner or later, the Congress is going to have to deal with cable and set the country straight on what the national policy is for this medium and how it's going to be regulated.

BARNHILL: It seems that public broadcasting, perhaps, inappropriately goes into the public affairs sector with programming when the commercial operations tend to give us that service. Yet, that service is questioned as to the integrity that it might be able to achieve.

WHITEHEAD: Well, let me dispose of the public broadcasting thing by saying that two wrongs don't make a right. Let me say what I said about news at Sigma Delta Chi in Indianapolis. The basic thrust of my remarks when I got to that section, was that the broadcaster (local station manager, licensee or network president) be a responsible leader, who will undertake to program his frequency in a responsible way and reflect the public interest. Now, that has been the concept since the beginning. What I said was that this Administration is going to propose and actively work for a License Renewal Bill that takes *away* Government powers, that insulates the broadcasters from even the communities having recourse against him. The first half of my speech in Indianapolis was directed to the rationale that the First Amendment should apply completely and fully to broadcasting. Now, as you all know, that was widely reported and I'm sure you got the thrust that we were very much pro First Amendment. So having said that the First Amendment ought to apply, having said that the only way to do that is to minimize these Government controls, and then having said that the broadcaster should do things on a more voluntary basis, I felt constrained to say, that from a First Amendment standpoint (with its concerns for free speech and free press), that there was probably no area more important for the broadcaster (in making sure that he was exercising his responsibility) than news. That's really what the free speech and free press provisions of the First Amendment were all about. Now, he ought to be applying that same responsibility in dealing with violence, and sex, and children's programming. He ought to be concerned about fraudulent or near-fraudulent advertising, but he also ought to be concerned with news. Where there are problems with news, where there is bias, where a newsman is guilty of elitist gossip or ideological plugola, the broadcaster, the broadcasting community (each licensee, all licensees collectively, each network president), *those* are the people who ought to exercise the checks and balances and bring the corrections to bear. If they are willing to do a conscientious and professional job of it, then we can continue to move in the direction I laid out. We can argue in the Congress, or to the public, that there ought to be less and less Government control, because the industry can handle these problems. So all that I was saying was that, where these things exist, the industry ought to pay attention to them and correct them itself. I have never made any evaluation of television news or network news. I'm not a professional journalist and I'm not capable of making that kind of evaluation, but some of you people are and you ought to be doing that. From my standpoint (and from your standpoint considering where I work), I think there should be no question that I should concern myself with the processes and not whether there is bias or not: processes whereby bias is identified and corrected; processes whereby the Government deals with bias; the processes whereby the Government deals with public service programming. I have tried to deal with these processes in a responsible way—in public television, by saying that the Government shouldn't be funding it, because it makes the whole of public television too controversial, invites political and Congressional intrusions. In the commercial media, where abuses occur, they ought to be corrected by a system of checks and balances within the industry. We should not allow the tremendous power that three television networks have *over* the television programming in this country (both entertainment and the news) to go unchecked. Unchecked monopoly power can be just as damaging to the purposes of the First Amendment as unchecked Government power. I don't think that I would argue that the answer to this problem is the networks and the local stations censoring the network new departments. *Negative* censorship is not a concept that we like in this country, and it's not a concept that we should foster either legally or informally. The key question, when it comes to network news—and I did single out network news (because of its tremendous power)—is that the local stations ought to execrise checks and balances there. The effort ought not to be *less* controversial programming; it ought not to be a narrowing of what they can say (certainly ought not to be a narrowing so that all they say is that Richard Nixon's a great guy every night), but they ought to be making sure that a wide enough range of points of view get on. The whole theory of the First Amendment is diversity. Give the people of this country a wide range of points of views, let them make up their own minds. Give them what they need to learn; don't try to teach them, don't try to cram some homogenized point of view down their throats. When you have that kind of control over network news, there is an *inevitable* tendency to narrow the scope, so that you have a rather narrow range of points of view. What we need to be concerned with, and what I was asking the local broadcasters and everbody else in the broadcasting industry to deal with, is an *opening up* to get more points of views on. The public has a right to know more than they know now. Let them make up their own minds.

Kasmire: One of the responses that networks have made about the December speech is that it suggested bias on the part of the network news operation. You weren't specific. Will you give us the specific example of ideological plugola that you've gleaned from a network news program?

Whitehead: Absolutely not. And I'll tell you why I won't. It's important. We're trying to provoke public discussion. We're trying to provoke serious consideration, and draw attention to some very important and very sensitive areas of our society and our government. Now, editorial aside, let me get in a little ideological plugola of my own. That's not the way I think an Administration would go about doing it if it really wanted to achieve some of the negative purposes that people suggest we have. It's much easier to do underhanded things if you do them in quiet, and when you don't provoke the press' interest. We have very consciously gone out to provoke the press' interest. We think these things ought to be discussed, that it's healthy to have them discussed. There seems to be a feeling that this Administration doesn't like the way some reporters or some television organizations report the news. There seems to be a feeling that this Administration is out to *get* people. The minute that I name an example of ideological plugola (be it a local station or a network, an anchor man, a specific incident, no matter what), all of this public discussion and consideration of competing issues is all going to go by the wayside. They will say it's Whitehead that's been dead against that, or that's Nixon's vendetta against that, and all of the discussion of the issues will be irretrievably lost. Furthermore, an awful lot of people in the broadcast business will rally around trying to save him, just as they tried to save Dan Schorr. They will justify every example I pick no matter how bad it is. Then I would have to start defending myself, and I hope that I've convinced you by now that that's not a constructive way for me to proceed.

Kasmire: I have another question. What were we trying to save Dan Schorr from?

Whitehead: Well . . . that's a good question.

Kasmire: Well, do you think you can?

Whitehead: I'm just saying that it becomes a *cause célèbre,* and the real facts, the real issues, get lost. Now . . . I don't know what the real issues in Dan Schorr's case were either, for that matter.

COHEN: We've got opportunity for just one more question, I believe. Let me give it to a professor, if you don't mind gentlemen. Charles Steinberg, from Hunter.

STEINBERG: Assuming that you are reluctant to give examples of ideological plugola, could you tell us what you meant when you use such a phrase? Plugola and payola were terms used in the 1959 quiz scandals. It meant generally that somebody paid to get something plugged on the air. Now is that your implication? Is that the inference you would like us to draw?

WHITEHEAD: No, no . . .

STEINBERG: If it isn't, without examples—and we can understand your reluctance to cite examples—could you define these phrases? What in your terms, in Whitehead's terms, what is elitist gossip, and what is an ideological plugola?

WHITEHEAD: I will endeavor to give a very simple explanation. As I understand the use of the words: payola is when someone is paid to plug something. Plugola is when some reporter or disc jockey plugs a product or something because it accrues to his own benefit, financially. Ideological plugola is simply the plugging of a point of view or a person's point of view because it conforms to the ideology and the politics of the reporter. Elitist, by my reading of the dictionary, is someone who is better than other people, usually by self-designation. So, it is someone who thinks that he's better than someone else. And gossip is when a bunch of people get together who think that they're better than other people, get together and trade points of view. When you get a fairly narrow, self-selected group of people who think that *they* know better than other people, and they begin to dispense over the air what they call "news analysis," but is, in fact, simply what they have picked up and agreed upon amongst themselves, that is elitist gossip.

STEINBERG: Then extrapolating this just one step further, this is what the networks are accused of?

WHITEHEAD: I think it would be a great stretch of the imagination to say that *that* kind of thing never occurred on network news. Certainly, I didn't mean to imply that those things happen every day on network news. I said, when it does occur, where are the checks and balances? Professionalism, as I understand it, involves self-questioning and improving yourself, and it means a willingness to listen to criticism from the outside and take that into account. It doesn't mean pulling into a little shell and saying:

"We are somehow a privileged group and the rest of the world doesn't have any right to criticize us." It means an "openness," a willingness to accept criticism and say: "We're not perfect. We could do better and we're always looking for ways to do better." I think there ought to be more examination by people such as yourselves in understanding the news process at work. How does the journalistic process work? Who are the keepers of professionalism? The people in the journalism schools ought to be the keepers of professionalism. It shouldn't be the Federal Government, and it shouldn't be the political process. You're the ones, I think, who ought to be asking what that means. What kind of abuses can occur in this very powerful electronic press mechanism that we have? And how can we make it better?

LABUNSKI: May I ask you if you can assure us that you have detected this ideological plugola on both sides of a given issue, both pro-Administration and anti-Administration? You don't have to quote the examples. Can you just tell us that you are aware of *both* kinds and not all in one direction?

WHITEHEAD: Yes sir.

LABUNSKI: Good. That's very reassuring.

WHITEHEAD: You didn't ask me which way the balance was.

PINKHAM: Certainly one reason there was so much reaction in the press about your speech in Indianapolis, was against the background of the attack on reporters and their sources. Was this an unhappy coincidence for you, or not?

WHITEHEAD: Yes, I think it's an unhappy coincidence. The issues we are dealing with are quite separate from the newsman's privilege issues. I think the reaction of some people in the press, insisting that the two are tied together, insisting on seeing a conspiracy between the State Court here and the Nixon Administration there, stretches things a bit and confuses the issues. I think that to the extent that the two have to be discussed, they ought to be discussed as professionally as possible, recognizing that the two are largely separate. The press is not under any siege in this country, and it doesn't do anybody any good—in particular, the press—to create that climate.

PINKHAM: Why, particularly, the press?

WHITEHEAD: Because I think that there's a great danger that there can be a "lash-back" against the press.

PINKHAM: From whom?

WHITEHEAD: From the public. The idea that newsmen should have absolute privilege is not something that most people would agree with. And I might cite an interesting statistic only because it is pertinent. When I gave that Indianapolis speech, I think you all saw the press coverage which was by-and-large misinterpreted, either purposely or inadvertently. The press interpreted what I said as follows: "I have a bill that will make the Federal Government the policemen of elitist gossip and ideological plugola. And if you want to get your license renewed, you're going to have to satisfy us." Now I hope that I've convinced you tonight, that that's not what my bill says. But, nonetheless, that's the way it was reported, and our mail (over the next few days) reflected, not a reading of my speech, but the press stories that the Nixon administration wants a bill that will hold the networks responsible for the contents of their news. It seems that 60% of the mail received was in *favor* of that concept. Now, that doesn't make it right, but it's just something I think everybody should think about.

Challenge V

Can an Incumbent Political Party "Capture" the Airwaves?

ALMOST FROM ITS inception, there was a realization that broadcasting was a mass medium far more powerful and persuasive—at least in reach if not in depth—than print. As a result, such disciplines as sociology, psychology and the developing discipline of communications each arrogated to itself the function of determining the effects of radio and television. Unfortunately, the results thus far have been ambiguous, particularly in the areas of television violence and television and political actions. Studies tend to conclude that many variables enter into the effects of mass media, that the phenomenon is not simply linear cause and effect, behavioristic stimulus and response. Prior experience, other social institutions, peer group influences, attitude or "set," disturbances in fidelity, problems of transmission are a few that have been discussed.

All of which makes more difficult any effort to evaluate the relationship between broadcasting and politics in terms of control of the air. There is widespread assent to the notion that those who have made up their minds about political choices are not about to undergo a political metamorphosis as the result of exposure to media messages. But there are also vast numbers who have *not* made up their minds, and in this arena the media seem to exert a formidable persuasive influence. Apart from elections, however, there is the question raised here of the power of the incumbent party. Can it "capture" the airwaves? The term has both implicit and explicit connotations. In an implicit sense, the party in power *does* capture the airwaves to a great extent. The President can request, and receive, prime time on the very shortest of notice. All three networks, as well as public broadcasting, bring program traffic to a stop and, in a very real sense, the incumbent has a captive audience. Those who do tune in to the networks have no place else to go. Furthermore, the party in power can—and does—occasionally create pseudo-events to command television coverage, and this is accepted as one of the facts of life of realpolitic.

Explicit control of the air poses an even graver problem. And that is clearly evident under authoritarian press systems, such as Russia and Red China, where the media and the government coalesce into a monolithic and propagandistic communications system. This, we have generally concluded, can't happen here. In the first place, our system grew out of the essential libertarian conviction that, however partisan or venal our government or our media might be, a self-righting process would prevail. And, in the second place, the government has said it encourages the media in their peremptory demand that they now operate in a spirit of free inquiry and social responsibility under the protection of the First Amendment, and in a pluralistic society.

Nevertheless, certain nagging truths persist. Incumbent Presidents, like Franklin D. Roosevelt in the thirties and Richard Nixon in two terms in office, have used the mass media of radio and television freely and often. So much so, in the case of President Nixon, that the opposition party complained of violations of fairness and was given time by CBS for a "loyal opposition" broadcast. The substance of the matter was the conviction that the President did not use air time for an informational address—a legitimate report to the people—but as an exercise in political public relations.

There is, of course, an ironic note to the relentless exposure of the Watergate matter on television and radio. Through an unusual chain of circumstances—purely fortuitous as it turned out—the people are now witnessing what the media can offer in the way of a critical examination of the practices of an incumbent party. But this was a mutation, an anomalous situation. Had the Watergate break-in not been discovered, had a forthright judge not meted out justice, who can say how far an incumbent party might have gone toward a more explicit capturing of the airwaves—to the ultimate erosion of the democratic process and the freedom of the media to perpetuate that process? It did not happen here. Could it have happened?

Dollars go a long way toward control. The "out" party simply did not have the unlimited funds available to the incumbents in the 1972 election campaign. And in this respect, perceptive viewers witnessed an advertising and promotion campaign—with both hard- and soft-sell spots and so-called "documentaries"—never before devised with comparable expertise and free-wheeling spending in the history of political campaigning. Is this not as direct a way as any other toward capturing the airwaves?

Or, will the Congress not only set a hard and firm limit on spending but finally rescind (not suspend), once and for all, the useless equal time provisions of Section 315 of the Communications Act?

One balancing factor to the possibility of capture by the incumbents has been post-broadcast analysis and interpretation by network news correspondents. But for reasons that appeared questionable to some, one network (CBS) briefly eliminated so-called "instant analysis" to the detriment, some believe, of the democratic process. Correspondents are trained, seasoned journalists. The press, in this country, has served as an important guardian of democratic rights, as well as in an important educational capacity. It may be asked whether cutting off discussion by experienced newsmen following a Presidential broadcast does not, in some way, erode the process of free flow of information. The days of "objective" journalism are gone, indeed, if they ever existed. As distinguished from editorializing, is there not a need for analysis by the electronic journalists—not next week, but immediately following a broadcast when public interest is at its optimum? For contrast, there is always the ultimate leverage of print. As Roper surveys show, most people now turn to television and trust its reliability. But even the television journalists agree that print is a vital supplement to broadcast news.

In any event, the question of political control is a critical challenge. Political campaigns are now waged in the environment of the electric media. Pseudo-events are staged by innovative advertising and publicity experts. And this aspect is probably the most serious challenge. For much of television tends to appeal, not to issues or substance, but to taste and to affective responses. It tends to stress personalities, not problems. The challenge to broadcasters is to resist the kind of image fabrication that characterizes modern electronic campaigning. The challenge to the Congress and to the Commission is to devise a structure that will not only make capture of the airwaves impossible, but that will also offer the opposition opportunity for reasonable exposure by the broadcast media.

CHALLENGE V

Producer: James Hirsch (Television and Communication Consultant)

Moderator: Charles Tower (Corinthian Broadcasting)

Panel: Lawrence Rogers II (Taft Broadcasting Co.); Russell C. Tornabene (National Broadcasting Company)

Question and Answer (in order): Richard J. Goggin, Sr. (New York University); Charles E. Phillips (Emerson College); Phillip A. Macomber (Kent State University); Phillip S. Gelb (Bronx Community College); C. A. Kellner (Marshall University); Kenneth Harwood (Temple University); Keith W. Mielke (Indiana University); Alfred L. Plant (Block Drug Company)

TOWER: The subject here this morning is an important one, and I'll read it quickly. The premise: Television has an enormous ability to affect national and international policies so that coverage is commanded and even friendly. Thus, months before a Presidential election or even the conventions, the public can be influenced at the will of the incumbent perhaps to an overwhelming advantage. *Question:* What form of impartial regulation can be established to neutralize this advantage and to permit the "out" an even break? Had I written this (and I didn't), I think I might have asked a preliminary question: Does this enormous ability exist, and if so, precisely what is its nature and historical antecedent? Bud Rogers has been in every phase of the broadcasting business, and perhaps more so than any other executive in the business today. I think it's enough to say that he is one of the most articulate, concerned spokesman for broadcasting industry that we have. His many contributions over the years are well known and we're lucky to have him in this business.

ROGERS: There are a number of reasons why I failed to prepare an advance text to deliver to you. First, I consider that premise that Chuck Tower just read shaky at best, and the only acceptable answer to the question of what machinery should be set up is: Nothing, No-how by Nobody. Well, I discussed the subject in advance with Dick Salant (President of CBS News) who is an absent member of our Panel, and we already agreed that it would be very difficult to take twelve or fifteen minutes to say nothing, which is the answer to the question as it was asked. On the other hand, I can reflect, and I'm sure that you'll agree with me, that I've known many people—academicians, politicians and journalists—who talk seemingly forever and still say nothing. I imagine that there will be a lot of divergent views on this general subject that we are discussing, and if you take enough exception to my temerity we may have a seminar yet. With brief reference to the dinner speaker last night (Clay T. Whitehead), and his predecessor in the field of bombast (Spiro Agnew), the Nixon

Administration has made one thing perfectly clear and that is that it doesn't like network television, and the Administration burns down the barn in the effort to get rid of suspected rats. The Administration doesn't seem to care; and I find it at least wryly amusing that a fellow whose professional affiliation is with a company named Taft should use a simile coined by Adlai Stevenson to discuss a Republican administration, but that is neither here nor there. In one form or another, the problem or problems we're discussing have always existed. There are those who believe, and I agree with this, that an adversary position between Government and the Press is precisely the correct position with respect to the rights of the people, and in this sense I use the word "press" to include all the media. The electronic media as part of the generic term "press" is not exactly accurate, because the electronic press broadcasts news that is not in fact entitled to the same adversary position with government as is the printed press, and we all know why. The quick and easy manner is that the Supreme Court in the *Red Lion* case decreed by unanimous vote that the Fairness Doctrine is consistent with the First Amendment. But I believe that this is mere window-dressing for the real reason, namely, that the Government has a licensing power which, if it were used to its fullest potential, could literally command compliance with Government's views as to how the news should be handled. Incidentally, there is an awful lot that can be discussed on the subject of the licensing power, and the "whys" of it. The regulatory body still adheres to the classic principle for the original establishment of the Communications Act, the technical shortage of frequencies. This is so much hog-wash in the light of today's facts, since a quick count yesterday indicated that there are more than 8,600 radio and television stations on the air (including the educational assignments) in the United States today, or one for approximately every 24,000 men, women and children. If we have a shortage, it's of newspapers and magazines, not radio and television stations. But, that's another subject.

For all the hue and cry on the subject of the adversary position between the Government and the Press, in every Administration since Washington's, the Executive has not yet succeeded in imposing its will on the Press. And I suggest that the surest way to bring about such a result, would be to establish regulatory machinery to prevent it. It seems to me that it's a lot easier for a powerful central government, whether by subterfuge or *coup d'etat,* to seize control of existing machinery than it is to stamp out all vestiges of opposition in the absence of such machinery. I for one, believe in reducing the regulatory bonds on broadcasting, not increasing them. Strangely enough, as if to re-enforce the Supreme Court, the so-called Fairness Doctrine already provides exactly the machinery which the question contemplates, and yet, everyone here presumably hates the Fairness Doctrine. Well, at the risk of committing heresay, I would like to say a word or two in behalf of the Fairness Doctrine. For one thing, it's much fairer than taking away all of broadcasting's cigarette advertising while leaving it to all the other media, while at the same time, the same Government that took away the money goes on subsidizing the growing of cigarette tobacco out of the same taxes paid by broadcasters, among others. So this is by way of saying that the attacks on the media come from every direction. As Shakespeare put it, they come not as single spies, but by battalions. But that's still another seminar and I'll get back to the point.

The Fairness Doctrine provides exactly the machinery the question seeks. If an incumbent uses up too much airtime to press his dictatorial concepts on the gullible public, then the licensee is already required to provide, nay, even to seek out the opportunity of those of opposing views to get in their licks. And neither the doctrine nor it's keeper, the FCC, has specified whether these opponents must be political "outs," office holders, network commentators or even elitist gossips. Well, gentlemen and ladies, to be ever mindful of the impeding Twenty-Eighth Amendment, how will it be? We already have the machinery—the Fairness Doctrine—The Supreme Court has already ruled eight to one that the Fairness Doctrine is okay with them and how do you feel about that? The premise is serious.

There must be another reason for getting rid of the Fairness Doctrine: namely, it doesn't work. You can't have it both ways is what I'm getting at, and I'm afraid that this is exactly what all governments want sooner or later. They want everything both ways. They want lower taxes so they'll be loved, and more money to spend to insure their power. They want more opportunity to tell their story and less opportunity for their opponents to refute them. All, of course, in the name of free speech or public safety, depending upon which side of the issues they are on at the moment.

I'd like to mention that Dave Brinkley gave the most concise analysis of this problem I've ever heard. He said that, like Gertrude Stein talking about writers, the only three things that a politician needs is praise, praise, and praise, and then David went on to say that history is replete with examples of politicians who've seized absolute power and muzzled the press, but there never yet has been a single example of the press seizing power and muzzling politicans. Now back to business. I have a couple of odd theories on this general subject and I'd like to try them out on you.

The first is that the Fairness Doctrine, in spite of what I've just said about it, has never really hurt anybody. Of course, I'd like to see it struck down by the Courts, but for a different reason. I consider it totally —well, almost totally—unnecessary. If I've learned anything about broadcast news in over a quarter of a century of involvement in it, it is that the American public simply does not respond well to unfairness. Fairness in TV and radio or the press, whether in news or in anything else, is good because it is right, and among other things, it is good for business. And, I've got another pet theory. That is, despite all the bleatings of my political co-religionists to the contrary, including Barry Goldwater, Spiro Agnew and Tom Whitehead, I'll let you in on a secret: there is no Eastern liberal establishment conspiracy in news or any other type of conspiracy for that matter. There is, in my opinion, a distinctly liberal or left-leaning or whatever you call it, coloration to almost everybody who makes his living writing, picturing and reporting news in whatever form, and what's so mysterious about this? Almost every professional news person, or nonprofessional news person for that matter, I have ever met considers himself an artist. Like most artists, he is intrigued with abstract problems and the problems of humanity and especially the problems of individual people. If he were a concrete-problem-solver or, as the industrial psychologists say, if he were achievement- or goal-oriented, he'd be a salesman or a manager, he wouldn't be a newsman.

Now this, I state, is a condition of Man, so why don't we get over arguing about it? On the other hand, I have some other observations on these characters in question. During the Moscow summit, I took a three-week sabbatical from concrete-problem-solving and goal-orientation to be a newsman or, at least, an observer of newsmen and of the events and of the reporters. For more than two weeks, I lived cheek-by-jowl, twenty or more hours a day, with about two-hundred news people including some of the more famous targets from Washington. And I might say parenthetically one of my colleagues among the two hundred is sitting to my left, Mr. Tornabene, who's an old and dear friend of mine, and I hadn't expected him to be on this panel when I put this particular thought on paper, so I assume that he's going to hit me with a water glass by the time I finish. However, you can choose your poison. I made an electrifying discovery about these two-hundred people that followed the President to Salzburg, Moscow, Kiev, Teheran and Warsaw. They're people, that's what they are. Just plain people. Just the same as two-hundred plumbers, two-hundred salesmen, two-hundred athletes or two-hundred professors, they are all people and they break down into broad categories just as all people do. Some, a very small percentage, are both brilliant and dedicated and hardworking. A larger group are not as smart, but they work pretty hard. The largest group of all, maybe half, are not very smart at all and they are kind of lazy. Then there's a category of hard-working dummies. Finally, there's another small group who are both lazy and stupid. Now you can supply your own percentages. I think the same break-down applies to all sorts of people, although one of my academic friends that I tried this out on last week, said that he had never heard of a smart plumber. I replied: "Hell, my plumber is very smart. I never heard of a smart professor."

Rather than attribute media problems to political points of view, I suggest that they are attributable to the caliber of the reporter. The ones that I characterized as stupid and lazy may be a pain in the neck, but they really don't cause any trouble. They never have enough ambition to do so. The most dangerous are the hard-working dummies, and the most numerous are the smart, lazy ones. They really create the worst day-by-day problems, because their stock-in-trade is not to bother to uncover evidence, but to wait until they pick up a smattering of ignorance in the bar or from a pool report and then to send into their paper the first thing that occurs to them at their typewriters. Thus, whether we're talking about the Moscow summit or elsewhere, there are always numbers of real stories that remain largely uncovered or ill-covered because the bulk of the reporters are either: (a) too stupid to recognize them, (b) too lazy to cover them, or (c) too bored to perceive their own opportunities for originality.

At any rate, that's what I think the problem is. If all the coverage of the great events could be limited to those people that I've characterized as brilliant and dedicated we wouldn't have any of these problems, obviously. But I used this supposition to illustrate how impossible is the problem of solution. Who's going to make the choice? And by whose standards? It's much like the old story, the best kind of government, and obviously, the most efficient form of government, is a benevolent despotism. But how, one might ask, can we be certain that despot will remain benevolent? And, of course, I've got the answer to that too: only if I am the despot. No, I don't believe new machinery to guarantee fairness is the answer. We have the machinery now. In the minds of most people, it doesn't work. And why will it never work? Because I believe both fairness and bias, like beauty, rest mostly in the eye of the beholder.

TOWER: Thank you, very much. Russ Tornabene is a late starter here and is very nice to pinch-hit at the last minute for Dick Salant and I guess this is NBC's contribution to CBS. There are probably others that I'm not aware of, but at any event, we are really fortunate to have Russ here. He's a long-time veteran of NBC News, has handled all sorts of assignments and, I'm told, very well for NBC. He now is in charge of the Radio News Division.

TORNABENE: You're absolutely right, Bud Rogers. There were, on that trip, just a lot of plain people, because that's what journalists are. I don't know about the plumbers. I would say that they are very smart people because, you notice, there is always a plumber's helper. And I would agree also that the correspondents break down into various groups, and most of them are reporting what comes to them, and that's because a reporter's first thought is an impression—an impression of what is happening and this stays with him and becomes part of his transmission of information. That's not surprising either, and so it becomes rather subjective.

I'm not going to tackle much more than the obvious in some quickly prepared remarks, but I hope that this can provide a lead into some discussion. Broadcasters, obviously, are carrying a very heavy burden in the seventies. We attempt to inform the public with very sophisticated tools of electronic journalism, but without sufficient understanding by the general public of how broadcast newsmen go about getting news on the air, how news is presented the way it is and what the journalistic challenge is, as differentiated from the entertainment side of broadcasting. Politicians well know this. They know what broadcasting is about, how to use it and about public attitudes and public knowledge on broadcasting of news. Politicians need public support for their legislative, judicial and administrative activities. Now, in seeking this support, they believe that a measure of control of the content of these activities is imperative. Not secrecy at all times, per se, but certainly control of the content of information of political activities. Therefore, any challenge to the control of the content must, they believe, be embattled and there develops what Bud referred to as the "natural adversary conflict between politics and journalism." This fact is not new, but it takes on a new meaning now with a greater effort made to control news, and yet, it's not new.

The Alien and Sedition Acts, sponsored by President John Adams in 1798, terrorized a great many people who believed in freedom of expression. Now, there have been innumerable efforts since the beginning of this Republic to control what is read by the public and in more recent times, of course, what is heard and what is seen, for the effort at censorship is aimed at the receiver. Politicians know the first rule about politics: You must be in power to use power. Power to pass laws, to rule in the courts, to administer administrative law, such as the President of the United States can do, and does. Power to regulate, as Bud pointed out, power to license. As a practical matter, why should a senator want his connection with a wealthy supporter known to the general public? Because that public might not like that activity and might vote him out of office. Out of power. Therefore, as a practical matter in the raw world of power, the politician wants only good news told about him and bad news told about his opponents. Again, it's obvious, but worth mentioning. Is this over-simplified? No. Not enough of the obvious forces in our society are discussed, and not enough so that the general public knows how public policy is made, who makes it, under what conditions and what the public's own role is in making this policy.

So, we have by tradition and by law in the United States a system of election of men and women to public office, or appointment to public office, or assignment to positions of responsibility and power, and a challenge to institutions, rapid change and change to accomodate change. Now sometimes, examples of attempt to control the content of news provide insight into the day-to-day struggle to tell what is happening to people, because, isn't that what news is—what's happening to people? And, I'll give you an example: When Secretary of State Dulles began conducting occasional news conferences which were permitted to be filmed and taped, after each conference—a few hours after, one or two hours—I would receive a phone call from one of his Public Relations Aides who would list the sentences that Dulles had answered in his responses to answers to questions, and the man would attempt to eliminate words in the transcript. But he would also want to *add* information. Now, we didn't have anyone on the staff that sounded like John Foster Dulles, so it was impossible for us to do it, and I explained this every time the man called.

We are students of human behavior, or we wouldn't be in this business and we see a country that is quite concerned, beset with fears and dreams, and I am struck by some of the things that Bud said in terms of people who don't respond well to unfairness. A very good point. Americans like to see the best in their country, their traditions, their laws, their leaders and their politicians so they will rationalize, and these dreams become the basis for acceptance of myths. I go back to what I said in the beginning: they don't know how we do our business and we've done a terrible public relations job in informing the public about why we do what we do. We have our job cut out for us, and maybe all of this challenge from Washington is going to prompt us to do that job. I hope it does. Politicians know very well how to get into news, how to get space in the paper, time on the air. When the politician is in office and he wants to remain in office, he is a very creative man in manufacturing ways of getting favorable publicity. When he puts what he thinks is a good bill in the hopper, the public must learn about it, or else he'll have no benefit from it, and if he loses a point in the rough game of politics, then he tries to assure that this can be turned around so that it isn't detrimental to him.

As I said before, you really can't use power unless you have it. But at the same time, there is a . . . I'm sure all of us have found this by study of history . . . there is a measure of cynicism in the politician's code. There sure is enough of it in our own business, but they are our targets for today. It says: The public is not very sophisticated about these things, therefore, let experts, as the politicians, decide what is good for them, but let us make these decisions and carry on this business without the interference of those who would oppose us. This attitude obviously leads to secrecy—from Town Hall meetings, to zoning changes, to Presidential activities. One President recently called Americans "children" and that's not difficult to understand, given a life-long nurturing of an attitude about the public as incapable humans who must have politicians to lead them (that is, the public as children and the politicians, as parents). It may be shocking to some people that newsmen tell them what is wrong in society, but it is up to the people and their leaders to fix it. Yet, we in broadcast news get the greatest amount of shrapnel when we go the one step further by stating what's wrong and adding: Here's how it can be solved. How dare we do that! There will be a lot of provocative comment, I hope, here today about the role of the news in broadcasting, the role of broadcast news in society, but I volunteer this thought: Politics is a volunteer occupation and so is broadcast news.

CHALLENGE V: QUESTION AND ANSWER SESSION

TOWER: I think, as with all such things, it's really a question of defining the problem, and this is a problem that really needs some careful definition. There's a lot of talk about this one, but I think you have to get to the cases of just what are you talking about, what kind of uses, for example, what kinds of activity are involved in this particular problem. Obviously crucial is the extent of the impact both before and after the advent of television. Historically, you could look at incumbents running for office in terms of how they fared afterwards as related to before. I think there is quite a bit of interesting information there that somebody could spend some time on and come up with some statistical insights. It would make a fairly nice area of investigation for a Master's thesis. For example, the activities relating to, and results of, the elections since 1950, the Eisenhower '56 election, the LBJ election and so forth. I think careful analysis in those areas is valuable. I think a very important area of investigation would be, since the charge particularly comes up with the Nixon Administration, what have been his uses of the media that might relate to this problem. What are the differences here, if any? Can you quantitatively or qualitatively come up with some differences that shed light on this problem? I think a third basic question is just why is it a problem? What's wrong here? What is the impact? I suppose it's possible that a party can give itself greater continuity and power and so forth. And then, important in all these problems, is the extent of the harm. Just what is the extent of the harm here? Who is damaged and how are they damaged and to what extent? What is the interest of society in terms of how severely it is affected, and what should be done about it, which was the central question in the outline?

GOGGIN: Broadcasters react in different ways to a Nicholas Johnson and a Clay Whitehead, and the reactions—including the emotional—of the broadcasters have been colored or affected by the different personal styles of Johnson and Whitehead, as well as the contents of their pronouncements. Considering them as Government officials, how do you measure and counter the distinct and relative alleged dangers of such individuals, insofar as what they stand for, or at least what they say they stand for?

ROGERS:　It's such a deep, philosophical question that it's going to take a little meandering on my part to come to grips with it. I suppose the best way I could try to attack that question, is to analyze what I perceive to be the basic difference between the positions represented by Nick Johnson and Clay Whitehead, as well as what I perceive to be the differences in their official functions. And I think having said that, I'll start in reverse order. Johnson is an appointee for a seven-year term by the President to the administrative regulation of a specific piece of legislation. Whitehead is the Head of an Executive Branch Office which was created by Congress, and therefore Whitehead is accountable to the Legislative Branch as well as his boss in the Executive Department. He is not charged with the responsibility to administer an existing set of laws, and his boss is the President of the United States. Johnson's boss, if you can call it that, is jointly the Congress' Committees of Communications, Sub-Committees of the Commerce Committees of the House and Senate. So they are two totally different breeds of cat in terms of what they are there to do. To finish off that end of my answer, in a seminar (Taft management meeting) that Whitehead had with my management group, barely a week after his famous Indianapolis speech, he was asked by one of my managers: What was the excuse for his job, and how long was it going to go on? That was roughly the question. Whitehead's response was that how long it would go on would probably be a function of the Congress and the next Administration, because it would go on until Congress abolished it, since Congress had authorized it. And it was certainly no intention on the part of this Administration to abolish it, and the reason for it, was purely and simply the fact that in this age of the explosion of technology, the President of the United States felt the need to have some means of expression of the development of communications policy and FCC was not it, because the instant the President appointed an FCC Commissioner, he stopped working for the President and started working for Congress.

As for their position on things, it seems perfectly evident to me, and I'll make no mistake as to the one that I favor, that Johnson is a protected anarchist who has decided for reasons that are satisfactory to him, at least, that the issue of public access (that is to say, the ability of any member of the public at any time to say whatever he pleases over any transmitter that he happens to want to talk over) is a legitimate function of our democracy and was contemplated by the Communications Act. Having read the draft legislation that Whitehead's group proposes to get through Congress, they believe exactly the opposite of this. Namely, that there is a professional function, akin to journalism, that not only can but must be served by the licensees of radio and television stations, and how they go about serving that function is their responsibility and is not the responsibility of the likes of Nick Johnson to tell him how.

TORNABENE: There are similarities between the two men in terms of their recognition of the tremendous potential of influence over public thought, and both would have an increase in regulation.

TOWER: I'd just like to observe this; both are obviously very bright and very articulate men, both are suggesting some significant changes from different points of view. In dealing with an industry as complicated as broadcasting, or with any other area of life that is complicated and has developed over a long period of time, I think there is a danger, particularly among people who are really very bright, to draw conclusions rather quickly. Our system of broadcasting isn't written in the sky, and it may not be eternal but on the other hand, it is not accidental either. A system like broadcasting in a country like ours and a society like ours, fits together through an enormously complex process of pressures and compromises and bits and pieces. It responds to something, and when you think about changing—and all institutions change and some need pushing in the direction of change—you have to be careful that you really understand where it's coming from, what it has responded to and what it's about. There is a tendency on the part of people who come into something quickly to believe that they perceive the totality of it. Basic complicated institutions don't lend themselves to that kind of simplification, and I think to get a "gut" understanding of something is very important before you start talking about basic changes. Now Nick Johnson and Clay Whitehead are talking about different kinds of changes, but Chuck Colson has made some statements recently and he is a tough-minded, tough-talking politician. He's a bright man, and he's after certain objectives, but those objectives have in them a certain philosophy of change about broadcasting and rather substantial changes and some of the things that Whitehead said, relate to it.

PHILLIPS: In the sense that a popular hero, or the party that has the best PR can capture the airwaves, there's no problem here. What I want to know is, does the machinery exist that the party in power could, in fact, capture the airways the way De Gaulle did in France under the RTF or as has happened in the Communist countries?

TORNABENE: No.

TOWER: No danger?

TORNABENE: There's always danger, but it doesn't exist now and I think that if we'll do our job, it won't.

ROGERS: Can I footnote that? I want to go back to try and respond further to that, Mr. Phillips, and Mr. Goggin's question earlier. In asking it, he referred to the emotional response of broadcasting to the Whitehead speech. Not everybody was emotional in response to it, and I think what's germane to your question is this: the Whitehead speech, for whatever reason, was a political, saber-rattling blast that was calculated to have some result, and I'm not sure what that was. It bears absolutely no relationship, living, dead or otherwise, to the legislation that has been proposed. In fact, if anything, it says some of the opposite things from what the legislation says. I never got terribly emotional about it for one reason, and that is the fact that in specific answer to your question, the Communications Act, no matter how it might be violated here and there by the Courts and the White House (or attempted to be violated by the White House), no matter how much it may be skirted by wicked and money-grubbing licensees, is a jealously guarded function of Congress, and all the power under the Communications Act is in Congress. My own guess as to where this war is heading, is smack into the arena that is now being expanded and refined for the classic confrontation between the White House and Congress on the issue of the usurpation of the balance of power. I don't think that anybody who watches the jockeying for position in Washington on a regular basis will dispute the fact that there is a big battle brewing on that issue right now. It will come to light in the legislative proposals of the Administration and the unwillingness of Congress to be the bell-cow of the Administration, and this particular issue is going to get in it, because Congress is not about to let go of anything that they perceive to be as enormously powerful as control of the nation's electronic press. I think it is just as simple as that, and I think the longer the White House persists in attempting to make that grab, the more resistance they'll build in Congress, regardless of who's right.

MACOMBER: In answering Mr. Phillips' question, you responded very pointedly from a commercial point of view. Would you care to suggest whether the White House could take over public broadcasting in this manner, as opposed to commercial broadcasting?

ROGERS: Well, I don't know whether I could come to grips with it in such direct terms. I'm not sufficiently conversant with all the facts in the matter to talk about it. I must say, however, that irrespective of any

position—political, commercial or otherwise—I find it a little bit difficult to follow the line of reasoning which Mr. Whitehead repeatedly said
his boss and the Administration want to accomplish—that is to eliminate
the Government influence in what goes out over the airways, where commercial broadcasting is concerned. If that is what they want to accomplish
as far as public broadcasting is concerned, and the first step is to take it
over and control what goes out over the air—I don't understand this.

GELB: I've got a question but I would like to preface it with a story. At
our college two or three years ago, a dissident group took over for a
couple of days, on a bi-lingual issue, closed the college, and held the president at knife-point. They had locked out the rest of us. A faculty group
came to me and said: "Gelb, you teach a course in non-violent Democratic procedures. Will you go in there and get those crazy kids out?"
My scholarly answer was something like: "Drop dead." But seriously,
this is basic to my question and that is: The time to start making use of
systems of non-violent, democratic, guaranteed, built-in checks and balances, is *long before* there is a show-down and you're running scared. I
don't accept your answer that no President can take over. If his job is to
take over to get re-elected, he is in a position similar to DeGaulle's. Now,
you just can't dismiss it. There is a real danger here. And what I'm asking
is what has the media, the press or Taft Broadcasting done to make the
system of non-violent, democratic checks and balances, understandable,
workable and meaningful before now? And hopefully, what will you do
for a non-violent, problem-solving system in the future?

ROGERS: May I beg that question with a reply question? Will you explain
to me the landslide for a Republican Congress that Mr. Nixon was unable to bring in as a result of this control in the 1972 election?

GELB: I'm not going to depend on my explanation, or yours, of what is
going to occur in the future. Particularly if Nixon can really gain control.
I heard an awful lot of scared silence there last night. I mean that silence
told me more than the questions.

ROGERS: Scared silence about what?

GELB: When Whitehead was speaking.

ROGERS: Well, I'll be perfectly blunt with you. If you're asking why I
didn't ask a question it was the fact that the day he made that speech I
called him at his office and said: "I want you to come and sit down in a
snake pit with thirty members of my executive staff so that we can find out
what the hell you're talking about."

GELB: That wasn't my question, my question . . .

ROGERS: . . . And, your question was what am I doing about it.

GELB: No. Media! What are media doing so that the broadcasting system can have guaranteed, built-in checks and balances?

ROGERS: The media are putting on a product which apparently various members of the White House guard don't like, and I think that's the best proof positive right there. I don't think Congress is going to take this lying down because, in terms of my narrow commercial interests—which is to say, the protection of my stockholders equity—I have to be concerned about whether or not we can get a renewal bill such as the one White-head proposes. I have to be concerned about getting such a bill passed. I have to be concerned about going through the gibberish that Whitehead gave us at our meeting, and again last night, on the subject of how do you develop this marvelous new world of cable in the face of the fact that the copyright law has not been amended since 1909. The only performance rights that are enumerated in the copyright law of 1909, is for player piano rolls, and the present law provides a situation where I can pay millions of dollars for rights to Hollywood films, or re-runs of network pro-grams, or the creation of programs of our own, and a cable operator can pick them up, pipe them into homes and sell them, and not even share my copyright fee. That concerns me, and these are the things that we're trying for: the long-range development of some kind of stable industry. And I can tell you, in terms of my lack of success in getting those things done, that I detect something of a much harder nosed atti-tude in Congress against positions taken by the White House than I have detected anytime over the past twenty years. I would belabor the issue if I told you I believe something else, but I don't. I believe that this war is going to come to a head in this Congress, and I don't think the White House is going to win it.

GELB: Let me just re-state my original position very briefly. One of my students at NYU did a study. He found that word "democracy," and the use or portrayal of democratic processes in the mass media, was 90% negative. Democracy was always related to words like "corruption." In other words, the very procedures that are needed now by the media, have been continually down-graded, and down-graded systematically by these same media for generations.

ROGERS: Well, I don't know if I agree with that. In the first place I think that it is awfully easy to make a fetish of the word "democracy." The fact of the matter is, we don't have a democracy, we have a repre-

sentative Republic, and I don't think that the media would serve any
useful purpose by telling people that we're going to run the Government by popular referendum on every local issue that comes up, because
we don't. What we do is elect representatives and they decide these
things. If you don't like what they are doing, you throw them out and
do it over again.

TORNABENE: I think commercial broadcasters are losing their self-consciousness. For a long time they made profits, and there seemed to be a
great deal of reluctance to tell the public about the role of broadcasting in
society. I think that they are losing this self-consciousness and I think it
will be a good thing to inform the public what broadcasting does, and
that will be a great benefit, because it will meet this problem head on.

KELLNER: I think that most of us in the room are aware of the pitfalls
of over-regulation. I'd like to go to something that Mr. Tornabene said
that we talked about here the last few days at great length. He said the
public doesn't understand its real role. Let's turn that to the Fairness
Doctrine. Is this why we have a Fairness Doctrine? I'd like to have you
gentlemen examine this. What is the purpose of the Fairness Doctrine?
Is it the lack of understanding of the role of the public? Or is it the
broadcaster who doesn't understand his role? What is the basis for the
Fairness Doctrine?

TORNABENE: The Fairness Doctrine is an attitude by regulators that there
is a safety valve needed in this tremendous pressure tank, and some outlet
other than the one that they thought was provided.

ROGERS: It would seem to me that the elitist attitude in government
circles is probably the underlying cause for this. There is an attitude on the
part of many people that we, whoever we are, know better than the people,
what's good for them. I often hear it said, and have heard for a lifetime,
that the broadcasters and advertisers down-grade the American people by
underestimating their intelligence. I believe the broadcasters and the
advertisers probably have a greater respect for the intelligence of the
people than the regulators who consistently adopt the attitude that it
would be well for government to make all peoples' decisions for them, that
Big Brother should keep people from making mistakes and falling on their
faces. I think this is the underlying attitude that gave rise to the Fairness
Doctrine. When I said that the Fairness Doctrine is almost totally unnecessary, it was because it's incapable of definition in the final analysis,
or of complete enforcement. But no one who fulfills the professional
role of a broadcasting operation can fail to learn very quickly that if you

grind the same axe very long, you begin to hear from the public about it, because they are just a lot smarter than the regulators think they are.

HARWOOD: This is addressed to the Panel members jointly. Some people say that television, radio and the press have a great effect on the way voters vote. Others say these media have almost no effect. In the light of that, would you comment on the public importance of preferential rates of charge for political advertising on the air.

TORNABENE: I'd like to throw that one to Bud, because he's in the area of selling time and I'm not.

ROGERS: Well, I'm not sure that I understand the question. I can tell you, if what you're talking about is a practice, or an alleged practice, on the part of the broadcasting fraternity for scaling up the rate because here comes a politician—that was eliminated by Federal Law in an Amendment to the Communications Act at least fifteen years ago. It was called the McFarland Act in which it was made illegal, and we all know what illegal means—you won't get your license renewed. It was illegal to charge any politician any differently from any commercial advertiser for the same unit of time under the same circumstances. That has recently been amended to the point where the broadcaster is required by statute to provide whatever is its lowest so-called "end rate" on his rate card to politicians on the theory that the appearance of a candidate for public office in paid political advertising is somehow inextricably tied to the public interest and therefore it must be as cheap as is possible to get. So for this reason, we have a check-and-balance system that is probably more successful than the Fairness Doctrine. We no longer have broadcasters suspected of loading up their cash drawer during campaign time. The fact of the matter is that they have to sell a spot that might go for a thousand bucks to some politician for two hundred dollars, and it's a very painful experience.

MIELKE: The question relates to the general problem of "Outs" getting access to the media, and particularly relates to the types of mechanisms you might employ to maximize the rationality of access of the out groups as opposed to access of those who had a publicity gimmick. What are the policies and practices that you employ to give access to "Out" groups in ways that can give access to the most reasonable manifestation of those "Out" groups as opposed to the most publicity worthy manifestations of those "Out" groups?

TORNABENE: There arc three aspects here. One must be: it must be

news. It must be important, and it must be interesting. The first test that
you must ask is whether it is news. It has to be presented in an atmosphere
of balance and of fairness. Of course, newspapers for years have been
very careful in lining up their columns in terms of length and size of
pictures. We try to do this to a certain extent in broadcasting, especially
in our major evening television news shows during a campaign, but it's very
difficult. And especially this past year when we had many surrogates for
the President rather than the President himself. We didn't receive too much
criticism from the general public that we were partial toward McGovern,
because we had him on more, which says something, because the measure
was news—he was generating more news per day. I think that, if we
can stand the test of balance of fairness, we can come through. We certainly did this time.

ROGERS: I think it is important to point out that there is widespread and
continual confusion in the minds not only of the public and the politicians,
but of broadcasters themselves, of the difference between Section 315
which speaks to the rights of candidates for election, and the Fairness
Doctrine. Section 315 was a total nightmare, because it says very specifically that if, during a bona fide campaign for election, a bona fide
candidate makes an appearance on the air, then all candidates for the
same office in the same election are entitled to the same exposure. Well,
this becomes a logistical problem of almost unbelievable magnitude,
especially when you think in terms of primary campaigns where you might
have the two major parties with multiple choice candidates, or you might
have four parties with candidates for nine seats on city council all at the
same time. So, it becomes really a terrible problem. A major exemption
was passed by the same law that chopped our political prices down, which
enables you to put a candidate for office on a news program as long as it is a
bona fide news event, without triggering any obligation. In other instances,
you assign a half hour on Monday night, two weeks before the election
and you pre-empt the network program. You put all eight candidates on
there for four minutes each, or something of the sort, and then when they
come around and the richest one wants to buy a lot of time, you say:
"Sorry, I haven't got anything to sell." That's another device that is now
being used very widely. And then still another device, which most of our
stations are now doing, is, in highly selective races, using editorial endorsements. The station uses an editorial to endorse a candidate for a specific
office. Obviously, every time that happens, that opponent gets an opportunity, either himself or through a surrogate and gets his licks in. These
techniques are being developed because of the dynamism that Chuck mentioned. We're in a new industry which is achieving a first blush of adulthood but the change keeps going on.

PLANT: I'm a member of the IRTS Board, and I'm one of the people who suggested this topic. I have a question for the faculty. I have been greatly concerned that any incumbent Administration can control the news and make the news. I think the word "capture" has misled us a little bit. I'm not talking about capturing the airways in the sense that DeGaulle captures them. I am, however, talking about controlling the news and making the news in the same way that Nixon was able to do it, and quite properly—this summer when he went to Russia, and to China, and when he had a joint session of Congress in prime time. For two weeks, the American public was exposed to the incumbent Administration. Now, it could have been a Democratic Administration and they could have done exactly the same thing, but it seems to me that the election might very well have been won back in July rather than in November. If this is so, what do we do about it? And the question is for you. I'd hoped that we would get a response and I hope that you'll go back and think about that, and come back and tell us what can be done so that there isn't an automatic renewal of the Presidency after the first four years. If that is so, maybe we ought to consider whether we shouldn't change the entire system. As I'm sure many of you know, Rex Tugwell, among others, has suggested a six-year presidency—just one term. If we really have an eight-year presidency now, at least we ought to know it and we ought to face up to it, and I hope you'll think about it and perhaps come up with some answers that will be useful.

Challenge VI

Is Broadcast Programming Only for the Mass Audience? Is It Mirror or Telescope?

THE IMPLICATIONS of this challenge are critical, indeed. They embrace so wide a range of possibilities and alternatives as to constitute the substance of a volume in itself. And the question of what the thrust of radio and television programming should aim to accomplish is really central to the function of broadcasting as the most extensive of the mass media. Involved are such related questions as the pragmatic basis for program decisions, the effect of the medium, the matter of value judgments and taste, the whole area of social responsibility.

The immediate answers to the questions posed would seem quite simple—even simplistic. Nor would there appear to be any area of disagreement. Broadcasting executives not only agree they have an inherent responsibility to program for cultural and other minorities, but assert that they do so. Further, if there is more diversity in non-commercial television, the broadcasting industry should have little difficulty in transferring to itself such catholicity. As for social acceptability, the NBA Code states clearly that, since broadcasting is a family medium which comes as a guest in the home, there are limits to what is socially acceptable program behavior. Yes, parameters can be established, but with considerable difficulty. Finally, with respect to outside supervision, the issue easily becomes polarized. The broadcaster believes that the exercise of responsibility makes outside supervision unnecessary. Yet, in the news area, would there not be a kind of indirect supervision exercised by the recently established press council to investigate, but not adjudicate, complaints of biased programming? And, if there were "supervision" who would do the supervising—and who would evaluate the supervisors?

Upon closer observation, therefore, neither the question nor the answer are simple—if, indeed, there are any categorical answers. The dynamics of the medium tend to reflect social change. The conviction that mass media reflect the social environment even more than they influence it, that the public is inclined to accept the familiar rather than seek out the challenge of the new is generally accepted by communications research—although perhaps it is time that these convictions were themselves challenged and re-examined.

Several facets of broadcasting should be considered, for they are unique to the American system and not duplicated anywhere. Television and radio reach no circumscribed public, as do other media. Even the newspaper has its geographical limitations. But broadcasting reaches virtually everyone, everywhere, and cuts across the widest possible spectrum of demographics—age, religion, social and economic strata, among other categories. Because the medium reaches everybody, in a sense, the broadcaster has remained convinced that the way to program is by "cultural democracy" which means giving the public what it wants. In this way, the medium functions best in a pluralistic society. What the people want, then, is what they view, and they seem to like and accept what is available. Certain staples, such as situation comedies, westerns and action-adventure programs tend to achieve high Nielsen and ARB ratings and thus are duplicated year after year in variations of certain themes.

But this discourages cultural diversity. It neglects cultural minority needs. It does not address itself to such normative considerations as whether what the public wants is necessarily consistent with, or germane to, its needs. Was it not William S. Paley, Chairman of CBS, who, when he determined to schedule serious music on the Network was admonished that there was no audience for such programs as opera or symphony. Mr. Paley reportedly replied, "Then we'll create one!"

But another aspect of our system of broadcasting is also significant and obtrusive. The media are supported by advertisers. The viewer has little investment other than the purchase and maintenance of the receiver, although there is now the option of pay cable in some areas. Hence, since this kind of libertarianism appears to be the most feasible method of protecting broadcasting from control by government, the consequences must be accepted realistically. The advertiser wants the largest possible audience at the most realistic cost per thousand, and this situation results in programming which is essentially entertainment-oriented. In these times, there are few institutional advertisers who will sponsor a one or two hour dramatic or cultural special, let alone a regularly scheduled series. Thus, the dilemma of the program executives is clear and the results have been equally clear. Television, say its critics, caters to mass taste, tries to please everyone, stoops to the lowest common denominator. The result is emasculation and blandness.

But not so fast. Two other factors must be considered at this juncture. First, there is the concept of demographics. If television need not program for mass audiences, if it is shown that special programs, pinpointing special audiences, will sell certain products, there could be a vast change in programming orientation toward vastly improved quality. This has already begun to happen with the unprecedented decision to cancel popular programs with high audience shares because the advertiser was not reaching the largest audience. And there is another encouraging factor—perhaps the most encouraging of all. Television is beginning to assume a bolder look. There is, for example, something to be said against programming an *All in the Family* because it may tend to reinforce bigotry. But there is also much to be said for the *idea,* the very changing concept, that television can tackle subjects and portray characters beyond the conventionally accepted stereotypes. In a medium like broadcasting, there are obviously limits of taste that do not apply to other media. But there is still a wide range of subjects that can be handled with taste and intelligence. The medium also has a responsibility to confront these areas, to experiment with greater boldness and, on occasion, even to take risks. As the success of *The Waltons* has shown, even programming of honesty and simplicity, revealing real people in ordinary situations, can build an appreciative audience. The answer to the question originally posed is probably that there is no need for the alternatives of either mirror or telescope. Broadcasting should be—and can be—both.

CHALLENGE VI

Producer: George Simko (Benton and Bowles)

Moderator: Roderick D. Rightmire (Ohio University)

Panel: Giraud Chester (Goodson-Todman); A. Frank Reel (Metromedia Producers Corp.); Irwin Segelstein (Columbia Broadcasting System)

Question and Answer (in order): Chuck Baker (University of Georgia); Richard Barnhill (Syracuse University); Peter K. Pringle (University of Florida); William Hawes (University of Houston); Bertram Barer (California State University, Northridge)

RIGHTMIRE: This is Challenge VI: Is Broadcast Programming Only for the Mass Audience, Is It Mirror or Telescope? Those are not necessarily the same, and I think our Panel will speak about the differences as we go along. Is there a responsibility to program to more limited audiences and tastes rather than just the mass? Can the diversity found in public broadcasting be transferred to commercial success? Is there a limit beyond which program content and subject matter cannot go, lest it become socially unacceptable? How can we establish parameters? Is there present or potential need for supervision from outside the industry? Let us introduce our first Panel Member, Jerry Chester, Executive Vice President, Goodson-Todman.

CHESTER: This is an interesting moment in time to be discussing this question, because we are now at the culmination of a period of approximately twenty years during which the broadcasting industry has been seek-and developing a new image of itself and its function. It wasn't until about 1953 that an awareness developed that broadcasting might have a greater potential than simply repeating the pattern that had existed for the previous twenty years in radio. That is, that a television network might provide a broad-ranging service of entertainment and of information, breaking away from a past of unbroken entertainment programming fifty-two weeks a year. They might find ways of developing new sources of economic support. This expressed itself in a variety of new program patterns, "specials" in entertainment for example, which made it possible for Hollywood performers to come to television on an occasional basis; to put on programs of deliberately limited appeal such as *Romeo and Juliet,* twenty years ago or *Hamlet,* and this year, *Much Ado About Nothing.*

But that's a spread of twenty years, and *Much Ado About Nothing* probably would not have gone on if there hadn't been that prior history of experimenting in that direction. Those movements and actions took place as a result of vision and ideas on the part of some leaders in the business—notably at NBC in the early years, followed by CBS. Now, there were other self-images of television at that time. One of them was held at the American Broadcasting Company, during the years that it was trying to establish itself as a competitive medium, and that was simply to be the neighborhood movie house and to provide a program schedule made up of films—film series mainly supplied by Warner Bros. In looking back on this twenty-year period, it is interesting to see that all three national networks now have the same vision. They want to provide a service that is reasonably broad-based, to attempt within their economic realities to provide a mixture of entertainment for some limited publics and a program schedule basically designed for the largest publics they can reach to support the economic base of their operation.

There has been a gradual process of putting public affairs programming into prime time. Last week, CBS preempted its Thursday night movie and put on an hour of Henry Kisssinger followed by an hour of Lyndon Johnson. In doing so, the people at CBS knew they were going to get by far the smallest ratings of the evening. None of these things would have happened without the history that preceded them in terms of the network's sense of its mission and its obligation. I think these developments took place because there were leaders in the industry who had a vision of what was possible and who were smart enough to develop new economic sources of support. We now pretty much take such matters for granted. The reality of the commercial business is something of which I'm sure all of you are aware—that if you don't maintain your economic base by providing a large basic circulation—the sources of income to underwrite your program schedule are gradually going to deteriorate. There has been an increase in the number of television sets, an increase in the number of stations and an advance in technological developments. To some extent these developments may release us from the tyranny of appealing only to one audience almost all of the time. I'm referring to cable television. Admittedly, it is still a fringe area, but it opens up the possibility of appealing to more limited audiences, with a different economic base.

The second aspect of the question in defining what is the responsibility of a network and of a station and how they will carry out their responsibility has been a matter of how fast you can move. There were programs twenty years ago that were considered pioneering programs— we put on *Medic* with Richard Boone at NBC and we showed an operation on camera, and that was considered much too strong. It wasn't a matter of bad taste, but of what the public was accustomed to see without prior notice. We've made enormous advances there, largely because our society has changed so much. Ten years ago somebody asked me whether I thought there were any sales possibilities in television for the film *La Dolce Vita.* My response at that time was negative. I just couldn't imagine it. I was completely wrong: tastes have changed, and acceptability standards have changed. When I saw *Last Tango in Paris,* I found myself saying, what are the television possibilities of *Last Tango in Paris?* How many years will it be before this is acceptable? I think that what happens within that framework of trying to meet and not offend public taste has been that producers step forward here and there with an adventursome move, and if the public reaction is not too overwhelmingly negative, a lesson is learned.

In terms of advancing frontiers of taste and whether or not television is reflecting or leading taste, the program, *Maude,* is, a good case in point. In my household *Maude* is a very popular program. I have small children, seven and nine, and I watch *Maude* with them. As a former network executive, I find myself saying: "Really, should this show be on at eight o'clock at night?", and I'm struck by the adventursomeness of the CBS management. As I watch it with my children, I say: "Well, half of it is going right by them and they're really not understanding it. . . ."

COMMENT: Except Jerry, that it's seven o'clock in the midwest.

CHESTER: That's what I'm thinking of in terms of the scheduling. The kind of material that's on *Maude* and *All in the Family* was unthinkable five or ten years ago. And that's really the process by which the frontiers are extended, and that comes about because individuals—producers, and executives, who have some sense of responsibility and desire to lead—put pressure in that direction and sometimes they make mistakes, but sometimes they do succeed in advancing the frontiers. Now, there is always a large body of people in any industry who are very conservative and don't want to make any waves and will repeat what's happened before. If something is acceptable in *Maude,* it will turn up elsewhere. It'll be script material for another show.

I remember, it wasn't so long ago (at NBC), when we gave a black entertainer his own show. That was Nat "King" Cole in the prime-time schedule—and it took a lot of guts to do that. There was great concern about clearance in the Southern part of the country, as to whether the program would be carried by the stations. All that's gone by the wayside. Has anybody made a submission for a new series with a black woman detective in the lead? You know that, if you have an hour series with three leads, there'll be two men and one woman, and probably one of the men will be black—that's almost become a stereotype now, and at some point we'll break away from that.

RIGHTMIRE: Thank you very much. Jerry Chester has given us a kind of historical perspective on changing tastes and changing images and the business aspects. Frank Reel, President of Metromedia Producers Corporation, is going to tackle, as his contribution to the Panel, the economics of this question.

REEL: Thank you. Let me begin where I think Jerry Chester left off, and maybe reverse this coin a little bit. Listening to Jerry, I realize that he had done an excellent job just now of describing some of the great advances in television and some of the things that are being done that are fine and different. And yet we all know, facing reality, that one of the great complaints about television, and I'm talking particularly about prime time television—because we simply don't have time to go into the whole field, let's limit it to the most dramatic—is that there is a sameness about it. And I believe that's where this question that we're discussing came from.

Is broadcast programming only for the mass audience? Is it a mirror or something else—a telescope? I would have to say this among other things: the company that I preside over produces such programming as the Jacques Cousteau specials. For six years we did the National Geographic specials. We've done *The Making of the President* for three or four-year terms. But the point is, that these programs, like *Romeo and Juliet,* like that marvelous *Much Ado About Nothing,* are specials. They are not the ordinary, day-to-day, bread-and-butter series about which people do complain as having too much of a sameness in their appeal. Not that these series aren't good—they are. I, too, like *Maude, All in the Family* and many others. I think there are some wonderful programs on television— regular series fare—but, I think we must admit that there is some justification to the claim of sameness, because perforce for economic reasons, these programs do appeal to pretty much the same type of people; not the great majority because there is no such thing. I don't think there is a great majority in this country—it's too diverse. We're a country of many, many, many minorities. But I do believe that, by definition, the great bulk of television is aimed at the largest "single" minority that fits the pattern that the advertiser is looking for.

And let's get into that for a moment. I know of no better way than to take the question that underlies this challenge. Just the first couple of sentences will almost tell you the whole story if you analyze it. The premise for this discussion reads: are commercial radio and television systems based on special and exclusive licensing, but financed by private investment—advertising? Presently, this system supports, and I think this is the key word, several thousand radio, and several hundred—now underline that word—several hundred television stations, plus at least (and that's an interesting phrase) three networks in each medium. Those numbers are the key to what we are talking about. In the main, the premise goes on, programming decisions are based almost entirely on popularity in order to attract advertising.

Now, how does this work and what's it all about? Companies like ours, and many others, produce programming which we sell to the networks. The networks take this programming and they, in turn, sell it to advertisers by way of spot announcements or sometimes in groups, and yet, in reality, what they sell the advertisers is not the program at all. They sell *you* to the advertiser. They sell the audience. They sell numbers, because the advertiser judges his "buy" by what he calls "cost per thousand;" dollars per thousand. How many dollars per thousands of viewers per minute of commercial does this show cost, or this spot announcement? So that the more viewers, the lower the cost, the greater the efficiency, to use the language of the advertising business. Results are based on the fact that the three networks, who are the purchasers, competing with one another, are looking for the greatest number of viewers. Now analyze that and refine it further, because it isn't even that simple.

But let's just start with a certain number of viewers. I said a moment ago that the key to this discussion is in the numbers. There are several thousand radio stations, but only several hundred television stations. Why? It's an engineering phenomenon. When television was first licensed in this country by the Federal Communications Commission, they used only the VHF spectrum which had been fairly well established with only thirteen possible channels—really only twelve, because one was reserved by the Government. For engineering reasons, you can't have the same channel closer than two-hundred or two-hundred-fifty miles from the other or you have overlap—you can have a Channel 5 in New York and in Washington, but you can't have one in Philadelphia or Baltimore. You can have one in Boston but you can't have one in Providence, Hartford, New Haven and so forth. There would be an overlap problem, so that there are a limited number of these channels. Those of you who live in New York or Los Angeles are treated to seven VHF stations. We're very lucky. Those of you who come from any place else in the country know that that isn't the case anywhere else. There are only eighteen cities that have as many as four VHF stations. Most of the cities of this country have three or less.

As a matter of fact, there aren't even three whole networks, because the ABC network is unable to clear as many stations as CBS and NBC, due to the fact that in many cities there are only two stations or, in some, only one. Now, I've been talking about VHF stations. There are UHF stations, but we don't have time to talk about why they are not economically viable to purchasers of the kind of programming that could compete on this basis with the others. If you want to get into that question later, I will be glad to discuss it. But let's just take my word for it for the moment. You have to ignore, by and large, with a few exceptions, the UHF stations as viable purchasers of either syndicated or network programming, in its first run, for economic reasons.

So, we have three networks. Probably your immediate reaction to that is, well, that's a tri-opoly. It has tremendous economic power. We're getting close to the dirty word "monopoly" and this is very dangerous and this is very powerful. That's not what I'm talking about. Quite the reverse. The problem arises because of competition among these three, and the fact that there are only three competing, so that you cannot, with the costs that exist in this industry, you simply cannot appeal to more than the largest single, mass minority audience that the advertisers want. Think of radio for a moment; New York City has dozens of radio stations. You can have a WQXR that has purely classical music. You'd have a news station, you can have a talk station, a rock station, you'd have a middle-of-the-road station. You cannot have that in television. It just can't work as long as we have this limitation of three "theatres" in which to have the property. We used to think that the only thing that was important was getting what we called "big numbers, big ratings," but over the last five or ten years (less than ten years, over the last five years probably), the science of demographics has grown up, so now the advertiser is much more interested in the kinds of audience he gets. He wants to reach the people who buy products. And who are they? We're told they are women from ages eighteen to forty-nine, so that the appeal is even narrower. Most programming, most staple programming (and I'm leaving out the specials and the exceptions, and believe me, there are many of them) is aimed at the women aged eighteen to forty-nine, so that you have an additional impetus for the "sameness" that people do complain about. What's the answer? I'm told we don't have to offer solutions, merely point to the problem, but let's think about a few possible solutions. As a matter of fact, again I turn to the premise, because the question posed is, and I quote: "Is there a responsibility to program to more limited audiences and tastes, rather than just the Mass?"

Is there a responsibility? Well, let's think about industry in general for a moment. Forget television. We'll come back to that. I read an article recently by Milton Freedman, the economist at the University of Chicago. He points out that all of this talk about responsibility of corporate executives for improving the general welfare is misplaced. For example: should a corporation that might be concerned with the ecology worry about the ecology? Should the corporate leaders, should the chairmen of the boards, should the president of the corporation, should the active administrators be concerned at the expense of their stockholders to protect the ecology? Or to be anti-inflationary? Professor Freedman's answer was, "No," because that's not their function. As a matter of fact, these are all very controversial issues. By what right does the administrator of a corporation take the stockholders' money, deplete it by reason of adherence to what he thinks would be good for the ecology? The stockholder might believe otherwise. Professor Freedman asked this question: What would happen to the labor leader who said to his membership: "Fellows, we're not going after an increase this year because it's inflationary?" To ask the question is to answer it. The logical result of Professor Freedman's argument, I'm afraid, was to reach a conclusion that he has always professed to be opposed to, namely: greater Government action, because the answer is that these correctives should not come from within the corporation, they should come from the body politic as a whole, or from the Government agency. And this, of course, leads only to more of the kind of state socialism that Professor Freedman expresses himself as being opposed to.

But in the television industry, we have something a little different. We have an industry that by its definition is a product of Government.

It's licensed by the Government. The air waves that it uses presumedly start in the ownership of the people; and the licenses—these priceless licenses—are given free by our Federal Communications Commission. But—since we're talking about programming—would any of us sit still for a moment and say that that Governmental agency should dictate the content of the programming? Whenever you get into this ground, you're in very shaky territory and you'll run all the way . . . you'll run the gamut from the problems that arise when the FCC says, as they did a few months ago, that they thought *Wild Kingdom* was a good enough program to allow for certain exceptions, to the kind of wild and dangerous statement that came from the OTP chairman when he indicated that he thought that the stations should be careful of the news content from the networks because it was, "elitist gossip," rather than news. This is an area that we can debate and we can discuss, but we enter with grave trepidation. So, it seems to me that the one thing that must be avoided is the government that exercises the responsibility to talk about programming or to dictate programming, and if there's an answer, the answer must be in increasing, if possible, the number of theatres available to show the product. That can be done without changing the present set-up, in the view of some people, by simply opening up time, and I'm referring now to prime time access role experiment. A lot of things are wrong with it, and yet the reason for it, the reason why it's existing, the reason why it may continue (with changes perhaps), is precisely because there's a feeling on the part of people that we've got to create more theatres than simply just the three that we have.

Another possible solution is one that is completely impractical, and that is the substitution of UHF throughout the country for VHF and the doing away with all the VHF, to put all stations on an equality as UHF. I think it's completely impractical, because it's too late. The networks have five owned-and-operated stations in the largest cities. The company that I'm with exists by reason of its ownership and operation of stations in large cities that are VHF's. Companies like Westinghouse, like Storer, like all the great newspapers in this country are concerned with this, and I think it's completely impractical but it would answer the question. And the third possibility, of course, is the strengthening of public television, so that perhaps it could be made into the kind of viable competitor that the BBC is in England.

In closing, let me just bring this into perspective by reading something that I want to share with you because I thought it was rather interesting. It may be that all I'm saying is that there is nothing new under the sun, but George Bernard Shaw in his preface to *Arms and the Man,* which first appeared in 1894, wrote the following about the London stage:

> Authors must not expect managers to invest many thousands of pounds in plays, however fine, which will clearly not attract perfectly

commonplace people. Playwriting and theatrical management on the present commercial basis are businesses like other businesses, depending on the patronage of great numbers of very ordinary customers. When the managers and authors study the wants of these customers, they succeed, when they do not, they fail. A public-spirited manager, or author, with a keen, artistic conscience may choose to pursue his business with minimum of profit and a maximum of social usefulness by keeping as close as he can to the highest marketable limit of quality and constantly feeling for an extension of that limit through the advance of popular culture. An unscrupulous manager or author may aim simply at the maximum of profit with a minimum of risk. Between them, there is plenty of room for most talents to breathe freely.

But he was talking about the London stage. There were how many theatres? Twenty, thirty, fifty or more? We're talking about three theatres. Even with twenty, thirty to fifty theatres the appeal had to be to the masses of one sort or another. With three theatres, the appeal must be to the masses. The problem with only three theatres is that we're limited to a very small single group of these masses and anything, I submit, that can extend that limit of theatres, is a step in the right direction.

RIGHTMIRE: Thank you. I will now introduce Irwin Segelstein, Vice President of Program Administration, CBS-TV Network.*

SEGELSTEIN: Thank you. Some of the thoughts here seem a little global. Most of the attitudes you'll hear from me are my own personal point of view. If you're a program executive, you never speak for the company because you may not be working there when you get back. Perhaps, if you'll let me tick off my answers to some of the questions raised in the premise or in the Challenge—a new word for "subject"—I think that you will find that most of the answers are platitudes and I suspect that most of the questions are platitudes, so there will probably be no surprises. Is broadcast programming only for the mass audience? A question like that would have been posed a few years ago: is it for the program or is it for the mass? Now we are saying: Is it *only* for the mass? Is it mirror or is it telescope? I think it is primarily for the mass. There are opportunities to do other thangs, and we *do* do them. A very simple illustration: obviously, *Captain Kangaroo* is not programmed for mass audience, it's programmed for a very targeted audience, and so I think, it is a mirror. The drive for large audiences has recently brought broadcast programming into areas and subject matters that represent breaks with the tradition of current social

* Mr. Segelstein is now President, Columbia Records.

acceptability. However, whatever changes you've seen, we're not talking about Bill Balance and sex radio. I think the drive for large audiences was not what motivated *All in the Family* and since I was there, I do know something about that. It was an attempt to do something new. As a matter of fact, most of the opinion in the Program Department at CBS and perhaps at the network management levels, was that it wouldn't reach large audiences. If a show goes on in January, in midseason, it usually expresses a network's feeling that it has greater risk potential up and down. So the more explosive shows generally find their way on the networks in mid-season. It struck us as something worth doing as an important, funny show and it was scheduled for that reason with a great deal of feeling that it wouldn't survive. To show you how professional we are, we were more surprised than most.

Is there a responsibility to program more for limited audiences? Of course there is, and you expect my answer to be yes. We do have a responsibility or desire to make some part of our schedule reflective of minority appetites and tastes. All program executives that I know will tell you that they feel they could be doing a better job in drama, dance, music, public affairs and documentaries. Can diversity found at public broadcasting be transferred to commercial success? Occasionally. Certainly though, its existence, apart from its own purposes, becomes another tool in your reading of, or in our reading of, what's taking place. What you see on the cover of *Time* magazine, or what you read in *Harper's,* and what you've seen at the theatre, or what movies you've seen, or which performers seem to be getting some attention what happens in a narrower-gauge appeal situation like public television . . . all this does have a very pragmatic work-a-day effect on the people who work in television network programming.

Is there a limit beyond which program content and subject matter can go? I think every program executive believes the answer is, "Yes, there is a limit." It is something that comes into the home, and as I said, it's a platitude and you know the answer.

Can we establish parameters? I don't know. It's very difficult. We have to make those fine-line decisions. Our Program Practices head has gone on the road with a little sample case of problems he has. It's a chalk talk and film lecture in which he shows a scene from *The Sergeant*. Rod Steiger plays a homosexual sergeant in the army. Now in effect, he's groping for answers. I was told that there had been moments on the show that scared the networks silly. And it's difficult to gauge, except by way of response and your own subjective judgment whether we are manipulating, or changing or offending.

What has happened is that, in the last five years, we have seen television changes in *Laugh-In, All in the Family,* and *Maude.* Each of these has built its own context. And after some initial flurry, people accept the contextual thing or a joke in that context, that they would not accept on the Dick Van Dyke show. It's been spoken of before, perhaps some of you know about it, but there is very little feedback on *All in the Family,* except for perhaps the most extreme comments. But on the Van Dyke show last season, we did a show in which he is visited, in a tasteful conventional situation comedy format, by a priest who has left the Church and is with a nun who has left the order. The two of them were on their way to Mexico to get married. It plays out as straight situation comedy. We had more mail on that, and Van Dyke did late night appearances to apologize for having done the show. They simply would not accept on the Van Dyke show, in its context, what they will accept on *Maude.* Now do we establish parameters? It's very difficult—step by step—and if we do try to do something new and different, we are going to make mistakes and we will hear from an outraged public about the mistakes.

The last question, of course, is one that I gather has unanimity in the industry. I don't think anybody at this end of the table believes in the need for outside supervision. Behind all of it, is a question as to some guilt about mass audience, about popularity. It's a question that arises primarily in upper middle class or upper income living rooms and in seminars—some peculiar feeling of guilt about large popularity. So that we take it out of this context and, because I work in a network, obviously you might suspect that my point of view is biased. I have found that if I go to talk to Paul Fox, who is head of BBC One, he is upset because he's accused of being too popular. I go to work every morning with a gentleman who works at Channel 13 in New York. I'll swear to you he knows the New York rating numbers every morning of *All in the Family* and is informed on the Knapp Committee hearings. He is counting the box office as readily as Joe Papp does at the Winter Garden and as readily as we do at commercial networks.

In effect, we are going through this discussion of what is popularity and why is it wrong to be popular? Why are we guilty if we do reach a large audience? I have never found that the kind of choices we make of the programs we schedule, has had to do with advertiser considerations. Nobody has ever said to me that these shows have advertiser appeal, although I am aware that there are demographic considerations. When we put a schedule together, we put it together in show-business terms, purely and simply, with an attempt in the basic schedule to reach an audience and to satisfy hopefully a large audience, not to sell a product or all the things we seem to be accused of. The issue is how many people can we reach with this program whose purpose is to entertain? And we make our choices on the ability to entertain a large number of people. Now, clearly, it's not only for the mass audience, because we fail a lot. I mean, there are shows we put on the schedule that clearly don't reach the mass audience even though our intention was to do so. And then, let me raise just one small thought—we know very little in terms of what effect television has on the audience and vice versa. We make assumptions. We lead a little and we push a little, and there is feedback. We really don't know about the extent of the most recent and publicized violence on television situation. We are perfectly willing to have somebody tell us precisely what research is, so that we can act accordingly, but nobody can really tell us that accurately, can they?

If you go to your local art house and find there is a Stan Laurel revival, it's a cult. Isn't it mass appeal and wasn't it intended to be? Is Dick Van Dyke merely a favorite performer and is Stan Laurel now a cult? Are the Harold Lloyd movies of the twenties, which were intended to be mass, now mass or have they passed into some cult? Will Carol Burnett, who is a 43-share show . . . , about which we could ask whether she appeals too largely to the mass . . . be shown at the Museum of Modern Art in New York ten years from today? We will think how charming it is, and how wonderful it is that we, the elite, can love her at the Museum. I don't have a lot of answers, I have a lot of questions.

CHALLENGE VI: QUESTION AND ANSWER SESSION

BAKER: This is addressed to Mr. Segelstein. You commented on the guilt you had on programming to the masses, when in fact you do program at CBS very nobly to the minority audiences, the small target audiences. We have a situation in the Atlanta market where the CBS affiliate carries *Camera Three* at 6:30 in the morning, and some cultural specials come along and never get cleared at all. Does this give you a sense of frustration?

SEGELSTEIN: Yes.

BAKER: What are you going to do about it?

SEGELSTEIN: Clearance is a very serious problem. Frank referred to ABC having clearance problems. I'm happy you mentioned *Camera Three*. Clearance has become a very serious problem for networks. In the days when somebody refused to clear a half hour at 10:30 at night, and put their news and movie early, it became a simple matter to define. There is an erosion of clearance now and peculiar DB's. Even in New York on a company-owned station, Channel 2, DB's on a Sunday afternoon, a family and children's program, but they put it on at another time. So clearance is becoming a problem. To counteract, we sell harder. We write notes. We put shows on closed circuit. We try to get the press in the local market into the local station to see the show for the worthwhile things, so that the station is either embarrassed or made more aware of what we are offering. We hope to get clearance that way.

BARNHILL: I am not going to quarrel with this, I'd just like to have it clarified. You say that in deciding programming, you use show-business terms or criteria—not advertising—but you do consider demographics. Is there a conflict in that logic?

SEGELSTEIN: Yes, there is some conflict. It is not as critical a problem in making program decisions. It may be more critical perhaps in an earlier stage of program development where you're choosing programs. A program development man may have to make some fine-line choices. But when the programs are in, and when you are ready to schedule—the choices are made on intuitive and subjective and show-business bases. I mentioned show business because one of the dilemmas of programming is that at one end of the business a whole group of salesmen are walking up and down the street selling guarantees of audiences, cost per thousand, efficiency and demographics. At the other end are a bunch of obese, bearded, middle-aged executives trying to find shows and there is a kind of inconsistency in that problem. We're really in show business at one end and we're in advertising at the other. Now that's kind of a tightrope.

PRINGLE: My question is directed towards Mr. Segelstein, too. I'm not clear on one point you made. It was when you were discussing the point that you don't always program for the largest audience, and you mentioned specifically *All in the Family*. You didn't really expect a large audience, in fact you said you were quite surprised. I'd like you to explain that statement in light of the fact that the program idea had already been tried and tested in Britain under the title *Until Death Us Do Part* and had been found to be a very successful formula and even today tops the British ratings whenever it's on the air.

SEGELSTEIN: I guess I was guilty of hyperbole. I had seen three episodes of *Until Death Us Do Part,* and I thought it was funny. I thought perhaps it was too British. ABC had made two pilots of *All in the Family.* They had examined the pilots, thought they were lacking in terms of popular appeal, and passed them. The agent on the package happened to remember our interest in *Until Death Us Do Part,* and brought us one of the ABC pilots. We had questions. We knew it could work, we knew it could explode. We also knew it could bomb. It was not one of those safe shows, which would seek a safe level of audience. I really don't think I can add any more to it than that. I don't think we can take the English experience and translate it directly to American television.

HAWES: Mr. Reel, it seems to me that inflation is killing product. Do you see any way in which the cost of programming, that is product, could be deflated?

REEL: Well, yes, of course. The cost of programming doesn't need to be as high as it is. *All in the Family* is about as good an example as one can find. I don't know what the program costs were when it first went on the air, but I dare say it was one of the lower-cost programs. I could make a guess that I don't want to make and I think I would be within a few thousand dollars of where it hit, which is probably a third of what the network has to pay for it today because of the success. Programming does not need to cost as much as it does, and those of us who have been programming for syndication realize this. I'll just give you one example of how this can work. We have just completed a pilot film which is geared for the prime-time access period and we aren't sure there is going to be a prime-time access period. It's a show that involves network actors, Bob Denver, Forrest Tucker, Jeannine Riley, Laury Sanders, all from network shows. It's produced by a network producer, Mr. Sherwood Schwartz who produces *The Brady Bunch*. It's written by a network writer. It's full network quality in every sense of the word. If there is no prime-time access, we will take it to the networks and it will cost half again as much if it is sold to a network, simply because the contracts with the actors, the director, the writers and with the producer say so. We are able to get much lower prices for the work of these very same people if the show is in syndication than if it goes network. One reason is that, if it goes to a network, the network will only buy 13 episodes and then maybe a few more, maybe up to 17, and then maybe up to as high as 22 or 24. Whereas, if it goes into syndication, we can guarantee these people 26 episodes and that makes a tremendous difference. But basically, the answer to your question is "yes." The same program can be done for less money.

BARER: Recently, there has been a furor about minority access to program conception. How do you deal with your conception of minority access to those programs? Is the movement on to serve particular minorities, with particular kinds of programs?

SEGELSTEIN: Well, you are really touching on one of the most difficult areas. Part of it has to do with the basic topic we are talking about. If television is a mass audience, in what way should it specifically direct itself to minority or ethnic group audiences as opposed to minority tastes? There is some feeling that this is a problem of how to take network television prime time and devote it exclusively towards some narrow segment of the audience. We are asking society to be active rather than passive, we are telling our kids to get involved. As a result, there is a constant barrage of pressure from every organized and unorganized segment of society. One of the ways we do it is simply to try to seek help from some of the groups which have a constructive point of view for us in terms of raising problems and providing expert consultants. If we were going to do *Sounder* as a TV feature, it would have to be produced, directed and acted by black people—forget the producer, that's a financial function—but the creative function would have to be done by people who know the material. And that's the only way we can do it.

REEL: As Irwin has pointed out, whether it's a black minority, or whatever other considerations in picking programs, the network, as I understand it, takes a very broad view . . . certainly this network does. But there is another problem, and it isn't only in picking the program . . . it's whether you keep it on, and I'm speaking now again of the staple series. I will give you an example. Lawrence Welk was on a network for years with huge numbers. He was cancelled because he appealed only to a minority audience, and it was not that attractive to advertisers. It so happened by accident that it was knocked off the year the prime time rule came into effect, so that it immediately went into syndication and is on 187 stations. But the network that had dropped it apparently felt that it did not want to have a portion of the evening devoted to that older audience, because of the flow-of-audience theory that they would lose the younger people. So that, regardless of the reasons of how these programs are picked, you also have to consider what reasons compel them to remain.

CHESTER: I think that is an important point. We have had a number of programs cancelled by CBS that had long runs: *What's My Line, To Tell The Truth, Password.* Interestingly enough, we found it possible to re-introduce all of them to the public. I am making this comment because heretofore the only means by which one could reach the public was through the three door-ways of the networks. When the programs were terminated by the networks they were, for all practical purposes, dead unless they were filmed series. We did find it possible, through syndication, to appeal directly to 150 or 200 different stations and to explore a different marketplace. Whether or not the network had been correct in its decision to terminate, and whether or not reasons were special to the time period, what was significant was that there was a public still interested in these programs. We are now going into the fifth and sixth years of new production of programs that had a previous life on the networks and, interestingly enough, as the wheel turns (having overcome the psychological problem of "once a show is cancelled, it must never again have a new existence") we have been able to reintroduce directly to the networks themselves new versions of shows that had been previously successful. The marketplace has been somewhat broadened. One thing you must keep in mind that is so different about the television business in contrast with publishing, Broadway or motion pictures is that you don't have, as a program producer, direct access to an audience. You have an intermediary, whether it's the network or the station. Even if you wanted to invest your own money without limit, you still do not have direct access to an audience. You can be a fool and put up a million dollars for a Broadway show, rent a theatre and determine for yourself whether the investment was wise in terms of the box office result. Or you could be a vanity publisher and bring out a book, and it may catch on. But you cannot do that in broadcasting. You have an intermediary whose judgment will determine whether or not you have access to the audience. Now we have to deal with these realities. The realities are changing somewhat, and I think that is encouraging, both the broadening of the market place and the greater flexibility of thought. Now, as to whether or not a Lawrence Welk show might have gone down the drain if its cancellation had not been timed exactly with the advent of the prime access rule, we do not know. I may not be a fan of the show and you may not be a fan of the show but the real question is: should the public which derived great personal satisfaction from that show, be deprived of any opportunity whatsoever of seeing it?

RIGHTMIRE: May I just ask Frank and Jerry for their opinions as to whether they think ABC now considers cancelling Lawrence Welk a mistake in light of their troubles on Saturday night.

CHESTER: I don't think they are unhappy about dropping it, because they want to have a young image. On the other hand, it might have been useful to have had it sold out and to have that revenue.

Challenge VII

Special Audiences . . .
Special Treatment?

THE THRUST OF this challenge goes directly to the heart of a question that has absorbed the attention of the government, the broadcaster and many diverse publics—academicians, special interest organizations and professional critics. It is the arresting and very difficult area of responsibility in mass communication, and particularly in media so pervasive and evanescent as radio and television. The challenge has been made more acute by the formation and trenchant public opinion campaigns of Action For Children's Television—a singular example of applied consumerism whose case, on the face of it, is without blemish or rebuttal but whose assumptions and special pleading have not always been based on the most careful of research or, indeed, on as thorough an understanding of American broadcasting as might have been obtained.

The responsibility of the broadcaster is clear-cut and yet ambiguous. And this peculiar phenomenon exists because of the nature of the medium, and it is what distinguishes it from the other communicative arts. Broadcasting insists it must operate under the social responsibility theory which states, quite simply, that the networks and stations alone must be willing to take total responsibility for what they broadcast. At the same time, in order to have this freedom of communication, the broadcaster also operates in a climate of libertarianism in that the industry is privately operated for profit, even while it performs a public service. At the same time, and to complicate matters even more, broadcasting cannot operate with the total freedom of print, because the spectrum space is limited, broadcast licenses involve a tremendously valuable national resource and the media must conform to parameters of the "public interest, convenience and necessity."

If the broadcast media are all things to all men in the programming objectives, they are equally ambiguous in their forensic obligation.

There is little to be argued about the assumption that children constitute a very special public. But there has been considerable discussion relating to whether this unique segment of the television audience should receive special programming *without supporting advertising revenues.* The supporters of ACT (Action For Children's Television) both in and out of the FCC are convinced that all commercials must be interdicted that programming for children must be underwritten by the networks as a public service and necessity, that this drastic change would dramatically improve programming because there would be no need to sell products. Others, perhaps more realistically, take into consideration the economic pragmatism of the medium and advocate a harder look at commercials, with the elimination of those that may be deleterious in their effect on children.

At the same time—and apart from the economic issue—the broadcaster insists that he has been responsive to the needs of this special audience. Witness *Captain Kangaroo* (elimination of show-how commercials). Witness *Fat Albert and the Cosby Kids.* Witness the calling in of "experts" from the university campus—educational psychologists and sociologists—to insure that the quality of programs for children is healthy and sound. And, witness the hiring of specially trained ambassadors who establish liaison with ACT and other groups in order to underscore that something positive *is* being done about children. Finally, see the Television Code, section 3, entitled "Responsibility Toward Children." There, the industry clearly states its awareness of this special public. In the Code, those who subscribe explicitly agree that children's programs must "afford opportunities for cultural growth," must enhance the "moral, social and ethical ideals characteristic of American life," and must eschew material "which is excessively violent."

But these affirmative declarations raise gnawing doubts. There is first the legitimate suspicion, raised in some quarters, that committees of educators and special educational consultants are mere public relations contrivances. With radical changes in commercial standards and the complete elimination of shabby action-adventure-violence programs and vapid comedy cartoons, in favor of genuine quality programming, there would be no need for persuasive communications. And, second, a more literal pursuit of the goal enunciated in the NAB Code would also eliminate much of the criticism that consumer and educational groups, as well as many psychologists, direct against the quality of programs for children. The feeling is all too prevalent—rightly or wrongly—that too little genuine effort is made to improve children's programming; that, when improvements are made, they accrue only as a result of an admonition from the Chairman of the

FCC or when such groups as ACT show that they can exert influence in Washington and on public opinion.

A little less polarization and a little more accommodation might seem to be in order. This would involve a more realistic understanding of the nature of American broadcasting by those who are critical. But it would also involve a more realistic and cooperative attitude on the part of the broadcaster—which would mean scrapping the public relations dodge in favor of carefully selected advertisers, total elimination of questionable programs and a genuine effort to purvey children's programs of high quality. There are many able people in the cartoon factories whose considerable abilities can be utilized in the direction of programs that children will find enlightening, as well as delightful.

CHALLENGE VII

Producer: Diane Sass (Kaiser Broadcasting)

Moderator: Phillip A. Macomber (Kent State University)

Panel: Elizabeth Roberts (Federal Communications Commission); George Newi (American Broadcasting Company); Walter Bartlett (Avco Broadcasting); Richard Block (Kaiser Broadcasting)

Question and Answer (*in order*): Keith W. Mielke (Indiana University); C. A. Kellner (Marshall University); J. M. Ripley (University of Kentucky)

MACOMBER: The premise for Challenge VII is that children are special. Accordingly they should not be regarded as marketing targets. Broadcasters should be required to provide appropriate entertainment, information, educational programming for children at their sole costs without commercial messages aimed at the children. And the question: "Is it the responsibility of broadcasters to provide special programming without support from advertising revenue for special segments of the audience?" This is our seventh challenge, and for this challenge Diane Sass of Kaiser Broadcasting, who could not be with us this afternoon, has put together a very good panel. Dick Block, Elizabeth Roberts, Walt Bartlett and George Newi are here to speak with us and I think we'll find them very interesting. I've asked Miss Roberts if she'll be our first speaker.

ROBERTS: For the past eighteen months I have been closely associated with the problems of children and television, both as a parent of a three-and-a-half-year old and as a concerned professional. I should say at the outset that my statements are not the official FCC position. As a matter of fact, there are not any official FCC positions at all to this date. They're just simply my own opinions and findings. I've come to the belief that the problems of children's television can perhaps be summarized best as analogous to those posed by an attractive nuisance. Just as society holds a property owner having an attractive nuisance as being responsible for the injuries of a trespassing child, so should it act possibly in relation to the current broadcasting fare. The core of the attractive nuisance doctrine is that, lacking mature judgment, children may be attracted to potentially dangerous situations, and protective measures are therefore necessary. Children are indeed a special audience. First of all, they watch an enormous amount of television. The National Commission on the Causes and Prevention of Violence reported that all surveys indicate that American children and youth spend from one-quarter to one-half of their waking hours watching television. Figures vary depending on which study you want to use, but a conservative estimate would be that by the time the child is sixteen-years old, he has watched from twelve- to fifteen-thousand hours of television during which time he has received something like two-hundred and-fifty- to three-hundred-thousand commercial messages.

While the figures are staggering, even the numbers don't say enough. Lyle and Hoffman in the Surgeon General's Report, said: "The importance of television viewing for the child transcends the actual time spent watching." Children learn a great deal from what they watch. Television has a powerful effect on their learning process and it teaches moral and social values. While children, as do adults, turn to television for passive reasons—relaxation, relief from boredom, loneliness—incidental observational learning is taking place.

I don't want to debate here what I've heard debated so often, whether or not television is important to an individual child's decisions, whether it will make him buy a gun or overthrow the system. I'm willing to admit that there are many other important influences on a child's behavior. What I do want to determine is that television is one important influence of life. Young children, two to seven, are particularly susceptible, because their life experience is so narrow. What is seen on television for them is particularly real. As children grow, their motivation for watching television becomes more purposeful. Many adolescents rely on television to learn about real life roles. This is especially true of those children who are not well integrated into family and school life. Children are also a unique audience for the broadcaster, because of the wide range of developmental levels. The developmental levels between two and twelve are more diverse

than at any other time of growth. They cannot be lumped together and
have their needs met. Using industry demographics, I project that it would
be easier to design a program to meet the needs of all eighteen- to forty-
nine-year olds than it would be to program adequately for all two- to
twelve-year olds.

Results of the work of people like Piaget and Erickson have made
many psychologists agree that the child is not just a miniature, although
somehow less wise, adult. He is a different being, with a distinctive mental
structure which is qualitatively different from that of an adult. We've
heard a lot during the last year, at least I have, about the fantasy-reality
problem for children when they watch television. This is a particularly
important aspect of the pre-schooler's adaptation to television viewing.
What they see is absolutely real. By kindergarten age, say five or six, they
can usually tell that the animated figures are not real, or that news programs are somehow more real than advertisements. But perception and
understanding of the full extent of television pseudo-reality takes much
longer for the young child. It is safer to assume he will simply accept as
fact the pseudo-real world he sees on television programs and in commercials. Children are not mature enough to make effective consumer
judgments. For example, a child of seven truly believes that water poured
from one container to another gains or loses in quantity depending on the
size of the container. Certainly this determines how he perceives products
advertised. Children lack sophisticated math ideas. Even though a young
child can count to twenty, he has no conception of certain fundamental math
premises. He may think a set of five contains more than a set of eight if
the physical arrangement takes on certain forms, so that price quotations or
showing pieces of a toy or game, are confusing to the child. Young children
have no sense of sequence. This would mean that they can't distinguish or
separate the commercial from the program content. And still another
example is that young children don't have a very sophisticated sense of
speed, so that all those speed racers in the commercials are fast and enticing.

Even though the child is developing various stages of reasoning, he
forms what he considers to be moral judgments, but he does so on a
completely different basis from most adults. What is right for him is ful-
filling commands in an identifiable person, satisfying an immediate need or
gratification. Until the age of six or seven, children have difficulty in
understanding both motive and consequence of an action. It was suggested by research in the Surgeon General's report that a young child
may be more influenced by the act itself than by an understanding of its
intention or its aftermath. Even the eight to eleven year olds while they
are capable of fairly subtle mental operations, are still strongly tied to con-
crete situations. He reasons best around immediate present objects and
fails to take into account the unseen possibility inherent in a situation.

This, of course, influences his view of program motivation, his susceptibility to value formation and his consumer judgments.

Our nation has long recognized that childhood is a particularly vulnerable time of life. Child labor laws have been enacted, we protect them in their business deals by holding their contracts voidable. The Supreme Court has recognized that children are a special class with regard to protection from obscene materials, and the lists goes on. Children are special and different. Since children comprise a significant part of the community to be served by the broadcaster, and since the broadcasting industry plays a significant role in the child's life, it seems to follow that the broadcaster must meet the needs and interests of the child audience.

What are the current problems as they have polarized during the last several years? First of all, Action for Children's Television and other advocate groups, have looked at what is, and is not, available for children. They began by looking at Saturday morning where the major bulk of production effort and time with programs designed for children is to be found, certainly the bulk of network programming. However, this does not make up prime time for children. It makes up only fifteen per cent of the average child's weekly viewing. Most children are watching most of their television in the early and late afternoons and the early evening hours. Action for Children's Television and other advocates maintain that there is very little designed for children during the time periods which they are watching. In the market where there is an independent station, that station may well be programming for children. However, what they're showing is usually off-network re-runs of adult situation comedies or syndicated cartoon shows. Interestingly enough, some of these cartoon shows were removed from network television fare several years ago as being "too violent." If you look at the afternoon programming for children, you can easily get the impression that what was good for us two, five or even ten years ago, is somehow now appropriate for children. Action for Children's Television is also concerned with age specific programming. They maintain, first of all, that children are an inappropriate group to advertise to because of their lack of consumer ability. But they also maintain that it's the pressures of advertising that affects the quality of programming that children receive. From their point of view, as long as programming must collect a large audience that includes the entire range from two to twelve, and must deliver this to the advertisers, programs will continue to be based on the lowest common denominator. Only, they insist, by relieving programs of that advertising pressure, can improvements be made. In their view, it is this artificial constraint that seeks to capture all ages in order to meet the needs of advertisers, rather than viewers, that prevents a considerable programming talent from being used with the child in mind. Advocates have maintained that they are not against entertainment programming. They are concerned, however, with the lack of diversity in children's programs. The NAB code states that television should give the child a view of the world at large. Where is this in children's programs, they ask? They maintain that you cannot produce educationally stimulating programs for children from two to twelve. You must target a developmental group. The children's programs that are most often pointed to with acclaim —*Sesame Street, Electric Company, Mr. Rogers' Neighborhood*—all target a portion of the two- to twelve-year-old audience. This of course fragments the child audience and thus it becomes important for business, and not for programming, reasons to avoid educational and diverse programs. These are three of the major concerns of ACT and the problems in most of the letters that I receive at the FCC center on: lack of week-day afternoon programming designed for children; lack of specific age programming; and a lack of a diverse program schedule over-all for the parent to choose from. In the view of the advocates, there is no effective means open to the individual household to alleviate the problem. Their only alternative is turning off the television set entirely, and this, to them, points out the great failure of American broadcasting to meet the needs of children. I said at the outset that, in my judgment, the bulk of programming and advertising for children is analogous to an attractive nuisance, a dangerous condition. In law, an attractive nuisance is a term applied to a device or condition which is at once alluring and potentially dangerous to well-being. Especially to one whose years preclude him from the experience, discretion and caution enjoyed by older persons, because he cannot see the risks. In the critic's view, children cannot be the sole judge of what is best for them, and parental control cannot be effective when the problem is pervasive and not an isolated one. The answer that they see is a basic change in the nature of children's programming and how it is financed.

MACOMBER: Thank you very much, Elizabeth. Our next speaker will be from the Network, Mr. George Newi, Vice-President of Daytime Sales for ABC Television Network.

NEWI: I think Ms. Roberts has stated the problem clearly, and I'll try to give you a Network Sales point of view on it and deal just with children. I couldn't get past the premise of non-commercial television either, so I'll restrict my remarks to that. And a part of the premise is that children are special. There is no question about that. Children deserve very special consideration in the minds of broadcasters and they're getting it. Many of those attacking children's television would have you believe that we're ogres, that we're dragging children, kicking and screaming, to the altar of exploitation to be sacrificed to the great greed of the advertisers, and that broadcasters bear and feel no responsibility for children other than delivering them at the best cost per thousand. All that is simply not true, and I hope to prove it to you.

In another part of the premise is the proposition that broadcasters alone should bear the cost of providing children's programming. Inherent in this is the assumption that advertising and marketing to children is bad. I don't think it's wrong. I do think we should point out more clearly that in addition—and its primary function is to provide funds for programming—commercials are accepted and enjoyed by children for what they are. A report to the Surgeon General's Advisory Committee in 1972 says that commercials serve as part of a child's training for adulthood and frequently teach children about consumerism and product evaluation, and that even second-graders clearly understood that commercials were trying to sell and that by fourth grade, children could understand a good commercial and a bad commercial—when it was misleading and when it was truthful. The rights of broadcasters to profit from children's programming are often questioned, too, and I see nothing wrong with the profit factor in this area. No one seems to be saying that manufacturers of children's clothing or that their retailers shouldn't make a profit on this essential item, and I don't see anybody saying that toy and game makers shouldn't be entitled to a profit, and I don't see anybody saying Walt Disney Productions shouldn't make a profit on Disneyland, or that the movies on Saturday afternoon are not entitled to a profit. And even the private schools that teach our children are entitled to a profit—not that very many make a profit. Some say that not only is it wrong for broadcasters to make a profit on children's programming, but that it's our responsibility to bear the cost of such a programming with no hope of financial return on the investment. The loss involved in absorbing these costs simply means less funds for other such important areas of broadcasting, as news, public affairs and general development of programs for better television. Some say that corporations should provide the funds on a grant basis with no advertising and no return. Not only are corporations, as far as I see, not ready to provide those vast sums, but I ask by what right should they be asked to do so. In fact, the loss of such advertising would lead them to seek alternate and probably less efficient means of selling their products and in turn could mean higher prices to the consumer for those products. And some say foundations would provide the money. I don't think this source is a bottomless well. If the money were put into the three television networks and local stations, it would probably be diverted from some other projects, such as children's television workshop and public broadcasting which benefit greatly from these funds now. Diluting the dollars would mean that no one would have enough money to do the job right. And speaking of public broadcasting, the idea of federal funds as a means of financing children's programming can best be judged by the cloudy and unstable condition that public broadcasting is now in. The extending of government funding to the three networks and local stations could be disastrous. In short, advertising to children is a viable and a practical marketing method and one which allows television to provide programming to children. The alternate sources of funding which have been suggested would provide neither the dollars nor the stability we currently enjoy and would result in a lowering of the quality of television in general.

Coupled with the broadcaster's right to sell advertising, however, is the responsibility to provide a balanced and uplifting schedule of children's programming. I don't believe, as some do, that Saturday mornings should be wall-to-wall informational educational programming. I look at my kids, and after five days of school and pressures to perform in class, as well as home work, and the general burdens of growing up for a seven- or eight-year-old, and I think he is entitled to a few hours on Saturday morning to seek out the kind of entertainment he chooses and he wants. It's our responsibility to make this entertainment of the best quality possible. It's also our responsibility to provide a balance of informational and enlightening programming for children. And I think that now as never before, broadcasters are aware of this responsibility, and they're meeting it. On Saturday and Sunday mornings, CBS, for example, is providing a three-minute news program for children every half hour. ABC has a three-minute show teaching the multiplication tables through the use of animation and rock music, and that plays every hour. NBC provides a one-minute letter and spelling program which pops up throughout its Saturday schedule. All these short programs appear within the heart of the entertainment schedules of the networks in order to maximize the audience and to take advantage of that large audience. And in the longer program form *Kid Power, Make a Wish, Children's Film Festival, Talking With A Giant, Children's Theatre* and *Fat Albert,* among others, are providing informational and enlightening programs covering a wide range of such subjects as social questions, behavior problems, self identity, nature, science, government, current events and so forth. And during the week, Monday through Friday, *Captain Kangaroo* has provided informational programming to the pre-schoolers, and recently ABC's *After School Specials,* on a once-a-month basis in the afternoon about four-thirty, have provided quality programs aimed at the eight- to fourteen-year-olds and they deal with such subjects as history, literature, health and conservation and they are tied into the schools through an extensive plan, using study guides and teacher's guides.

While we're talking about programs directed toward specific age groups, let's discuss the practicality of the theory. This is a very difficult thing for commercial television to accomplish. It is a mass medium, even for children. Distinctions can be made between pre-school and six- to twelve-year-olds in terms of program content, but we haven't been able to find a clear distinction of program preferences between six- and nine-year-olds or ten- to twelve-year-olds or an eight-year-old and an eleven-year-old, and even if we knew what programs appealed to these two school-age groups, we'd have no assurance that we were reaching our target audience. Very often, more than one child is viewing the set, and generally it's the older child who controls viewing, so that a program aimed at a six- to nine-year-old may be tuned out by his twelve-year-old brother, because it doesn't appeal to him, and the six- to nine-year-olds would not get to see the show anyway. This is also true of pre-school programming. The best time to reach two- to five-year-olds seems to be during the early morning hours of school days, before the set becomes controlled by older children or adults. Right now two excellent programs, *Captain Kangaroo* and *Sesame Street* fill those time periods, as well as several local shows. Study and research into the areas of specific age programming should continue, but on the basis of what we know today, it appears that the best course for commercial television to follow is one of programming to a broad age-group among children, leaning somewhat to the older end of the six- to twelve-year-old scale. The younger children still get entertainment and informational value, our research shows, because they are interested in characters and situations that are older than themselves. And recently two of our programs, *Multiplication Rock* and *The Afternoon Specials,* among numerous other local programs, won awards from Action for Children's Television which Ms. Roberts mentioned, and I see this as a positive step in the rhetoric between these groups and the broadcasters. I think that rewards for taking constructive action in this area will accomplish much more than the acrimony that has existed in the past. I also think these groups are performing an important service in our area; although I disagree with most of their proposals, and doubt that they accurately reflect the majority of the people in America (A recent study showed that fifty-two per cent of the public was satisfied with Saturday programming; only thirteen per cent was dissatisfied and the remainder had no opinion). Nevertheless, these groups made broadcasters increasingly aware of their obligations and, in part, are responsible for some of the necessary changes we've made. Among the improvements that we've accomplished in the past few years are the deletion of violence for its own sake and I think that you can see that if you look at Saturday morning these days.

There is a tighter regulation of commercial content which is vital and this gets to the idea of misleading commercials. The amount of non-program time, which primarily means commercial time, has been reduced. There has been an over-all upgrading of children's programming, not only on the air, but what is equally important, and maybe more important, in the minds of broadcasting executives. These things came about from within the broadcast industry and not by outside regulation. However, broadcasting is responsive to public reaction. Programs stay on the air because people like them; programs go off the air because people don't watch them. Children's programming and commercials have improved because people wanted them improved and we're listening to the public and acting on what we feel are their areas of importance. I think that the entire rhetoric should continue between the groups and the broadcasters, and I think there is a lot of benefit for everyone in it, but we should try to achieve a little better balance of understanding and responsibility and reality. Thank you.

MACOMBER: Thank you, George. I'm now going to turn to a fellow Ohioan for our next presentation. Mr. Walter Bartlett who is the Senior Vice-President of the Avco System.

BARTLETT: Liz has spoken about the points made by many of the critics of broadcasting, George has covered what a network can do that has a great amount of money and potential far surpassing that of an independent or a group of stations. I would like to talk to you from our viewpoint, contrary to some of the points that have been raised thus far, and I'd like to use one of Liz's statements that I believe she attributed to ACT that says the pressures of advertising affect type and quality of programming. I think that's very true, but I'd turn it the other way. If you get one thing out of my remarks, I will say to you that, if we took advertising away from the current children's programming, we would end up with poorer quality programs for children. I do agree with her contention that children without question are special but let me give you some other special groups—why single out children?

Minority groups are special too—Blacks, Chinese, Spanish-speaking Americans. All of them have an intense need for programming to tell their story, and we cannot do that in unsupported, unadvertised programming. Add religious groups, they're special too. It might surprise you to know that Avco Broadcasting has telecast many religious specials—sponsored—and I'm not talking now about paid religion, because we don't accept that. In Cincinnati, for example, we have a very high Catholic percentage of the population. We've carried twenty-two programs in the last twelve years on special events of the Catholic Church in Cincinnati, all sponsored. These have included four installations of Archbishops, two Requiem Masses of two Archbishops who have died, and one Golden Jubilee and they have all been sponsored. Because they were sponsored, we were able to present good top quality remote coverage of the event— and I'm talking about only a single station. Today, women are special to us; not only are they demanding more active parts in our programming decisions, more active coverage in our programming, but the government tells us that we must program for women and that we must report our activities on their behalf in making them a part of television coverage. In the Mid-West, the farmer is special. We've got to continue special farm programming; the Appalachian poor are obviously important to those of us from Ohio, and a few of the other less fortunate areas that are represented here today. Anti-pollution is important. Talking to the kids who are involved with dope is extremely important. Political discussion is important to all of us. All of us, you and I, are indeed special people. Programming on television today should be devoted to us, as well as to children.

I think that when you go through the extensive lists of all groups that should be served as well as children in television programming today you can readily see why the average station cannot afford to program for *all* these groups let alone one group, without commercial revenue. I believe these points are all true. I believe that the individual broadcaster today is trying his very best to entertain, to inform, to educate and to stimulate. And if these groups and their programs are special, then where would the advertiser and where would the broadcaster be without advertising revenue? Let us remember one basic tenet. Every time I go to a college campus, I try to emphasize this to the kids, because it is hard for them to understand: This great broadcasting system that we have today is very simple. Money comes from advertisers. With that we buy our programming, our news efforts and our ability to serve our public, and at the bottom line, hopefully, are some bucks for the stockholders and for the people who own our companies. We've built a great broadcasting system in this country through free enterprise, through advertising, and I would suggest that it should be very carefully analyzed before any action is taken by the FCC or any other governmental group to restrict certain portions of advertising from commercials, or to edict to individual stations that they must carry "X" hours per day without advertising.

How has Avco Broadcasting treated this problem? I think that we have treated it fairly well. As George mentioned, the activist groups in children's programming who have criticized us, have performed a very worthwhile service. About three years ago we started, at our stations, seminars with our management to analyze what we were doing in children's programming. We hired Dr. Bernard and Louise Guerney from Pennsylvania State College. They are child psychologists and they have advised us over the past several years. We developed a group of special programs that we air once a month, in prime time, designed to serve the family. Let me give you the basic approach we developed. First, we determined our target audience would be the six- to fifteen-year-olds, a group largely overlooked in television offerings. Second, we decided upon a series of prime-time specials, as opposed to a daytime strip, in order that the children and parents could share in the viewing and learning experience. Third, our schedule calls for programming the specials once a month during the school year and development of in-school plans so that teachers and educators could help promote viewing of the shows. Fourth, obviously since a prime-time viewing period was to be used, programs had to be of superior quality. I emphasize the words "superior quality," with considerable entertainment as well as educational appeal. Since we were after superior quality, obviously this was an expensive undertaking. We first decided to sell advertising in the programs, but with carefully selected and checked advertisements. We do check the messages before they go in. Secondly, we were delighted to receive the participation and support of Meredith Broadcasting. Why? Because it provided us with another source of thinking from another outstanding broadcaster in the country to contribute to the idea and development of our plans, and because it gave us money for better quality children's programming. This series has been extremely successful in attracting family audiences, and principally children. It's been successful in working with schools for educational purposes and for providing a new and interesting pilot approach to children's programming which has been applauded by educators, groups such as ACT and members of the FCC.

Time is too short for me to list or get into all the other activities that our stations do in serving their communities and that are supported by advertising. But very obviously, all the areas that I covered before— minority programming, anti-pollution, anti-drug—are quality efforts that we try to accomplish through well-thought-out, well-planned programmed series, and they are supported by commercial advertising. Advertising permits us to do a better quality job. I believe, for one, that much of the programming that is described by the critics of the current children's programming, is being done on educational television stations and should be done on educational television stations. We believe that so strongly that Avco Broadcasting subscribes to one educational station alone thousands of dollars a year to support their activities in that area.

I would like to leave with you another thought on what individual stations can do and can't do in this area. Our stations, being in the top fifty markets, can afford to spend additional money for a particular program such as this, despite the fact that we would lose money. It would not be a happy solution with us, but we could afford it. But let's get into the markets that are in the top one-hundred, and I'm sure Mr. Block will speak to the independents and to the U's. It may surprise some of you to know that there are still many, many commercial television stations in the United States that are marginal and unprofitable. If the FCC or any governmental group put the burden on them of buying additional programming, of creating additional programming without advertising within that programming to support it, what quality programming do you think would be achieved?

In summary, to re-emphasize my point, I believe commercial broadcasting can improve its children's programming; I believe we are making serious attempts to improve our commercial programming; I believe that for many of us the very warm, strong advertiser support that we have been able to engender with our programming ideas for children, has permitted this to expand and certainly has resulted in greater program quality; and I believe that any approach that would say, as an edict, that we must carry "X" hours without advertising would defeat the entire approach of most broadcast groups to improve the quality of what our children see. Thank you.

MACOMBER: Thank you, very much Walter. Our next speaker is Dick Block, with the Kaiser System, and I think he can give us insight as to the independent and the UHF station.

BLOCK: Let me first put into perspective where we are and what we do. I don't have to make my reasons explicit as to why I'm with commercial broadcasting. At the moment, we're telecasting in six of the top eight markets and we hope to add another one within a month or so which will give us seven stations in the top eight. Our stations happen to be UHF's, but if you're in Boston, or Philadelphia, or Cleveland or anywhere on this earth, it doesn't matter . . . the only place to go for *other* than commercial network service is UHF. At five-thirty, local time today, according to Ace Kellner's former rating service, ARB, somewhere in excess of one million children will be watching our stations and they'll be watching such programs as *The Flintstones, Speed Racer, Three Stooges,* and *The Munsters* and programs of that ilk. The facts of life in a market situation where there are more than three stations for the most part is that the network affiliates opt to go to other kinds of programs in so-called early fringe. This has occurred in the last five to ten years with the increases in network news, the increase of local news service and the advent of Mike Douglas' desk-and-couch kind of program, as well as our series of network programs that appeal to the eighteen to forty-nine adults, which is *Big Valley* and *Star Trek.* So that children are left in a situation that Paul Klein, who was the research director of NBC described, and you must be familiar with his theory of the Least Objectionable Program for a child. It will not be Mike Douglas, it will not be *Big Valley,* it will be a situation comedy kind of program—the durable *Lucy* or *Munsters* or *Flintstones.* If you recall, the *Flintstones* was at seven-thirty and had a very large adult audience when it first started on the air. With the exception of the fourth quarter, children's programming, even in the independent market, even in a market as large as Boston or Detroit or Los Angeles, is not particularly interesting commercially. The bulk of the business is done in the fourth quarter of the year—that's when the heavy investments from the toy companies come in. The other products marketed toward children do not make a particularly profitable nine months for the rest of the year. In the situation comedies to which Liz did allude—be it *Lucy* or, as she said, the ones kept or thrown off the network—we find the broadcasters quite often don't want the children to watch those programs. They're just as happy if the audience has a higher adult content, because this is marketable. So that's generally the situation.

Let me crank in one other relevant point as you think it over and ponder. To develop programming that's competitive from a youngster's standpoint requires somewhere in the neighborhood of from $90,000 to $135,000 per half hour. That is impossible in the current structure, and the foreseeable economic structure of the independent stations. The network can do that if they wanted to put a program on at six o'clock, but I hardly think it would be in the public interest to see *Eyewitness News* go off Channel 7 at six and be supplanted by *Sesame Street.* So I can say that over the last seven years or so independent services, mostly on UHF, have developed in twenty-five of the top twenty-seven markets. This delivers potentially more than half of the population of the United States. Our hope and belief is that, as these stations can join into kinds of networks, they will be able to support new kinds of programming and that certainly is where we think the major change will come from. Yes, we do think there should be some after-school programs for children. We don't think that the audience should not be served, we think it can be done well and that is where our plan goes. You might also think about the feasibility of the interim period, because the revolution in programming doesn't come without a tremendous investment and I certainly cite *Sesame Street* and I believe it cost an excess of $600,000 for the development of the first years of *Sesame Street.* So I leave you and submit these to you, since this is for the record, the only commercial that I will say is that we do think that we're doing quite a bit to give children a richer experience than five years ago, and we plan to increase in richness over the years.

CHALLENGE VII: QUESTION AND ANSWER SESSION

MACOMBER: Thank you Dick. We're now prepared to accept your questions.

MIELKE: I'd like to address this to Mr. Newi. You said that pressure groups have made broadcasters aware of their obligation. I would appreciate it if you would reconcile that statement with the description in

Broadcasting Magazine a few weeks ago which said that brownie-point shows—what one network executive calls them—are more and more finding their way into the children's programming schedules of ABC, CBS and NBC. These shows are designed as appeasement gestures, and expensive ones at that. And in the words of another television executive: to placate those who don't think we're living up to our responsibilities in the area of children's television—from the FCC, on the one hand, to ACT, on the other.

NEWI: Well, I think that there happen to be one or two opinions and it depends upon what you mean by "brownie-point" programs. I think there have been shows put on the air for that simple reason. But the quality of the shows is what reflects the growing sense of obligation on the part of the advertiser. It's not just putting on any old semi-documentary, semi-informative thing. I think the real values that you see now are in shows like *Kid Power* or *Multiplication Rock*. For example, *Multiplication Rock* is a three-minute show which costs us $15,000 to $20,000 per episode. Normally three minutes of animation should cost about $6,000 or $7,000. If we wanted to slough it off, we'd put on a cheap show and not go into all of the research—we've done a lot of research on this show with the Bank Street College of Education. I think this shows in the quality of the programs going on now the increasing awareness on the part of the broadcasters. It's very simple to put on a show that appears in the logs as a do-gooder program, but it's the quality that counts and I think that speaks for itself.

KELLNER: I believe that the present Monday through Friday afternoon network feeds are a good move on the part of the networks. And it does answer some of the questions Ms. Roberts raised about limiting our programming for children to Saturday morning. I would like to ask you, Mr. Newi, what kinds of problems do you have with the affiliates in getting them to accept and clear these programs, and do you have any knowledge about NBC and CBS's experience in its Monday–Friday offerings?

NEWI: In the afternoons, you mean?

KELLNER: Yes.

NEWI: The *After School Specials* that we're doing, which appear only once a month at this point, are not a regular series. They get tremendous clearance from our affiliates—98% of our stations, or 98% of the country, rather, is carrying these shows. The response from the affiliates has been tremendous. The problem really gets down to the fact that, if you want to do it on a day-in-day-out basis, networks have historically seen an erosion of their clearances in the late afternoon periods, even for women's programming for daytime television. Monday through Friday women's programming, used to run until five o'clock, and then the affiliates asked for the 4:30 time period back and didn't clear the shows, and eventually the network only programmed to 4:30. We see a strong erosion again in the 4:00 to 4:30 time period for women's programming. CBS has the biggest problem. I think their normal daytime network show will clear 93 or 94% of all U.S. TV homes in this station line-up. CBS's afternoon is down to about 78%, we are about 85% or 84% and going down, and NBC is in a little better position because they have a soap opera sponsored to carry it, and they're about 92%. The problem is a real erosion of network clearances in late afternoon. If we were to go to our stations and say, "All right, we're going to do this after-school special every day of the week," I think we would have big problems, and it's understandable from the station's standpoint. But it seems to me that, with the late night programming now provided by all three networks, stations don't have that much time to put on their own local programming, which is the great revenue maker, so we've lost a lot of clearances in the afternoon, we've got great clearances with the special on a once-a-month basis. I think we'd have big trouble if we did it every day.

BARTLETT: I happen to be primarily NBC in my station, Dr. Kellner. NBC spent $1 million providing a program called, *Me Too* to their affiliates. They recommended that it run from 4:30 to 5:00. I don't recall what their clearance was, but I doubt if it was 20% for some very, very important reasons for the broadcaster. Most stations from 4:30 to 6:30 can pinpoint approximately 35% to 50% of their total revenue—in this time period—that's their prime time. In a market that I looked at just last week of one of our stations, the ABC station was starting their programming at 3:30 and going to a movie and inheriting a tremendous amount of women eighteen to forty-nine for that movie, and was dominating the entire 3:30 til 6:30 audience in the time period. The CBS station was beginning their programming at 4:00 and going in with a movie and they were second in the market. Our NBC station happened to be following *Peyton Place* and *Another World: Somerset*. The only way they had a chance to compete with the two other commercial stations in the afternoons, was to go to a 3:30 start and to drop both *Peyton Place* and *Another World: Somerset*.

COMMENT: With the exception of Ms. Roberts, I have to say I'm amazed that the alternatives to the nation's number one resource is really a cop-out, not only from broadcasters, but perhaps from the citizens themselves. I don't think that we have to be the ones who solve the programming situation specifically for the pre-schooler, who before age six has watched in excess of five-thousand hours of television viewing. There is an international organization that meets every two years, and tries realistically to appraise the programming of ninety to ninety-five nations across the world. And yet, I do not see any serious attempt from broadcasters or educators to bring some of the creative programming which has been done (although it's not American) someplace else. My question is: Why don't broadcasters think of our number one resource as perhaps a priority item? I don't think that any of the programs you mentioned was geared for pre-schoolers.

BLOCK: We do a pre-school program called the *New Zoo Review*. This is a program that was taped about a year-and-a-half ago and it came into being because independent stations in the top markets—Metromedia, Kaiser, and the Chicago Tribune told the Mattell Toy Company, "Okay, we'll clear it for you." And when we did it, about sixty other stations cleared it for us. And this was the kind of pre-school program that came in at about a million-and-a-half dollars; it is a fairly good effort. There is a new one that we're working on together—this time it came in from *The Daily New,* and WGN group—called *Magic Garden* which will be going on the air there fairly soon and will reach the pre-schoolers in our stations mostly in the premium period—eleven to twelve o'clock. There is a great deal of the entertainment programs for pre-school, certainly they do watch television after school but we try to give them something besides entertainment in short informational units that Ithiel de Sola Pool, of MIT, gave the title "The Snipets." They are programs that tell things about environment, and how to use the telephone and what to do when you go to a doctor. We do take it quite seriously, and if you don't think we take the responsibilities seriously, then you're wrong. I wish there were a lot of quick easy solutions to doing all the things that we want. Probably by the time we get the next solution, they'll be more things we'll really want to do. But I think an awful lot of broadcasters such as the Avcos, the Kaisers, the Metromedias, the Merediths, the WGN's, the WPIX's— not to mention the networks—are seriously going about this. NBC was so serious that they chased the whole audience away on Saturday morning. We tried to do a special program called the *Live Wonderful World of Television*. It didn't work. We took elements from all over the world— Germany and Holland and Czechoslovakia—and we tried to get it sponsored on a cost basis. Some advertisers had problems, because they said we had Communism in the elements that we took in Czechoslovakia. The whole problem of education in this society is something we feel quite serious about, and we are sure you do, too.

ROBERTS: I would like to make three general statements that perhaps we can discuss. Fortunately, or unfortunately, the person you usually hear from is the concerned broadcaster. I submit that they make up 10% of the broadcasters in the country. I've seen what Avco is doing and it is very impressive. I've seen some of what Dick is doing and it, too, is impressive. I would submit that makes up still a very small minority of what's happening. You don't hear from the broadcaster who doesn't care. I think they make up the majority. Secondly, you addressed your question to pre-schoolers. I think Dick's point was well taken. What is available for pre-schoolers across the country, is generally better on weekdays. *Captain Kangaroo,* what's available through Public Broadcasting, *New Zoo Review,* which is a good pre-school program in syndication, *Romper Room,* a local show, and many local broadcasters are also doing pre-school programming very often on a sustaining basis. The concern of many advocate groups is that this is not true weekdays for school age children. What they have at their disposal is what Dick points out he's doing. It's *Speed Racer,* it's *Hogan's Heroes,* it's *Gilligan's Island,* it's *The Munsters.* I submit that these are not programs designed for the child. Finally, the thing that I've heard up here, and that I've heard so many times, is we are doing better. In fact, I think that's true. I think that children's television, both on weekends and the kind of efforts that have been made during the week, has improved. About eleven years ago, a man called Newton Minnow, then Chairman of the FCC, made a vast wasteland speech and in response to that, the networks and other broadcasters added *Reading Room, Mister Imagination,* a number of educational entertainment programs for children. In the time that Newton Minnow left the FCC and with maybe a year's leeway, these programs were all off the air and we came to a 1967-69 network schedule, that was almost exclusively super-hero—*Shazzam,* and *The Herculoids.* So, in fact, things are improving. The concern of the advocates is what happens when the pressure is off? Do you slide back into what is easiest to hold audience and attract an advertiser?

NEWI: I just wanted to make a point on the two to five pre-school situation. As I mentioned, the real problem seems to be to find that time of the day when you can get those children to be in front of the set and watch it without interference from parents or others, and you have *Captain Kangaroo* early in the morning. Nobody but the two- to five-year-olds really are watching that. *Sesame Street* has tremendous audiences in the two- to five-year-olds, because that is where the program is aimed. It doesn't have much of an audience beyond that and if you look, interestingly enough, to the ratings of *Sesame Street* nine to ten in the morning, versus four to five in the afternoons (as it runs in New York twice) the four to five presentation of *Sesame Street* probably gets (I don't know exactly the figure) about a third of the number of children that the morning one gets. And the two- to five-year-olds are counted in with those six- to eleven-year-olds that control the set now, and are watching *Wacky Racers, Super-*

man or something like that. You've got to find the time when those kids dominate the set and there isn't that much time, because the minute someone else gets in there, they're not going to stand for that two- to five-year-old programming and they're going to flick the set. This is being alleviated somewhat by multiset viewing, but it really is a problem. We've been trying to find a way to do a two- to five-year-old show, and from a cost standpoint that can always be worked out, but where to put it so you can reach them? We don't want to go against *Sesame Street,* and we don't want to go against *Captain Kangaroo,* and I think it would be wrong if we did.

RIPLEY: Ms. Roberts, at the beginning of your speech, you labeled several premises upon which your position was based. I wonder how you reconcile those premises with the Scott Ward study which found that children down to the pre-school ages are able to discern what a product is, what a commercial is, whether they're being appealed to, whether that has value to them or meaning to them?

ROBERTS: I don't have very much trouble reconciling with Scott Ward, since most of my premises were taken from his research primarily because of the limited amount of research there has been really on children and advertising. The comments I've taken are with children from the ages of two to seven. Before children have a great deal of trouble differentiating between program content and commercial content. So, they don't disagree with Mr. Ward at all. The concern is that there has not been that much extensive research for the older child, with what his viewing of commercials is. Like Scott Ward's conclusion with the limited amount of research that he did was that what we can say for certain is that they become cynical by the age of seven, eight or nine. The child disbelieves the advertisement. Now it's up to you to decide whether this is a positive or negative effect from advertising.

RIPLEY: Is that bad that they become cynical?

ROBERTS: Well, I think it depends on your viewpoint.

Challenge VIII

De-Regulation of Radio—Necessary?
... Evil? ... Now? ... Ever?

R ADIO HAS AT LEAST one uncompromising facet going for it. The medium refuses to be licked. There were those in the 1950's who did not hesitate to predict the demise of radio. These prophets of gloom simply could not believe that this original form of broadcasting would prevail while the new medium of television threatened to bestride the world of mass communications like a veritable colossus. Television did become the most powerful of all mass media, and the fortunate recipient of most of the advertising appropriations, but radio survived. And it prospered. It survived and prospered because it proved malleable and amenable to inevitable change, because millions listened to it and because technology—which usually rises to meet a need—provided the transistor. As a result, radio is still a household commodity—reaching out also to the car, the countryside, the street and the beaches. It is the one medium that can be taken virtually everywhere and will work almost anywhere. There are even those rebellious souls who prefer it to television for their news source, because its newscasts are frequent, succinct and unencumbered by images on the tube. It is "pure" news, straight and unadulterated—even though much of it is of the "rip and read" variety, deplored by those who feel that the wire services, however useful, have standardized and stereotyped our information flow.

Radio, then, has survived and much of it is flourishing. It may not be recognizable to those who still have total recall of the great days of network radio drama, comedy and variety. But it has metamorphosed into its own form for the seventies—whether its forte be all rock, all news, all classical music—or a combination. And radio receivers are still selling by the millions, and radio stations still are proving a tempting outlet for those investors who want to buy time.

The challenge to radio for the seventies, then, is not sheer survival. It is how to disentangle itself from a plethora of regulatory practices and standards which have become anachronistic since television made its appearance. Radio and television are broadcasting, but the similarity pretty much ends there. For one thing, so far as regulation is concerned, we are dealing in hundreds of television stations, but in thousands of radio stations. The mathematical differential in receivers is not as great, but it is substantial. Thus, the argument may well be made that the Federal Communications Commission ought to take a new look at radio, not only in justaposition to television, but also in terms of the vast differences between different stations and markets. And that is precisely what the Commission has been doing under the guidance of Commissioner Wiley who addresses himself to the question in this section. The prospects before the discussion panel seem confusing. Is radio to continue to be regulated as it is, or is it to be de-regulated entirely, or should it undergo re-regulation? If categorical conclusions are not reached by the various presentations and subsequent discussion panels, it is hoped that they have served to clarify to some degree a significant problem in contemporary mass communications.

Looking at the question from the perspective of broadcast history, the need for a new appraisal of regulatory practices becomes apparent. Not only is radio different from television, the radio broadcasting industry of this decade is not the same as that of the twenties, or the thirties or forties. Scientists have learned more about radio energy than they knew when experimental radio began. The social, political and economic environment has also changed. The process of encoding and decoding information goes on, but the systems have changed, society has changed, technology has changed. And all this suggests that regulatory practices should change.

Consider where mass communication has gone since Samuel F. B. Morse showed how telegraphy could transmit communication by means of electrical energy in 1844. Within thirty years, Bell had established an operating telephone, in 1877. A recounting of the complicated patent maneuvers that ensued among the industrial empires has been amply accomplished by historians and critics of our system of broadcasting. What is relevant in this context is the establishment of a system of regulation unique to no other mass medium. And it is the presence of many regulation practices which no longer seem relevant—log keeping and reporting systems for example—which has suggested the current re-appraisal of radio regulation by the FCC.

Unlike print, which was able to throw off the shackles of licensing, electric communication could not function without regulation almost from the start. In 1910, the Congress included wireless communications under the Interstate Commerce Act. In 1912, the Radio Act came about as a result of the sinking of the *Titanic,* but with no provision, unfortunately, for any genuine regulative power to inhere in the office of the Secretary of Commerce. Thus, regulation broke down from the start and continued in a state of chaos, while stations proliferated, until the Radio Act of 1927 which came about, oddly enough, more through the instigation of the industry than of the government. It was this Act, which became the basis for the Communications Act of 1934, under which broadcasting is currently regulated.

What the Radio Act did accomplish, however, was to set the regulatory climate for broadcasting, to lay down the basic philosophical as well as technological principles under which radio would serve "the public interest, convenience and necessity." Those basic concepts have not changed. The right of the public still transcends that of any individual. The air waves still belong to the people. Broadcasting is still a service that must be fairly distributed and used. Only those with unique qualifications, at least in theory, can use channels and those who do use channels operate under the free speech provisions of the First Amendment.

The basic regulatory philosophy, then, has not been changed. What may need to be changed, however, is the application of those basic principles to a medium such as radio which can hardly be asked to function under regulations which are anachronistic, tedious and, in the last analysis, not relevant to the way this medium functions in the seventies.

CHALLENGE VIII

Producer: Robert Liddel (Compton Advertising)

Moderator: * Maurie Webster (Columbia Broadcasting System)

Panel: Nicholas Gordon (National Broadcasting Company); Richard W. Jencks (Columbia Broadcasting System); Art Topol (Ogilvy and Mather), Dewey Yeager (The Nestlé Company)

Question and Answer (in order): William H. Cianci (Rider College); Thomas A. McCain (Ohio State University); C. A. Kellner (Marshall University); Robert P. Crawford

---

* Mr. Webster is now Executive Vice President of Compu/Net, Inc.

(Queens College); Charles E. Phillips (Emerson College); Charles W. Shipley (Southern Illinois University); Phillip S. Gelb (Bronx Community College); Saul N. Scher (University of Maine)

WEBSTER: Last night, Clay Whitehead didn't answer all of the questions that I guess everybody would have liked to put to him, but he did say, from a broadcaster's point of view, some very good things. He made one comment, if you recall, about the whole area of the de-regulation of radio which is what we're going to discuss here this afternoon. De-regulation of radio was the subject of the very first public speech which he made at an IRTS Newsmaker Luncheon sixteen months ago. And one of the things that he said then that I think is important is that it is time that we began to recognize that commercial radio is a medium that is totally different from television and that we start to de-regulate it. His proposal, if you recall, was that what they ought to do initially was to pick a couple of large cities where there were a number of broadcast stations, and then make the radio assignments or transfers, virtually on pro forma basis; that renewal applications would not be reviewed for programming or commercial practices and that the Fairness Doctrine, about which he said some things last night, should be, in those markets, either suspended or enforced very lightly. And this afternoon what we want to talk about is the whole challenge of the opportunity for de-regulation which he proposed sixteen months ago, and what that challenge really means. I don't have to tell you about the seventy-three hundred radio stations in the United States. I did look up some figures. In New York, you wouldn't be surprised to know that the ARB book lists ratings for forty different radio stations (AM and FM) but what might surprise you, as it did me, is that in Port Arthur-Beaumont, Texas, which is the one-hundredth market, they list seventeen different stations, and in addition to that, there are a number that you can hear but don't get measurable audiences. So, while it is not likely that it is either increase or decrease in those numbers that we've been talking about, de-regulation can have quite an effect. And the four panelists this afternoon will look at it from four different points of view. The first one is Nick Gordon who is the Vice President of Sales for the NBC Radio Network.

GORDON: There are currently about sixty-eight hundred commercial radio stations in the United States. About forty-four hundred of these are AM and the remainder twenty-four hundred are FM. To a very great extent, they are subject to the same regulations as are the seven-hundred commercial television stations in this country. It is my opinion that radio, particularly, given its multiplicity of voices, has too much regulation for the sake of regulation. Radio has a healthy, vigorous and competitive climate. Laissez-faire, therefore, will be a far better principle under which to operate—that is, regulation by the market place. There is too much Government, there is too much paper work, there are too many legal sophistries.

We in radio are in the news, the information, the entertainment business and most broadcasters, certainly, are responsible businessmen. Their own self-interest dictates a high level of public service, a high level of community involvement and a commitment to their industry—otherwise, no listeners, no ratings and no revenue. That's the most effective kind of regulation that I know, and the one most consistent with the principles of our Constitution. We always come back to this when we talk of our radio regulations. There are obvious technical reasons why there must be a limit to the number of radio stations which can exist. But this ought to be the only limiting factor on the number of facilities. As a competitor at NBC for the advertiser's dollar and for the listener's ear, the more radio there is, as far as we are concerned, the better. I will always get my reasonable share of revenue through salesmanship, and because I believe that our product is a superior opportunity for the advertiser. Further, I will always get my share of listeners, because I believe we offer a superior, timely, and attractive broadcast service. I do not believe that the listener should arbitrarily have his choice of radio broadcast service limited. For example, I don't see any reason why there should not be more than two all-news stations in New York, or only one in some other large city. I don't see why, for another example, there should not be more than two or three hard rock stations in a major market.

Radio is a personal medium, as witness the fact that thirty-three million radios are sold annually. Each owner of each radio continually makes his own choice as to what he is going to listen to and when he is going to do the listening, as well as *where* he is going to do the listening. Speaking selfishly for a moment, we know among the radio networks that we had two-thirds of all the radio listening, with only one-third of the number of stations, and frankly, I am more interested in people getting the radio habit and learning to discover what the medium will do for them and creating an aware and responsive group of listeners than I am in limiting their opportunities and their choices.

NBC's commitment to radio de-regulation is based essentially on the fact that radio regulations to some sixty-eight hundred commercial stations were written for a medium that had only some six hundred stations at the time that they were put into effect. It is a far different world today than it was in 1934, and frankly, the public's taste is the only valid, determining factor in which a radio station is going to be successful or not, and maybe that's the way it ought to be from a regulatory standpoint, considering the multiplicity of choices that most listeners have in most major cities. NBC supports these kinds of actions concerning de-regulation. Some of these, of course, apply equally to television. First of all: Longer license terms. Second: Greater license security for the responsible broadcaster. Third: Repeal of the equal time provision, at least for the offices of the President and Vice President. Fourth: Simplification and clarification, if not repeal, of the Fairness Doctrine, which was originally a concept for fair presentation of controversial public issues. It was administered on the basis, for a long time, that if the broadcaster's judgment was reasonable, the Commission did not question his decision. This is true even though the Commission, were it the broadcaster, might have taken a different action. It is not administered now on the basis that an action was reasonable, but *rather* on the basis of how the Commission thinks it should have been done. Also, it now involves, very often, line-by-line review, by the Commission, of content. And since the Commission is not staffed to analyze and review Fairness Doctrine pleadings on a detailed, sentence-by-sentence basis it is nonsense to believe that the analysis and review is anything more than perfunctory, at best. The FCC has about sixteen-hundred people on its staff. About three or four hundred of them are lawyers. About ten or fifteen of these normally work on Fairness material. As is obvious, any quantity of action under the Fairness Doctrine must totally paralyze the Commission and, what is worse, leave other important issues unresolved for months.

NBC also supports a tremendous simplification of license renewal procedures, although specific approaches of various broadcasters may, of course, differ from ourselves. In summary, after twenty years at NBC in our stations division and our television network, and now in our radio division, I am convinced that the industry's best regulator is its listeners and its advertisers since after all, they are the people we serve.

WEBSTER: Dick Jencks is the CBS Vice President in Washington. He's committed himself in public before on this issue of de-regulation and what he has to say, I'm sure, is important and knowledgeable.

JENCKS: I have a little difficulty at the outset in describing this question that we're discussing as either a challenge or a problem to be solved. Should radio be de-regulated? Should prisoners of war be released? Should kangaroos eat kumquats? It doesn't seem to me that there is any question that when you have, of all our media the most numerous—radio—a regulated medium, that it should be de-regulated. None of the conventional, liberal arguments for the regulation of licensed media really apply to radio in its present state. It is not scarce. As I said, it is more numerous than any other medium. In the top fifty television markets, there are an average of forty-five radio stations in each market. As has already been said here, the regulation that purports to take place in Washington, of radio, is *pro forma*. It must be, unless you're going to build within the FCC one of the really huge Washington bureaucracies. So why not recognize the fact and liberate radio more or less completely from all but the kind of regulation necessary to preserve the effective use of the spectrum and occasionally to throw out rascals who have character deficiencies that don't go to program content.

Now, I guess I'm supposed to give the specific Washington view of radio, and Washington pretty much forgets about radio most of the time, except, of course, that the President doesn't. It's his primary medium now and seems to work very well for him. It does seem to me that the most important thing that's happening in Washington, in a communications way, is the fall-out from Mr. Whitehead's Indianapolis speech in December, and to me the most interesting fall-out from that speech is the fact that it has made some of the most enthusiastic regulators of the media, for the first time, doubtful of their premises. The active regulators, until very recently, have been talking about the Fairness Doctrine as if it were a way of enhancing (I think that's the word) the First Amendment. And they have regarded regulation of content as being benign and even affirmatively desirable. The Whitehead attack upon the media, followed by those of Colson and others in the Administration, has forced a change of mind, at least among some of these people, and it has now occurred to them that the regulators will not, in the final analysis, necessarily be people like themselves, but might be people with quite different views. So I think that this attitude in Washington will lend itself to permitting an experiment with de-regulation of the medium. And of course, Dr. Whitehead himself called for such an experiment a year ago last fall. One of the most interesting things about his Indianapolis speech is that while he now wishes to enshrine the Fairness Doctrine as the central plank of license renewal in this country, only a year and a half ago he was saying let's experimentally see if we can do away with it in radio. I think he was right the first time. Now, the paper we were given to discuss asks us to comment on what might happen to radio, and all that I can say is that one of the reasons that we experiment and innovate is to see what would happen, and one of the reasons we make human progress is that we have the curiosity to see what would happen. I can guarantee you this, some radio stations would be worse, perhaps, than most are now. Some would be better. That seems to me to be a desirable change, however, because that would give us a greater range for the public to choose from, give them a chance to reject the worst for the better. It would permit innovative radio people to devise new formats and ways of using radio—permit radio, in the words of Chairman MacDonald of the House Commerce Committee—to define its own audience, in the same way that the people who put together *New*

York Magazine were able to say: "We want to reach a certain audience. We think we know how." And I suggest to you, that the magazine could not have been started or pursued successfully if they also had to worry about another problem: how will the Government feel about my magazine? I think we need that kind of innovation in radio. I think we need the new Pulitzers and, if you please, Hearsts and Henry Luces. I don't think you're getting them now, and I think that as teachers of journalism, you ought to be among the most interested in attracting these young into this very powerful and flexible medium.

WEBSTER: Thank you, Dick. I'm not sure that I heard him correctly last night, but I think that Whitehead is off the Fairness Doctrine now. Our third speaker this afternoon is the Vice President in charge of Media and Broadcast at Ogilvy and Mather, one of the major agencies in New York, Art Topol.

TOPOL: I guess, like everyone on the panel, it seems that I should come out against any form of regulation by an outside body and we should always provide more opportunities for innovation and experimentation in broadcasting. But from an advertising point of view, the more choices (and we have plently of them now in radio) that we allow on the scene, the lower the cost. And that would make it a very sound advertising purchase, except that the more choices we have, the smaller and smaller the audience is going to be for each of the outlets that currently exists. Therefore, we feel that there should be some kind of controlling factor so that it remains as a viable medium. *Variety* just the other day said that: "Radio right now is probably the best media buy around today." And from an agency point of view, we concur. It is. We think that radio right now is going through another transitional period. A period of image. Where does it really fit in the entire advertising spectrum? What purpose is it serving besides being an individual medium? One that you can carry around in your breast pocket. One that you have in your kitchen and your bathroom. But is it really serving more than that function? We think that if it stays the way it is, it will continue to serve that function. If we keep adding more outlets, we're going to have a smaller and smaller audience. As an example, in 1972, the advertising activity for radio started out vigorously during the early part of the year and then it faded. And it even faded during the political period even though the President was using the medium very heavily. It seemed that the other advertisers walked away from the medium, so that the activity for the total year was really not impressive as compared to what was happening to the total advertising economy, where television had its best year, I guess, since 1950. We at Ogilvy suspect that these conditions that have continued so far into 1973, will continue for the entire year. And we feel that the reasons for the abundance of these availabilities is not only the number of outlets, but basically the number of outlets that have been created by the true, competitive emergence of FM.

To the listener, FM is just another radio station providing a similar service that other stations in the market provide. The audience equality of stations within a marketing area has also created the abundance of availabilities, whereas you have so many stations on the scene today that there are very few truly dominant ones. They're all within a pack. All serving their own function within that pack. Radio also is really the localizing medium. It is the voice of that community taste and of the groups within that community and where it is a strong national medium today is for special events, but radio is truly a local medium. I just came back from New Orleans yesterday, and the New Orleans paper listed (and Maurie alluded to it in Beaumont) twenty-four radio stations, and fourteen of them have different formats. I don't think the city itself could support many more than it has right now, if it's even supporting these twenty-four with fourteen different variations of formats. Therefore, I feel that if radio were de-regulated the market place would be further inundated, creating more voices and more sounds for listener's ears. And this you might say is healthy, but to an advertiser, we don't think it is. There are now already over seven-thousand radio stations and over 336-million radio sets. We don't think it would be an advantage to any of us to have more than what we have now, unless the need were truly created by public fanfare. The audience is not lacking for a variety of different formats, as for example, the New Orleans situation.

We have a pocket guide that we issue for our advertisers, and internally, for our own people. In this pocket guide, we list nine different radio programming formats and we indicate that each one of them has its own profile, its own different kind of personality. And if you want to reach a certain type of person, you should be buying a certain type of radio format. Different age, different sex, different household income. In these nine types, as we have categorized them, one of them is: contemporary top forty. Another one is: middle-of-the-road music, and we have standard music, and then good music, and classical and semi-classical music, country-western music, the all-talk show, the all-news stations, and then the Black stations. There are fourteen different programming types in New Orleans, and there's a radio programming profile that is published, and in that one they listed seventeen different programming variations by which one can classify a radio station. I think the public's tastes are truly being satisfied with all those different alternatives, and if there are more radio stations, how many other types could we really ever develop? Or would we just be duplicating what we have and, of course, that is the competition of our society—the one that is the best wins out. I think that right now we're doing that and we're doing it very successfully. We think that the current status of the medium is very healthy for the advertising dollar and if the audience was fractionalized any further, it would truly take a great deal of ingenuity and patience and planning on the part of an advertising agency even to buy radio, let alone plan on it. Right now, it is extremely difficult to plan radio. More and more stations are attempting to develop their own image in the radio spectrum and they're having difficulty doing it.

We're having the same difficulty in planning how to use the medium and in actually allocating our dollars to various marketing areas. As an example, we have created here for our planners, a planning guide. This is a massive book that our media planners go through before they write a media plan. In it is a section about twelve pages long on radio and how they should use it. The radio section of the planning guide is based on the top one-hundred television markets, not radio markets. Now, this has to affect the use of the smaller radio stations in the suburban areas and the smaller communities because they are now part of the television area which is much greater than a radio market area. These stations, from a national viewpoint, are being short-changed. They are being short changed from a research point of view. As Maurie says, the New York ARB is showing forty stations. I'm sure it doesn't include any of the stations in Fairfield County which is part of the New York metropolitan area or any of the stations that are up in Rockland County or Westchester or out on the Island, which are all part of the New York marketing area. And yet, they don't show up in that ARB service. At one time, the dial position of a radio station, and the power of the station from the technical viewpoint, were extremely important in making a radio buy. These factors today are not as vital as they once were. The type of person that the radio station is delivering is more important today than the technical advantages that a radio station has provided for listeners. Now, one of the things that I read in the material that we received on de-regulation was related to what I guess the Commissioner has referred to as "re-regulation" and this is the area that he is supposedly going into first, and that is making the bureaucratic procedures that the stations have to go through—all the various forms that they have to fill out to get their license renewals—very simplified. This will have no bearing on the advertising agency point of view. As I said, our job is to deliver to our advertiser the type of person—that male, that female, that teenager—who will buy his product. And we think that by de-regulating radio, that's not going to help our situation one iota.

WEBSTER: Thank you. I just noticed by looking through the program that Art Topol appears to be the first agency executive who has spoken here about agency problems or techniques of employing any of the broadcast media. He's made a good point, and you may have some questions that you'll want to ask him later because certainly, in terms of where the jobs are for the people that you are training now, radio with its multiplicity of stations has a lot of opportunities. I guess what we're really talking about is getting rid of the section of the course that deals with how to fill out the forms for the FCC. The advertisers, who of course, are the real key, are represented today quite well by Dewey Yeager who is the Advertising Manager of one of the big users of the medium, the Nestlé Company.

YEAGER: Just so you don't think that this whole presentation is completely fixed, I'm going to represent a slightly different point of view from Art, I think, in the two particular issues that he talked about. However, to position this, I would like to describe why the Nestlé Company might be considered a typical advertiser or a typical grocery advertiser. We are listed in the trade sources as among the top hundred advertisers, as we are among the top twenty-five food advertisers. We operate with approximately a 5% ratio of advertising dollars to total sales which is about par for the course in the grocery business. We are electronically oriented, that is to say, that approximately 85% of our advertising dollars go into television and radio. We are international, as are most of the major advertisers these days. We are represented in most of the free countries of the world.

And the next point that I would like to make and I think it is particularly important and pertinent to the subject that we are discussing: we are diversified. I'm not really selling products now, but I would like to take you through the rough line-up of products that we have. We are in the chocolate morsels for baking; we're in the coffee business, instant coffee business with Nescafe, Taster's Choice, Decaf and one or two minor brands. We are in the tea business with Nestea and tea mix products. We have a line of upscale products under a Crosse and Blackwell label. We have a line of cheese products both domestic and imported. Wispride would be the most important domestic one. I guess the best known imported one is Swiss Knight. More recently, we have gone into the wine business with an imported and a domestic wine operation, and lastly, with Deer Park, we're in the bottled water business. My point in all of this is that there are many different products in this diversified line and many different audiences. For example: for Quik, the target audience is kids. I know that in different parts of these meetings, we've talked about the kids' audience. That is the one we're after with Quik. You come to a tea product, and it's the housewife with maybe some secondary emphasis on other family members.

Which leads me to the same points what Art talked about before, but again from the advertiser's point of view—from, perhaps, a little more selfish standpoint. My first point is media efficiency, and to lead into this, I'd like to repeat the point that you probably are aware of, or certainly that this panel of speakers is aware of, and that is: that in 1970, 33% of the AM and combined AM/FM stations operated at a loss. This is not a good situation from the standpoint of the advertiser who is using the medium. In all cases, in our business activity, we want to see our suppliers make a profit—a reasonable profit. If they don't make a profit, the relationship doesn't last very long. So it's important that the medium makes a profit. No one has gone into a great deal of detail about the mirage of red tape and regulations that we're trying to de-regulate. I guess a couple were raised such as a longer license period, and I believe it is going from three to five years. One little thing that I stumbled on was that, right now, the regulations require that the engineer at the antenna site inspect that antenna every two hours. I believe the proposed amendment to that would be eight hours. As someone divorced from the thing, it would seem sort of silly to have someone running out to see if your antenna is up every two hours. So, we would hope that greatly increased efficiency among the radio operators would relate back to us in terms of perhaps lower costs and a happier relationship.

The other point is audience selection. And really, it is at some odds of the cost efficiency basis, because cost efficiency or the blind following of cost per thousand leads you out the window, whereby everything is completely on the dollar-and-cents basis. These days, our company (and we are not different from many, many others) is more interested in psychographics than demographics. It's life styles. And it gets back to the point I was making before about different products and different audiences. To us, it is more important to pay twice the cost per thousand for the best possible prospect. Radio has, and I think Art identified some, fourteen different groups. That's also important, and perhaps throwing the thing open to more and more operators can perhaps polarize some of those groups or make it easier for the advertiser to select the particular audience that he is after. Yes, and there could be more stations and that could be bad for the industry. On the other hand, I think we've found under our American laissez-faire system that it generally shakes down to the few who offer their radio audience and the industry the best for the dollar. So, in conclusion, I would like to say that we would welcome a more relaxed and a more liberal Government stance for those two reasons.

CHALLENGE VIII: QUESTION AND ANSWER SESSION

WEBSTER: Thank you, Dewey. You heard from two broadcasters, an agency man and an advertiser. There appears to be a certain degree of unanimity in what they said, and I'm not sure that this is shared by everybody out in front. The time now is here when you can ask questions.

CIANCI: I'm addressing my quesiton to both Mr. Gordon and Mr. Jencks. Mr. Gordon first said there was too much regulation, too much radio work, too much paper work. Mr. Jencks also said there was too much regulation. There seems to be an assumption here that there is a great emphasis placed upon the public. If there were a de-regulation of radio, there's a great emphasis placed upon the public in terms of having the knowledge to take action if radio does not live up to its public interest standards. It seems to me that you're probably referring to a small minority of the public, like the people in this room, the attentive public, the people who are up on the media and the regulations—what can be done; how to go about going to the FCC, complaining, etc. To me, the mass public has no idea of process of law or what things to do and, in fact, in the last ten years, you've had people like Nicholas Johnson, who have gone around and tried to tell the people, "Look, if you have a gripe, here is what you can do." So I don't know if I buy this idea that here should be a de-regulation of radio when the people don't know what to do if they have a gripe.

GORDON: Yet me show you, if I may, the principal way that radio ought to be regulated. And there are thirty-three million sets sold a year. This is a radio. This is a Sony transistor radio. This has revolutionized the industry, and the way this should be regulated at the station, is not serving your needs by doing that (transistor shut off). Because that really is what the transistor has made possible. There are five radios, average, in every home. There's a radio in every automobile. There's no possible way for Government, unless it's going to grow bigger and bigger, more expensive and more dangerous for all of us, to regulate every single thing that comes out and is received in this little box. We have no fear of anybody in this room or anybody in this country, marching into our stations, either our affiliated stations or our owned stations, and saying: "You're doing this, that or something else wrong." We welcome that because they at least spell our names right—which is the essence of audience. We have no fear of the listener or the advertiser.

JENCKS: Well I don't know if I can add much to that. I don't think that the public is unknowledgeable. I think that the public, as consumers, make choices with respect to every other commodity and service, and I think that they are perfectly capable of making choices as to radio. I simply think that they should have more choices. I think they would have more choices, if we were able to substantially de-regulate radio so far as program content is concerned.

McCAIN: Given that de-regulation comes in some form, Mr. Gordon and Mr. Jencks, I'd like you to address this issue. On what basis should the radio frequencies then be allocated? Assuming that there are going to be some new stations or some changes in existing facilities, what criterion should any regulatory body, which is only going to act like a policeman, use to allocate those frequencies, choosing from among competing applicants? Isn't that the same damn problem that we've got now?

JENCKS: Well, first of all, I think that the decision can be made without reference to the character of program content—fairness, unfairness or whatever, just as we decide which airline will serve two cities on the basis of considerations that do not go to any First Amendment matter. Now let me just also observe that, in practical effect, most radio licenses that change hands now, and therefore most people that you would characterize as "new radio licensees," are purely and simply people who have recently bought their radio stations from other people. That process will continue, and should, just as it does with respect to magazines, newspapers and other media. I don't know whether to agree with Art and his idea that there will be more radio stations under de-regulation. My guess is that there would be fewer, because I think competition would be fiercer if entrepreneurs had the opportunity to shape radio toward the special audiences they were trying to reach, so that would solve part of the problem. But if it did generate more stations, I think the Commission would just simply have to decide as it does now in the first instance, on the basis of capability, character, qualifications, financial stability and other aspects of a licensee's proposals, except that I would exclude them from the consideration of proposed programming.

KELLNER: Let me address the question to Mr. Topol and Mr. Yeager. Accepting Mr. Jenck's proposition that de-regulation of radio does not mean release on the part of the Commission of the assignment and efficient use of the spectrum and therefore *probably,* would not result in more radio stations, would you then be in favor of de-regulation of radio?

TOPOL: Radio regulation based on the airways and the availability of a free channel—I really can't visualize fewer stations. I think that, if there is an available channel for airway, someone's going to put up a transmitter and broadcast, and whether it be broadcasting to some select group that he or she has picked, or some private society, or some way, shape or form to get his viewpoint on the air, I think he's going to use it. So I can't visualize fewer stations than what the Government would allow. If the Government allows more, I think there'll just be more voices out there.

Regarding the point on the regulation, there were seven items that were listed in an FCC re-regulation program that they sent out, and some of these I've never heard of, but this is what I gather they were going to de-regulate: one of them was called meter reading, and I assume they think they are Con Ed or something like that. One is a transmitter inspection, which sounded crazy to me, too, when I read it. Then they have a list of station identification requirements in which, supposedly, the station has to identify itself every three minutes. If you listen to radio, they identify themselves practically every three seconds, because if you can remember their call letters or their channel numbers, it will show up better on the rating survey. Another is mechanical reproduction. One is called logging, in which they have to log everything that they do after a certain number of hours, or something like that. One is called program re-broadcasts, and the other is the filing of certain contracts. Now, as Dewey mentioned, if cutting out all these things would make the stations run better, that would then lower their costs to the advertiser, to the agency. I'm all in favor of that. That's fine if the re-regulation is going to help us in that way.

COMMENT: Art, you're beginning to understand our problems.

CRAWFORD: Following up some of the remarks, hopefully then, 33% of AM/FM stations might possibly wind up in the black, if they had greater opportunities and less restrictions and that kind of thing. I was interested in two things. Number One: where are the frequencies going to come from for new stations? And number Two: would Mr. Gordon welcome the opportunity to have more owned-and-operated radio stations with the network?

GORDON: In terms of more stations, we don't regard it as a threat. In fact, we're delighted to see a trend in the American universities to take advantage of the educational FM allocation possibility, which puts many services in many markets (where such might not exist). Nor do we regard as a threat, stations which presumably siphon off a younger audience. Any company that's a public company (as we are) and that presumably owes an obligation to its stockholders, looks at ownership of an asset, be it a radio station or a Hertz Rent-A-Car or whatever, based on return on investment and so, without speaking to the point of regulation or de-regulation, obviously my organization, as I'm sure CBS and ABC and every group owner, continually examines opportunity for ownership.

PHILLIPS: Assuming that the de-regulation increases the need for additional channels and for additional frequency assignments, would you favor the re-assignment or the re-allocation of the clear channel stations as local stations, now that apparently there is no real need for clear channel stations? And second do you favor the enforcement of the "one to a customer" rule for AM and FM stations to widen the ownership?

JENCKS: Well, in the first place, I emphatically don't accept the proposition that's been discussed here, that de-regulation would have any necessary connection with an increase in the number of stations. As I said before— I think probably the latter situation would occur—a decrease. As to the question of the one-to-a-market and other matters that have to do with concentration of control over the media, let it be perfectly clear that, in talking about de-regulation, I am not talking about the suspension of the antitrust laws or the laws governing concentration of power generally in this country. What I'm talking about is the removal of government control over content to the extent that we can achieve that, as well as the lessening of the burdensome and unnecessary technical and administrative regulations. Now, finally, on one-to-a-market, which is, as it were, an administrative aspect of the antitrust laws, I think that there is very serious doubt as to whether the one-to-the-market proceeding which as you know is still pending at the Commission, would in fact serve its intended purpose of bringing about greater diversity—more voices. The unhappy experience with WHDH in Boston suggests that the breaking up of joint media ownership can sometimes result in fewer voices in a community, and as television grabs off more and more retail business from newspapers in this decade, I think that the real concern in general in this area is the *reduction* in voices as a result of breaking up, let's say, newspaper-television or newspaper-radio combinations. So I think the answer to your question about one-to-a-market is that it may or may not be a good policy. I think that possibly there are some indications that it is not, and that there are certain kinds of station services which, if we want to keep them alive, we'll have to permit some degree of joint ownership. The Commission went that direction, of course, in a sense in preserving classical music in Washington by permitting joint programming on AM and FM in order to make economically possible the survival of a particular kind of program service. I don't think that we should fail to look for opportunities of that sort to improve diversity.

SHIPLEY: Given Mr. Gordon's four points in de-regulation, in which the second was greater license security; given Mr. Jenck's reiterated emphasis on regulation not including program content, and Mr. Yeager's reference to laissez-faire with de-regulation and the elimination of the weaker stations —and considering at the same time, the emphasis now on minority programming—would there be enough protection with de-regulation for minority tastes or audiences, such as classical music that you just referred to, Mr. Jencks? Realistically, when it was on a more competitive basis, with the government not having the power to bring about program balance, would that classical music station really disappear? And would we have more Bill Balances or more rock and roll, or would you suggest that it went to public stations?

JENCKS: I don't pretend to be a prophet or a seer, and I can't guarantee what would happen. All I say, is that it's worth an experiment to see what would happen, and if the experiment fails, then the experiment fails as experiments have failed before. But it does seem to me, particularly from the standpoint of minorities—and I mean not only racial and ethnic minorities, but other minority tastes—de-regulation in terms of program content ought to increase the options of the listener. It ought to make it more possible for community groups—Black and otherwise—to seek out and appeal to their own special audiences. That might mean establishing organs of opinion such as exist in the print media. We have none really in broadcasting *per se*. It might mean, in New York City—a great clothing center—a radio station devoted solely to fashion in the sense that *Women's Wear Daily* is devoted to that, or devoted solely to sports, or in many more cities than there are now, stations devoted solely to news, of which there are really very few, and only in a few large cities. I think that it would give entrepreneurs a chance to try those things without having to worry about balance. What we now do in terms of insisting on balance, is to insist that all radio stations shall be media of general circulation. That is as if we were to tell all magazines—*Yachting* as well as *Motor Boating* and *Road and Track*—that they all had to be general magazines. I think that's foolish. I think we should let them diversify, and some of them couldn't survive on a de-regulated, competitive and diversified basis. I know of nothing in the Constitution that requires us to have enterprises survive in a competitive market place.

WEBSTER: Dewey mentioned psychographics a little bit ago, when he was talking about the little marketing thing, and I'd like to get his reaction to this, because classical stations, and Black stations and so on, involve that.

YEAGER: Yes, exactly. And I didn't go very far into the life-style research, but we break down the audience—our target audiences—into about eight or nine different groups. Funny names for them. I think that one is called the "self-satisfied-traditionalist"—she's the gal who wears the white hat on Sunday, you know the type. But right now, it is difficult for us to identify these groups in radio. A part of it is the industry's lack of information, and secondly, I think it is the lack of polarization, or really pulling some of these groups together a little bit, along the lines that Dick just mentioned.

GELB: I have heard for two days that the Government represents a great, big, terrible giant, and I agree—although I thought our speaker last night, Mr. Whitehead, was a very likeable and personable, individual. But the fact is that he has a great deal of power. But, I kept saying to myself, we have elections . . . I can vote him out. Or, I have a Bill of Rights that guarantees me rights; I have a courts system; I have a legislative system to balance it; I have all these things going against that man's power. I think he can be contained. Now, I also view the broadcasting industry as a giant. In some respects it is more powerful than Mr. Whitehead. I thought that I had a Fairness Doctrine. I've learned today, or over the last few days, that the Fairness Doctrine is unfair, and there aren't going to be any regulations. And licensing, that made you responsible at least every few years or so for what you are doing, is now something that's passé. This is really a question for Mr. Gordon, because I wasn't satisfied with his answer to the first question. You tell me that all the recourse I have now is that I can turn you off or I can come into your station and get sore and you can kick me out and I can get arrested. I don't think that's sufficient as an influence to contain broadcasting. I'm not saying that you have to have a better answer, but, I certainly hope that you do.

GORDON: Well, I'm probably the only man in the room who's carrying a copy of this, and this is the Constitution of the United States and the Bill of Rights. We can look up what our rights are, and we discover that they are rights to operate without harming others, essentially. We don't wish to operate without public responsibility. We don't wish not to serve you, but radio, with these many, many, many voices (as Mr. Jencks has pointed out) given an opportunity, would probably serve better. I live in the Bronx. I regard WFUV as a community station, because in many way, it is able to serve the community. But were it permitted, as a commercial station, not to have to carry a certain quantity of news, a certain quantity of this, and a certain quantity of that, but rather to serve the citizens of Bronx County, perhaps that would be a better and more useful service for it—as the *Riverdale Press* serves the Northwest Bronx. I think that is essentially our point. We're not trying to be free of criticism, and we're not trying to operate in a vacuum, but we have discovered, because we are advertiser-supported, that probably the best means that the listener has of telling us that he doesn't like us, is to turn us off. Because then, we don't get any ratings, and at that point, we don't do much business. But we are not copping a plea to be permitted to operate in a climate without any sanctions. That is not our interest.

SCHER: How much balance does the FCC actually insist upon now from radio stations? It seems to me that the number of program categories on license renewal forms have been reduced, and the FCC also recognizes the idea of format and specialization in radio. Is that not true?

JENCKS: No doubt about it. The FCC has permitted, I think, a greater and greater degree of latitude in radio broadcasting. And it should. The fact that it has recognized this, does not persuade me that there not be even greater diversity and proliferation of formats and ideas in radio broadcasting. Indeed, it reinforces the view I have, that if we were to embark upon an experiment permitting greater latitude, we would have an even more exciting medium, more exciting young people going into it, a better mix all around.

WEBSTER: That concludes this part of the discussion. Some of you may have noticed that during the question-and-answer session, we had in the room the man who is more responsible for seeing that radio de-regulation happens, than anybody else—Commissioner Wiley of the FCC who is seated in the rear, and whom you'll hear later.

Address by
Commissioner Richard E. Wiley*

Federal Communications Commission

Introduction: Gene Accas (Leo Burnett USA)

Question and Answer (in order): Dan McGrath (D'Arcy-Mac-Manus & Masius); James A. Brown (University of Southern California); Philip Gelb (Bronx Community College); Jon T. Powell (Northern Illinois University); Richard T. Goggin, Sr. (New York University); K. Sue Cailteux (University of Kentucky); James W. Rhea (Oklahoma State University); Aaron Cohen (National Broadcasting Company)

ACCAS: Those who are students of administrative politics, are aware that the Federal Communications Commission subscribes wholeheartedly to tokenism. There is a Black Commissioner, a female Commissioner, and a Commissioner who wears a white hat. That is tokenism. We have the wearer of the white hat with us this evening. For those who haven't had the opportunity to spend time with him, let me swiftly do away with the "good guy" image that may have been created and tell you that he's a *very* nice guy; cooperative, earnest, interested, *interesting,* willing to listen, willing to learn. I had the tremendous presumption to tell him some months ago, he is the hope of the industry. It gives me a great pleasure to introduce Commissioner Richard E. Wiley.

---

* Commissioner Wiley has since been designated FCC Chairman.

WILEY: It is a distinct honor for me to be invited to address this out-standing Third Annual IRTS Faculty/Industry Seminar. Indeed, when I review the really impressive roster of distinguished officials who have participated in your programs, I feel a bit like the sixth wife of Henry the Eighth on her wedding night: I know what I am supposed to do. The only question is whether I can make it interesting!

Indeed, the composition of this audience, and the situs of this meeting, cause me to recall a recent event which occurred in the classroom of a prestigious Eastern university. It seems that the professor had decided to utilize a word association experiment with his students—he would mention a name and the students would orally respond with the first thoughts that came into their heads. The professor began with the name "Vietnam." And like the good collegians they were, the students responded in unison: "Get out." Next the professor called out: "Dr. Spock." And, to a man, the students hollered back: "Right on." Finally, the professor ventured the name: "Indianapolis 500." To which the students collectively replied: "They're innocent!"

I have an uneasy feeling that if, in like fashion, I were to call out the phrase "constructive regulation," very few of you might be impelled to shout back the hallowed name, "Federal Communications Commission." Instead, I am afraid your oral-Rorschach response might just be: "Mission Impossible." And yet, gentle academicians and other disbelievers, that is just what I am here to tell you tonight.

When you first address the issue of constructive action within any Federal Agency, I suppose you have to begin with the question: what are your goals—what should be the objective of federal regulation of the media? I suppose that an easy, perhaps overly simplistic, answer might be to bring about the best broadcasting system possible for the benefit of the American people. Having framed such a generalized response, one must then address the really high, hard question: by what means will such a goal be achieved? It is here that we encounter an important factor which lurks behind many well-documented administrative actions: personal philosophy. The continuum of thought as to broadcast regulation goes something like this. At one end are those who, pointing to the fact that broadcast frequencies are scarce natural resources *temporarily* consigned to the trust of Commission licensees and also to the alleged "special" impact, pervasiveness and importance of the media, would transform our current commercially-supported broadcast system into a public or eleemosynary medium primarily designed for the expression of individual viewpoints, private grievances, personal disputes, societal shortcomings and perhaps so-called counter-cultures.

At the other extreme, we have the people who lampoon the fundamental basis of our administrative authority—the alleged scarcity of frequencies—and argue that any regulation at all is necessarily an undesirable infringement on the First Amendment right of broadcast journalists, that only a modicum of technical rules can be tolerated, that the only good bureaucrat is a dead bureaucrat, and so forth.

Faced by this wide divergence of philosophy, what is a poor regulator to do in order to achieve his regulatory objective? Well, other than adhering to his *own* personal philosophy, I think one must begin by giving due consideration to certain "givens," the first and foremost of which is the Communications Act of 1934. When that Act was passed, Congress had a number of options concerning the type of broadcasting system we would have, options which mirrored the range from government control to permanent licenses to private individuals.

As you know, Congress did neither. Instead, our elected representatives created what I regard as a hybrid: a private, free enterprise system with limited-term licenses requiring service in the public interest. Necessarily, that kind of broadcast Minotaur, half-private and half-public, is a difficult one to administer with built-in and inevitable conflicts. And, necessarily also, such a system provides a natural environment for the development of the kind of divergent viewpoints as to appropriate nature and scope of regulation which we have discussed. Indeed, many of the subject-areas which you have explored in this conference developed as a result of this same basic dichotomy.

Nevertheless, I am convinced that the Minotaur can be housebroken —that constructive regulatory solutions to every such conflict or problem can be found. Indeed, my own experience has been that, when the Commission has set out to address one of these issues, there is no shortage of possible remedial alternatives. The thesis which I pursue tonight happily accords with my own regulatory philosophy and yet, at its heart, is very much a pragmatic one: that ultimate Commission determinations must be arrived at with some understanding of our basic system of broadcasting— or otherwise, at least in my opinion, they simply won't work. I am not saying that any decision which offends broadcasters should not be adopted —far from it. Nor am I saying that changes in our current system must be avoided. What I am trying to express is that regulation cannot be conducted in a vacuum, isolated and apart from the real world of commercial broadcasting in this country. In this connection, let me provide some "specifics" on several pertinent problem areas now before the Commission.

First of all, however, let me say at the outset that I am not about to deny the legitimacy of the theoretical basis for asserting Commission jurisdiction over broadcasting. Although one might argue that there are many more broadcast outlets than newspapers in this country, it is important to remember that, should I be rich enough and foolish enough, I could start a new morning newspaper tomorrow in Washington, D. C. No one could

stop me. However, I could not start a new TV station on Channel 9—
WTOP has the exclusive federal license there. So I believe the basis for
federal regulation does exist—and, indeed, it is one which the Supreme
Court originally recognized more than thirty years ago in explaining why
broadcasters, unlike newspapers, were to be regulated. "Unlike other modes
of expression," said the Court, "radio inherently is not available to all.
That is its unique characteristic, and that is why, unlike other modes of
expression, it is subject to government regulation."

From such a theoretical basis flow certain unavoidable facts of regulatory life for every broadcaster: renewals, the Fairness Doctrine and a close
relative called access and, finally, a massive and complex code of conduct:
the FCC rule book. Let me test out my thesis in each area.

Let's take renewals. For broadcasters, the issue of renewal is not a
theoretical question of administrative policy, to be nicely debated at conferences like this, but a very real question of life or death. Without renewal,
without a license to operate, the rest of the industry's problems become—
for the unfortunate—somewhat academic to say the least. And, in light
of the over two-hundred license challenges which have been filed with the
Commission, broadcasting today has become something of a hazardous
enterprise.

On the other hand, broadcasting's critics point out that challenges are
perfectly legal and often may be the vehicle for station improvement and
reformation. In any case, as they are loath to allege, the Commission
effectively rubber-stamps the vast majority of renewal applications.

I think this latter allegation requires a measure of analysis. Of course,
most broadcasters get renewed. There are, for example, over 7,000 radio
stations in this country, many of them in smaller markets. For them, the
incidence of license challenge is virtually non-existent. This is not to say
that, without challenge, such stations will be automatically renewed because the Commission does have its own standards in this regard. But
let's face it—with over 2,500 renewal applications to process every year,
the Commission of necessity must rely on "200 million attorneys general"
(as Chairman Burch recently put) to bring licensee derelictions to our attention. Moreover, and quite frankly, I personally think there is room, indeed
need, for some reasonable continuity of operation within the industry.
Without such stability, the resources—both human and financial—simply
will not be available to assure the delivery of a quality broadcast product
to the American people.

Accordingly, in the absence of clarifying Congressional action (which
the FCC would welcome), we are working on renewal procedures which
the Commission feels are consistent with our localized, privately operated
broadcast system. The primary emphasis is on the maintenance of a continuing dialogue between the licensee and his community of service. We

realize that the FCC, with its Washington location, its small staff and its limited budget, simply cannot resolve every conflict that some 8,000 licensees may have with their viewing or listening public. What we hope and desire is that objections to station operation will be brought to the attention of the local broadcaster (and not just on the eve of the renewal application), that such objections will be resolved at the local level and that appeals to the FCC will be made only as a last resort.

To my regulatory way of thinking, this is a policy which makes sense in terms of the realities of our broadcast system.

Let me turn now to the Fairness Doctrine, surely the most elusive and ephemeral Commission policy in force. Indeed, what the FCC has wrought, let no Commissioner attempt to render understandable. In substance, the Doctrine requires that the broadcaster provide coverage of controversial issues of public importance within his service area—and, further, that he afford reasonable opportunities for the expression of contrasting viewpoints on the issues he does choose to cover.

Stated in this manner, I personally believe that the Doctrine is neither repugnant nor an unconscionable infringement on a broadcaster's freedom or independence. Indeed, as a public fiduciary, it perhaps states the very essence of his trusteeship.

However, due to certain recent and, to my mind, unfortunate procedures (both administrative and judicial), the Doctrine has become increasingly difficult to implement and almost impossible to administer. Accordingly, the Commission initiated a broad-ranging inquiry into the purposes and effectiveness of the Doctrine, the first overall review of Fairness since its formalized inception in 1949. Out of this analysis, which is as yet incomplete due in large measure to an anticipated Supreme Court decision of which I will speak in a moment, we hope will come a Fairness Doctrine which is indeed "fair," which is understandable to the average broadcaster who must apply it in his everyday work, which is capable of consistent and intelligent regulatory enforcement and, finally, which contributes to keeping the American people reasonably informed on controversial issues of public importance.

Let me quickly sketch one representative problem with which we are grappling in this study and which was the subject of Challenge IV here: counter-commercials. As a result of the cigarette advertising case—in which the Commission first applied the Fairness Doctrine to commercials which "implicitly" argued a controversial public issue—broadcasters (and the FCC in turn) have been more and more deluged with demands for time to "answer" commercial announcements. Since this issue is still pending before us, it would be inappropriate for me to make any definitive pronouncements at this time. Nevertheless, I must confess that I have serious reservations about the advisability of such a proposal.

The reason for my concern can be simply stated. Commercial broadcasting, unlike so-called public television which is supported by federal and private grants and gifts, is solely dependent on advertising revenues for its financial base. Any deterioration of that base of support weakens the structure and endangers the continuation, much less the expansion, of public service programming. And, frankly, if a product can be advertised on radio and television only when accompanied by a countering message from your friendly local ombudsman on some supposedly relevant public issue, I think many businessmen are simply going to find another outlet for their advertising dollar—and presumably an unregulated one.

Moreover, where does the public interest lie in such a system? While one recent broadcasting critic has suggested that commercials may be more provocative and interesting than the programs themselves, many of us will agree, I think, that media advertising represents for most viewers primarily undesired interruptions. A constant by-play of ads and counter-ads would scarcely improve this situation. Moreover, I seriously question that a 30- or even 60-second spot is the appropriate forum for effectively "educating" the consuming public—if that, in fact, is the objective of the counter-advertiser. Instead, such a format inevitably leads to appeals which are brief, impulsive, often whimsical and sometimes even emotional—as advertising itself has clearly demonstrated.

Radio and television advertising, however, has one saving grace—it alone supplies the economic wherewithal to support the independent, free enterprise broadcast system which Congress created. And until the people's representatives dictate to the contrary, it seems clear that a detrimental restructuring of that system is neither within the mandate of the Federal Communications Commission nor, at least in the opinion of this Commissioner, in the public interest.

Another, and related issue, is access: the concept being that an individual or group should be able to buy time (or perhaps even get reasonable amounts of free time) to discuss a position on some subject important to him or them. For example, as you know, a group opposed to the War in Vietnam (*BEM*) asked Station WTOP in Washington if they could buy time to run spots in opposition to the war. WTOP's refusal to sell the time was upheld by the Commission which found that the station had, for Fairness Doctrine purposes, exhaustively covered all sides of the issue. However, the Court of Appeals for the District of Columbia (Opinion by Judge J. Skelly Wright) reversed the FCC, recognizing for the first time an "abridgable First Amendment right" to buy advertising time where the station otherwise engages in the sale of such time.

As then General Counsel of the Commission, I recommended that the case be taken to the Supreme Court because I felt that it conflicted with some thirty years of consistent regulatory policy—a policy upheld by the high Court as recently as the famous *Red Lion* case—that the broadcaster, under our system, is a public trustee serving for the benefit of his entire community. He, in his reviewable discretion, decides what controversial issues to cover, how to cover them, what format, what partisan spokesman, and so forth. No individual has a right to speak (i.e., access) —instead, as the Supreme Court said in *Red Lion,* it is ideas which have access under the Fairness Doctrine.

The *BEM* case has been argued in the Supreme Court and we await a decision. Again, candor compels me to say that a reversal of Judge Wright's opinion is necessary if we are to effectively preserve the licensee-controlled broadcasting system which we have known in this country. Whatever the faults and imperfections of this system, I believe that it is far preferable to the government controlling the broadcast agenda, a circumstance which I predict would follow, sure as night the day, the imposition of any demand access system on a limited spectrum medium. I say this because broadcasting, in a nation of two-hundred-million people, must still remain "inherently not available to all." Accordingly, someone's constitutional right to access would have to be, in Judge Wright's words, "abridged"— and I have a distinct feeling that the Commission would have to be the ultimate judge of the reasonableness of any such abridgment decision.

In short, a demand access system is simply not consistent with our present form of broadcasting.

There is one final aspect of regulation that I would like to mention which promises to bring change where necessary and recognizes the development of the broadcast industry over the past four decades. The Commission recently initiated a program of revised regulation (or "reregulation") of the broadcast industry. The hypothesis of this program is that while the industry, and public dependence on it, have changed dramatically over the past thirty years our regulatory philosophy has remained the same. For example, radio no longer is the creature it was during the twenties; it no longer represents a new and solitary form of broadcast communications. It is, today, one of many competing voices in an expanded communications network that includes television, CATV and the print media. The rules we drafted to govern the conduct of an infant now seem to stifle unnecessarily and frustrate the adult.

In addition, our rules and regulatory philosophy make little or no distinction between various broadcast services in different *markets.* Thus, our re-regulation program is analyzing whether small market radio demands the same regulatory treatment as major market television—and whether, in a market served by numerous broadcast voices, the public interest is best served by requiring that *all* stations meet certain programming obligations in precisely the same manner.

Re-regulation holds the promise of improved public service because it recognizes that government cannot stand still while the industry it regulates changes. Our plan is to evaluate the need for every FCC rule in terms of the 1973 state of the broadcast art and, if that need no longer exists, to eliminate the rule involved—not as a sop to the industry but out of an abiding belief that such "re-regulation" will lead to a reallocation of broadcast resources and, ultimately, to a better broadcast service to the American people.

In the final analysis, it seems to me that the public interest is better served by a regulatory philosophy that builds on the strength and existing foundation of our present-day system of broadcasting, rather than attempting to reconstitute or restructure that system into something it cannot be. In the areas which we have discussed—renewal policy, Fairness, Access, Re-regulation as well as others I could mention—practical, pragmatic solutions are available within the context of our free enterprise, public trustee broadcasting structure. And, to my way of thinking, these remedies are far and away to be preferred to others which would effect radical surgery on a service widely enjoyed and admired by the great majority of our citizenry.

Thus, viewed in this light, it seems to me that our other regulatory goal should be clear: a healthy, stable and viable industry, confident of its own place in serving the American public and secure in its knowledge that our role in government is designed to assist rather than hinder it in meeting the legitimate needs and concerns of the citizens of this country.

Thank you.

QUESTION AND ANSWER SESSION FOLLOWING WILEY ADDRESS

ACCAS: I wouldn't be a bit surprised but that there might be a question or two. I wouldn't even be surprised that Commissioner Wiley might be agreeable to answering them.

McGRATH: Commissioner, maybe you can't comment . . . but can you, or would you, predict what the outcome of the vote on the prime-time access rule will be?

WILEY: That is obviously something that we are currently studying, the comments are coming in, perhaps they're all in now. It's a very difficult issue. I was not on the Commission when it set out the great goal of trying to develop diverse programming sources and, ultimately, diverse programming. I think that was certainly the Commission's thinking. I think that Chairman Burch feels very strongly that the project was doomed at the outset and it certainly has been proven to be a failure. There are others, of course, who see it in different lights. I've been consistently quoted as being one of the three votes that is definitely for the repeal of the rule. I would like to assure you that I don't make my mind up on anything until I've seen all of the evidence and I'm going to await that. I would say that I'm not sure that the rule has really developed. What I would be interested in is some diversity of programming. I think it's an alternative that may not work if it's attempting to dictate to the American people the kind of programming that they should like. So, I'm uncertain that the rule will survive, but I think it still is an open question.

McGRATH: Are you suggesting that the half-hour every night will be returned to the networks?

WILEY: Well, certainly that's one alternative. But there are other alternatives that fall short of that. For example, there have been suggested that it would be returned to the networks, but with a condition. Judge Hooks would like to see it returned if they would program that half hour on local programs; programs of local interest, particularly, I suppose, focusing on minority interests. Others have suggested, as they did at the outset of the rule, that there should be a waiver, or an exemption, for news and documentaries, because that's good programming. It is programming that I personally like, and I suppose that's supposed to be worth something. But again, my own philosophy may be that that is not my decision to make. There's been a suggestion recently that CTW, the Children's Television Workshop, will put on a quality, half-hour children's program in that half hour. Bob Lee, one of the Commissioners, wants to see it go to twenty-one hours to give the networks more flexibility so that we get away from these waivers. I've been disturbed, frankly, by the waivers in which we've said that the *Wild Kingdom* is more important than the Olympics. I felt that not giving the three-and-a-half hours to the Olympics, something that happens once every four years and is of great interest to the American people and is really good programming, was just ridiculous. I dissented, but I'm not so sure that turning the half hour back to networks is the way to go either. So, I must admit that Im giving you an ambivalent answer, because my mind is ambivalent on it.

McGRATH: You may be aware, or maybe you're not, that the networks should be thrilled with the prospects of not having to program that half hour, because the total number of dollars in the network market place has remained constant or increased whereas the cost of programming has decreased 14%. In point of fact, economically the networks are making out like bandits on the prime-time access rule.

WILEY: Well, my understanding is that they don't want it back so that they suddenly get it for the fall season. I think that they are opposed to it generally, as they see it as a government intrusion into programming areas. Basically, as I say, the waiver route seems to have been something which we have used to make selections between a variety of programming. I think all of us would like to see more diversity on television. Here again, my alternative on children's television is not to withdraw the commercials, because I just think that's going to lead to poorer programming. It does take money. I'd like to see more diversity. Unfortunately, some networks have tried it and it hasn't worked out so well. I think that what all of us want is more diversity, more interesting programming.

BROWN: Commissioner, would you care to comment on whether, or to what extent, actions or statements of the OTP support or help some of the things that you are engaged in?

WILEY: Telecommunications in this country is an extremely complex, diversified area, with the technology pushing and dragging the law behind it. I think that with the diversity of problems that come before the FCC, come before the government really, the situation certainly dictates that the executive have some voice in this area. I've never felt that the existence of OTP is an infringement on the FCC's statutory responsibilities. And as long as it does not become an infringement, I find no problem at all with the OTP expressing the President's positions in many areas. And I think that, in many cases, it's been quite helpful. Let's think about re-regulation. Would we be doing this today if Clay Whitehead hadn't made a de-regulation speech at one time? Now, we transformed it, we changed it a bit and put it in slightly different form, and I think that was a good thing. But the original stimulus may have come from OTP. I think the fact that Mr. Whitehead has put forth the renewal bill, and that the FCC has commented and taken some different views in some areas, is constructive. I definitely disagree with the idea that we are just political appointees on the Commission. I am certainly a Republican—no question about that—but I've not yet had phone call number one from the White House, suggesting how I should vote. If the day comes when I am told to vote in a certain area, then I might look for another job.

COMMENT: What are the pragmatics of the solutions that you have to offer? Was the reference for the allocation of broadcast resources you are talking about a transference of existing resources, or expansion of existing facilities?

WILEY: No. I'll comment on the latter part of that first and then get back to your observation. No, I was talking about the fact that if we tell a person that he doesn't have to look at the meters every thirty minutes, but every three hours, if we change the whole way that you have to log, if we come up with a short form in radio renewals, if we come up with different kinds of ascertainments in different markets, there are obviously going to be some savings to the broadcaster. Indeed, I have received many poignant letters from very, very small broadcasters indicating precisely what the changes (which some lampoon today as being a "few crumbs") have meant to them in their everyday business, in terms of dollars and cents. It seems to me, that those dollars and cents ought to go into some better programming, some better service to the American people. I don't want to debate what better programming is. I would say this: I think people are going to look back on this period as perhaps a period of somewhat more enlightened regulation. In any case, one of less regulation and more emphasis on the strengths of the private sector. I would like to think that they would also not look back on this as a time when technical compliance and service to the American public went down too, because if it does— and I've said this to industry groups and I'm going to continue to do that —then I think that a different Commission will come along some day. It would have a different regulatory attitude, and I think would call for much more restrictive regulation, and I think industry would deserve it at that point. So, that is the kind of re-allocation that I'm talking about. Now as to your question as whether pragmatics are in the public interests, I'm not saying that one has always to decide that *is* before deciding what *should be*. I'm suggesting that I don't think that many of these suggestions (counter advertising, access, taking all commercials from children's television), really are realistic alternatives. And if it isn't realistic, I don't think that we ought to spend a lot of time on it trying to go one way or the other. Instead, we ought to look at the range of possibilities that makes some sense in terms of the type of broadcasting system we have. Now, if you want to change that, if you want to have a public system, that's one thing. But if you're going to have a commercial broadcasting system, it's going to have to be supported by advertising. As far as institutional advertising, foundation money, and government grants and all the rest of it are concerned, I just don't think the money is there. Also, I'm not sure I'd want the government funding all this programming anyway. Let's look at the public interest but let's try to take pragmatic alternatives, because, otherwise the Commission is just not going to succeed with those alternatives.

GELB: First, I want to say that I appreciate the opportunity of hearing you tonight because up until this moment, I was under the false interpretation that we had been lead to believe that you were the FCC Commissioner in charge of dissolving the FCC. And so because of that misinterpretation, I'd like to ask you a very naive question. Why don't your reasons for making changes, re-regulations in a small market radio also apply to television?

WILEY: Oh, they do. They do. In fact most of the real changes to date have also applied to television. The emphasis right now is on radio, because I think that's where the Commission's regulation really needs some changes. Radio really is a different animal than television. There are differences and we've got to start regulating with those differences in mind, but many of the changes will affect, and have affected, television.

GELB: Then there will be less regulation for television?

WILEY: Less regulation is probably what's going to happen, but we're not setting out with the idea of saying that less regulation is a goal. I happen to think that probably is not a bad idea, because I happen to be one who believes a lot in the strengths of the private sector. But what we're really saying—and I think this is the essence of good government—is for the government agency to take stock of the last twenty or thirty years and say: "What's on that Rule book? Is it still viable?" If you've ever seen a FCC Rule Book, you don't want to see it again. I'm an attorney and I work a twelve- or fourteen-hour day, but there's no way on God's green earth that I can keep up with those changing regulations and I don't have to sell spots, appear on the air, interview every local nabob in sight, and all the other things that broadcasters have to do.

GELB: I thought that you made a statement in your opening remarks that you felt that the changes in regulations in small market radio did not apply to TV.

WILEY: Oh, no. Many of the changes that we've made to date apply equally to television. No question about it. I just say right now, the initial impetus of the program is radio. Television, after all, is a form of broadcasting (like radio) and, obviously, we are in broadcasting re-regulation. But the emphasis is on radio at this point.

POWELL: I find very little to disagree with what you said. But if I could ask you a question, could you give us a time parameter for this? Are you talking about something you perceive within twenty-four months? Thirty-six months?

WILEY: I don't think it will ever cease. I think that re-regulation is a continuing process. In fact, Wally Johnson, our Chief of Broadcast Bureau, was once asked that very question. "Will I be able to see this before I die?" And Wally said, "It depends on how old you are." I have set about a two-year period as a watershed point, and I have phased this program. The first phase was those rules that we could change without any public comment. We didn't have to put out rule making. There were non-controversial changes which were just clearly things that we, as a Federal Agency, felt should be done and no one disagreed. Dr. Parker, indeed, of the United Church of Christ, has been a fine supporter of our program to date as one broadcasting critic. Then we're going into Phase Two which will be areas in which we've got to go out and get comment about such things as the short-form renewal, and a notice of inquiry on ascertainment. Should ascertainments be the same in all markets? How's our primer working out? Should there be different types of ascertainment in different markets? I believe in ascertainment. I believe it is the way to go, but I think that there are things about our current ascertainment policies that don't make sense, particularly in certain markets. I might mention another thing: automated transmitters. I think that's got to come. There certainly has to be an option to the broadcaster who wants to avoid a lot of the technical logging rules and what have you. On such things, we're going out for comment. Now Phase Three—down the trail a bit—are the so-called de-regulatory areas in which we might (if Congress would acquiesce or we find the legal authority) look at an area like New York City and try to determine whether we could put the Commission stamp—the complete stamp—of approval on fully-formatted radio. That's somewhat down the trail, and at each stage of the game, we're going to look at this carefully, and I'm not going to be impelled by private interests pushing on us. One noted broadcaster called our first action a couple of crumbs. I reacted to that by saying that it overlooks the historic significance of this program, and that is: here's an organ of government willing to look at its own regulation, and say, "Wait a minute. Does it make sense or not?" And I think that whatever we do is going to be a good thing. It's catching steam now. The "Hill" is hopping on it and, I think in two years, maybe we'll see some interesting changes.

GOGGIN: How do you feel about the Executive Branch of Government's recent activity (political and economic) insofar as public broadcasting is concerned? What are the implications of negation of the concepts of the "Fourth Network" and the statement that public broadcasting should not be involved in any substantial way in public service (public affairs programs) when any money came primarily from government funds?

WILEY: Well, first of all, you're asking me a political question. I'm not a politician. I'm a statesman. But I feel that when you do involve public funds, you get into a question really of trying to make a real effort to cover all the needs of the country, and I think that there is sometimes a tendency toward elitism. I know Judge Hooks feels this way. Programming doesn't always meet the needs of minority Americans. And I think that this is something that public television has really got to strive to do. Now whether or not it should be news or public affairs, I must say that I'm not the last word on that. I do think that it doesn't make a lot of sense to try and duplicate the work the networks do in this area, as far as coverage is concerned. But I really have not reached any definitive decision in my own mind, as to what should be the programming for public television, beyond those general guidelines.

CAILTEUX: You've been talking about re-regulation and public broadcasting as a dimension. Does the Commission intend to take a look at the rules and regulations as they apply to public broadcasting and re-regulate in that area or wait for some legislation?

WILEY: Well, it hasn't come up yet. And in all honesty, we've been so busy working on the commercial side of it that we've just not gotten to that. This may be something that is possible. When we get into ascertainment this is an area that we certainly might want to think about. If we're telling them to serve all of the community, then one of the ways they do it is to find out what the needs and interests are of those areas which they serve. So I think that is a possibility. But I must say in candor that we've not gotten to that point yet. At least, my little committee hasn't and keep in mind that I've got four or five people and we're certainly not the be-all and the end-all of the Commission's activities.

COMMENT: I don't have a question. I just want to say, thank you for a refreshing breath of fresh air from Washington.

WILEY: I don't think it's likely. That's my opinion. I think that other reflective of the majority thinking on the Commission.

RHEA: How likely is it that a broadcaster will be appointed to the Commission?

WILEY: I don't think it's likely. That's my opinion. I think that other interests are getting stronger—for example, the cable industry. I think that anybody that comes to the Commission has got to remember that the spectrum of problems that we've got before us is certainly far broader than broadcasting today. I looked over the Chairman's statement tonight, coming up on the plane, for our Over-Sight Hearing before Senator Pastore. It's just amazing the developments in the spectrum management field (and I'm spectrum management Commissioner) and in common carrier and all these diverse areas.

COMMENT: Where are the other guys?

WILEY: Well, when Commissioner Bartley retired, Dean Burch called me and said, "You're going to have to leave right away for New Orleans. You're going to be invested down there as Head of the Radio Technical Commission for Marine Service." So I went down and I really didn't know much about it. I was sitting there at lunch and it came time for the speaker. His topic was: "Data Telemetry on Tugboats." So maybe we'll have a tugboat captain as the next Commissioner.

COHEN: There seems to have been a definitive statement made from the OTP concerning satellite direct communications. It seems to be one of the only definitive statements we've heard in recent months. Is this in line with FCC opinion?

WILEY: Well, which statement are you referring to, precisely?

COHEN: Well, it seemed to rule it out in the twentieth century.

WILEY: Satellite to home, you mean?

COHEN: Yes.

WILEY: Well, I think that may be a statement that perhaps could be realistic in terms of the technological developments or the likelihood of this happening. I must admit that I've not studied that issue sufficiently to make a judgment. The whole area of satellites is one that we spend an awful lot of time with and I think that the Commission has certainly laid the groundwork for eventually getting to that with its domestic satellite policy. It is going to allow multiple entry and give a lot of new companies an opportunity to get into the business. I see a great development coming in communications, technology. When you think about the kinds of ways that we communicate with people, it's a little hard to decide exactly how it will develop. At this point all that I can say is that the new potential uses of the radio spectrum make this era of communication a particularly exciting one. Thank you very much.

Rapporteur Summaries
of Group Discussions

CLOSING PANEL: GROUP REPORTS

Rapporteurs: Phillip Gelb (Bronx Community College, City University of New York); Keith Mielke (Indiana University); James W. Rhea (Oklahoma State University)

COHEN: I'd like to thank the three group discussion leaders who worked in very close concert with our three Rapporteurs to pull together the reports that you are now going to hear: Bob Crawford from Queens College, Knox Haygood from the University of Alabama, and Ken Harwood from Temple University. Thank you very much for your participation. We will begin with the first Rapporteur, Phil Gelb, of Bronx Community College.

Challenge I—Public Television

GELB: The opening round started with a few light jabs, followed by some brief counter-punching, but the first ten minutes were mostly sparring around, until the group focused on three suggested public TV inevitabilities: One, there is always a government to deal with. Two, there are always funds to be raised. Three, someone has to run the show, or shows. The key question then became, how are decisions made in these key areas in public TV? And how are any checks or controls maintained on those who make these decisions? That seemed to be the general focus.

What are the checks and balances on these key decision-makers in public TV? The answers appeared in ten fairly specific and constructive suggestions, only a few of which might be considered at all novel or innovative; but, taken together as a package all of the following might present a very fine program for a specific public TV outlet or network—not only facing the inevitabilities of politics, power and money but also for continually maintaining checks and balances in these areas:

1. Establish and maintain local lobbyists and lobbying groups.
2. Encourage wider organized public action groups, such as ACT.
3. Establish either a regular coupon-clipping monthly donation fee and/or a regular licensing public TV tax fee, a la the BBC. It was stressed that a regular fee system from the public for public TV not only creates a no-strings-attached income but also, and perhaps what is even more important, creates an involved, vested-interest audience.
4. Try to use or establish town meetings in the local communities. These would not only be covered by public TV for broadcasts, but some of these public town meetings could deal directly with the programs and problems of public TV itself in that community.
5. Several pressuring checks and balances were brought out as not particularly successful, but maybe worth considering, such as: using big name groups like the ex-Hoving-Committee in New York, or using militant groups to picket and demonstrate.
6. Tighten local and regional station management communication with PBS and other national, and even international, entities in the field. In short, stabilize our own house.
7. Consider the possibilities of pay TV, coin box and of course cable TV funding, particularly for special situations, such as an auction or anything which involved media feedback.
8. All of these and more taken together should aim at a spirit of local community pride. WGBH in Boston was pointed out as an example of this. Public TV should be public-spirited.

Nine and ten, I think, are comparatively new suggestions.

9. This involved using the current controversy, on commercial TV needs, for public TV. Several members of the group felt that we should tread lightly on this conflict between the government and public TV, or at least be diplomatic. Others however, felt, that the current conflict could prove to be an excellent channel for calling both the existence and problems of public TV to more of the public. In short, controversy itself can be publicity, promotion and action.
10. One final suggestion started by relating public TV to a supermarket and/or to an experimental test track: a place not only for viewers to shop for variety and diversity—and this I think was an interesting idea—but also a place for commercial TV to do the same. In other words, a direct working relationship seemed to be in order between commercial and public TV in which public TV

would get funds, people and aid from commercial television; and commercial television would get lower cost experiments, a testing ground for innovations and possibly even specific programs and personalities for future commercial network TV use. Now, some of this has already occurred but what was suggested here was an actual planned, budgeted, long-range working relationship between public and commercial TV. Again it is the totality of what I'm saying here and the continuity of suggestions that the group felt could make the inescapable inevitabilities of public TV—power, politics and money—more liveable.

Challenge II—Television Aesthetics

The comments and insights can be summarized in three not too novel ideas: One, TV is too young for aesthetics. Such critical standards will be developed by others in some future time. Two, aesthetic standards are a purely personal matter. Depending on your point of view, that is "the final solution" of the aesthetic problem, or the ultimate cop-out—aesthetics are strictly personal. Three, aesthetic standards! What did they ever sell?

The last ten minutes of this session, however, were comparatively uncongenial. They were pointed and uncomfortable, but several exciting ideas came out of this short, but genuine give and take. First, the vocal majority felt that the aforementioned writing-off of aesthetic standards for television was a *carte blanche,* unchallenged go-ahead for whatever standards, norms or conventions exist now. In other words, TV or any man-made phenomenon abhors a vacuum even more than nature. Standards of some kind, existing formulas, conventions eventually become rationalized as aesthetics and the status quo just moves in or stays in and takes over. Now this may be what has happened already. In the first forty minutes, for example, the people who didn't think aesthetic standards were possible kept using words such as "good, great, lousy, terrible." What were these based on? "Standards" already exist! Most of us felt that the only question was: are the premises and standards of aesthetics good enough? And in the last few minutes of this session, aesthetic standards of TV became more of a goal, something possibly for us to search out and teach, something for producers to aim at. A few standards were even suggested, as specific TV shows and commercials were probed. For example, one standard was "human believability." Some characters on the Mary Tyler Moore show were cited, and the Alka-Seltzer commercial, in which something always went wrong and in less than a minute, a foolish, fat, middle-aged stereotype changed into a real human being, demanding your empathy and sympathy.

When the experts were pushed, we got "standards" on wordiness, artificiality, sense of movement, the real versus the canned feeling, something meaning more than it says, and levels of meaning. All these were touched upon in the last few restless minutes as relating to possible aesthetic standards for television.

Challenge III—Broadcast News, Is It Biased?

The group felt that Mr. Methvin and Mr. Wolf overlooked some bias in their formal presentation. Additional biases, real and/or potential, that broadcast newsmen evidently must face and overcome included these: The bias of selection. The bias of editing. The bias of summarizing and categorizing. The bias of journalism schools. The bias of phony objectivity and the bias of real objectivity. The bias of corporate and inside politics. The bias of advocacy. The bias of smugness. The academic bias and the anti-academic bias. The "I want to hold my job" bias. The bias of anticipated government intervention and surveillance. The big name or new wave biases. The bias of opinion as fact. And, of course, the bias of fact as opinion. The bias of having to talk with nothing to say. The bias of just three network news editors. The bias of statistics and numbers and ratings. The bias of thinking too much, and the bias of not thinking at all.

It was around this point that the Chairman politely interrupted to summarize. It would appear that broadcast news is biased, because life and people are biased. The solutions for such biases were not as easy or as quantitative as the problem. Some solutions were suggested:

One, maintain a large stable of clear biases in every newsroom, now and then even presenting the exact same story as seen through two opposing biases.

Two, instead of all "doing the same damned thing," one station could do a daily news show a few hours after the others, summarizing their sameness and pointing out the differences and oversights that all the other news shows omitted in that day's news.

Three, the networks might offer an alternative news half-hour at the end of each week, actually critically analyzing and even attacking their own news presentations during the past week.

Four, numerous comments added up to labeling virtually everything as commentary or interpretation.

Five, all of these suggestions to overcome bias seem to come down to humanizing the news, and presenting the humans broadcasting it as something other than infallible. For example, a retraction or correction-minute on the daily news show was suggested. No one in our group ever heard of a mistake in the history of broadcast news, since no one knew of anything in this area as ever being retracted or corrected. Only specials are fallible and occasionally allow the admission of mistakes. In summary, there seemed to be some feeling that the supreme bias of broadcast news is ultimately its assumed infallibility and untouchable power.

Challenge IV—Counter-advertising

In general, questions, usually critical, were directed at this session's guest, an advocate of counter-advertising. This tended to lead to a repetition of the same material brought out in the formal presentation. The only dissent here came when an industry spokesman pointed out that the counter-advertising quarter-hour would be costly to the station carrying it, since it would lose audiences before and after and could not draw more than a miniscule audience, even in prime time. A few in the group dissented, primarily, I think, because the industry spokesman said, "I assume we all agree that this could not draw." So several of us said, "No." We thought the counter-advertising program might draw for its very off-beat, crazy nature. And it was pointed out that, for several years, Italian TV's top-rated show was a half hour of commercials. The most succinct comment of the day occurred when a commercial sales manager was asked how he would feel selling counter-advertising spots. His succinct answer was, "I'd retch."

It was felt that the needs for counter-advertising could be met internally. For example a more enlightened industry would demand self-policing, conscientious responsibility and other internal self-regulation. I think everybody agreed, and I'm not being facetious here, that these "internal enlightenments" should be pursued. But it was a kind of dream that a vocal minority praised, while suggesting we put our efforts and faith into more built-in, measurable, outer checks and balances.

Challenge V—Can the Incumbent Capture the Airways?

This was our "but" session, which refers not to the seat of our ideas but to the synonym for "however." Incidentally, it really happened this way. Perhaps there weren't that many "buts," but the session actually followed a point-counter-point format. It was pointed out that the threat of the incumbent capturing the airways was very real. *But,* the President generally gets coverage because he's making real news. *But,* he times his real news for political purposes, such as the China visit a few months before the election. *But* the President then runs the risk of the visit either turning out badly or running contrary to the wide public anti-Communist feelings. *But,* it didn't happen that way. We did get balance. His motives were questioned, and the pro-Commie possibilities were probed. *But,* this was underplayed. The government can intimidate the media and control content. *But* is "that" capturing the media or even encroachment? *But,* don't the media encroach and intimidate with twelve cameras aimed at you, six mikes in the face and the power to edit? *But,* media newsmen still need protection! *But,* from what? *But* from everything, the government, any strong institutions, self-interest groups, the subtraction of newsmen's rights. The media need to tell the story of their own importance. *But* this would backfire as manipulative public relations. *But* civics classes in schools teach the value of media is now. *But,* civics classes are the least-regarded courses and the average high school student would vote against the Bill of Rights if you phrased it in day-to-day language. *But,* it is still the larger public's right to know what is at stake here. *But,* that's what Agnew said! *But,* should a vital idea be discarded just because Agnew said it? *But,* our Chairman pointed out, our time is up.

Challenge VI—Mass Audience

The Chairman's opening question here: "Is responsibility owed to the mass audience?" brought a vocal minority's resounding "Yes." This response was in answer to Mr. Segelstein's question, "What's wrong with popularity?" It was pointed out that mass audience popularity can be very wrong. What was brought out here, I think, was an academic idea, if you will excuse the expression, that popularity is wrong not because of program content, not because of elitist feelings, not because of Mr. Segelstein's upper middle-class-living-room attitudes, or for any reason connected with a popular item. The concepts and work of Colin Cherry in England and the French structuralists were cited, showing that popularity, *per se,* tends to create itself in its own image, while simultaneously creating the phenomenon of diminishing alternatives. I've been doing some research in this area myself. I call it The Law of Diminishing Alternatives, which is the greater the popularity of any form, even *Sesame Street,* the more the possible alternatives to this form become downgraded or denied. Now, this is a simultaneous activity.

Let me see if I can give some examples. The more television uses violence as a problem-solving method, the less desirable non-violence methods automatically become. This is nobody's intention. There is no conspiracy. This is a dynamics that, men like Colin Cherry say, occurs automatically. And this can be tested out in research. For example, in this conference, if you emphasize short, succinct, complete statements, the possibility of complex, longer incomplete statements is automatically downgraded. You simply can't have it both ways. There is a huge cost in popularity. For example, *The Dead End Kids* gave birth to the *Bowery Boys* and to *The East Side Kids* who still get prime youth time twenty to thirty years after these films were made. And this anti-adult, take-the-law-into-your-own-hands pattern really has not been broken on Saturday morning television for this particular age-group yet. The idea of the concept of diminishing alternatives is that popularity acts as a giant censor of the alternatives to the popular patterns.

We also mentioned that the industry tends to look at certain superficial changes as real changes or breakthroughs, such as changing the pigmentation of a detective in a detective series and that a more major change, such as a popular TV series built around the adventures of a female arbitrator—yes, "the arbitrator" could still capitalize on the real human drama conflicts and suspense of characters in current adventure shows—but the industry spokesman then pointed out that such a series would lack the essential "complete resolution" of the popular pattern where violence completely resolves everything. He did acknowledge, however, that TV cannot say that it can sell SupHose and then say, but we do not sell patterns and values. The question was then asked, is violence so popular, or are the media popularizing violence? Other questions restated this basic concept. For example, some people asserted that available supply tends to create demand. The industry spokesman said that a new show will be shaped by its antecedents. The need for television to fail more was cited. The observation was also made that the way one deals with this "responsibility" is that, if you don't like the six-and-a-half hours of patterned daily television, you can turn off your set. But a minority of the group felt this was not an adequate solution to this built-in patterning and censoring dynamics in this phenomenon of popularity itself. This is a fairly new concept, and it might be something that IRTS will want to probe in the future, this concept of popularity as a real danger in itself.

Challenge VII—Special Audience Treatment

This discussion focused on the need of children's audiences as meriting special attention. But the problem seemed to dissolve in a general consensus that perhaps TV's influence had been overrated. Personal testimony was given to the effect that "my psyche has not been terribly warped by Ovaltine commercials and Superman." It was also pointed out that, since small children watch TV one-third of all their waking hours, doing away with commercials seen by children would do away with one-third of all television commercials. It was felt that children are bothered only by commercials when the damned toy doesn't work. This led to an agreeable discussion built around the idea that TV really isn't so powerful, that it isn't such a bad influence. The suggestion of consensus here uncovered a single dissenter. Dissent was based on the view that nothing like television had occurred in human history and never had so little been said to so many so often, and perhaps our job was to be overly critical of this mammoth, unprecedented phenomenon. Some new lines of research were suggested, and consensus was successfully defeated.

Challenge VIII—De- and/or Re-regulation of Radio

The group was fortunate to have several station managers and FCC form-fillers among its members. Ten areas of existing FCC regulations were pointed out: program content—engineering requirement—on-air performance—economic injury—controversy—public service—sales—multiple ownership—owner qualifications—administrative requirements. It was felt that the endless, time-consuming red-taping bureaucratic procedures in most of these areas, if not all of them, could be cut down or eliminated. It was pointed out the situation had worsened in recent years. Radio stations lost money, but were hung on to as a valuable property to sell. Radio time was being traded for products and produce. Thirty-two out of 108 radio stations in Kentucky got temporary licenses leading to back-breaking law costs. The group again pointed to a consensus—de-regulate. Take all the regulations away. Again a lone dissenter, and not the same one (the dissenters were different): "You're putting us on. Doesn't the FCC offer some protection? Are you eliminating public interest, convenience and necessity too? No standards? No criteria? Is this what you're suggesting?" It was suggested that the market place would solve such problems, and then it was noted that the most pornographic station undoubtedly would have the biggest audience, and thus sell. Again, consensus was avoided and rethinking on this idea of de-regulation was going on as the last session ended.

In general, in all discussions the group seemed impressed by its ability to avoid a band-wagon effect. Members did stand alone and moved others from the pack. The feeling was expressed however, that even less agreement and less compatibility might lead to more creative alternatives. Essentially Broadcast-USA was a very pleasant mammoth, quite capable of inadvertently producing only those ideas it wanted to hear, even from us. *Unless,* it more consciously (and we more consciously) encouraged other views. The group also seemed to feel that "only the ideas radio/TV wants to hear" were fine ideas in general, but perhaps they were insufficient and inadequate for meeting the problems and challenges currently facing the industry and the nation.

COHEN: The second report will be presented by Keith Mielke of Indiana University.

MIELKE: We know from a long tradition of research in psychology the effects of serial learning experiments on retention of the middle position; whatever is said in the middle position will be mercifully forgotten within thirty minutes. There is also an additional danger, I think, in the combined role that's indicated by the title "Rapporteur," which I gather is a hybrid between a rap artist and a reporter. We know this because geneticists at Indiana University have for years been trying to cross-breed an abalone and a crocodile in the hopes of producing an abadile. However, there was something that went wrong with the experiment and what resulted instead was a crockobalony.

Challenge I, was the funding of public television. We discussed this issue from the point of view of how can funding be acquired without accepting, in the package, undue control over content. We felt it necessary to enumerate some assumptions on this. Assumption One: You cannot depend solely on foundation support for public television. Assumption Two: Some form of government funding is inevitable. Assumption Three: With funding, there is to be some degree of concern if we accept that premise. Assumption Four: Diversity of funding is desirable, particularly voluntary funding, directly by the audiences served by public television, as well as from various interested groups.

From that basis of assumptions, we came to four suggestions of how we might fund public broadcasting. One suggestion was to incorporate a consortium idea. This has precedent, for example, at National Instructional Television, where local groups pool their resources and make out of that pooled resource something analogous to centralized funding and centralized control and the concomitant economies of scale. For instance, at National Instructional Television, they will go to various groups and say, do you have a need for this kind of program; and, if the answer is "yes," do you want to jump into the pool with us to do it? And if that answer is "yes," then you have a collectivity here that is being served by a centrally produced, well-produced series of programs. The consortium idea may be an alternative source of funding and control—management control—for public broadcasting, it was suggested. There are a variety of ways that were suggested for the collection and utilization of voluntary contributions. One of these was a form similar to the income tax form contribution to political parties where, by checking a box, there can be a small amount contributed that way on a very large scale. It was also suggested that the telephone company could conceivably collect an additional dollar a month or dollar a year, whatever the fund, because the collection machinery is there and well established. It was finally suggested that CATV could have additional billing services, with a spin-off of some of that funding to public broadcasting. We thought that there could be a form of revenue sharing here which is sort of reversing the reverse flow of dollars to and from local communities to Washington. It was pointed out that there are already monies at the state level being used for public television operations.

With *Challenge II,* aesthetics, we had as many problems as did the first group. We questioned whether a question of aesthetics can seriously be applied to commercial television. We thought that it might, but we noted that the one-shot nature of television—it's here today and it's gone tomorrow—the ephemeral nature of the product, made serious aesthetic critical analysis extremely difficult. However, there was thought to be some underlying practical benefit to taking aesthetics seriously. Mr. Crowther was our resource person and he was saying that the true understanding, the true grappling with aesthetic principles ought to have the effect of producing superior programs, involving, compelling programs, and that could not help but be an advantage for the television medium. We got into a discussion of whether in aesthetics we're talking about a quality of the stimulus or a quality of the response. My thesis was that, if we're talking about a quality of the response or making a prediction of behavioral effects, we might as well look to principles of psychological testing, as well as to principles of aesthetics. In general, I was stereotyped as a damned scientist who wants to run around with a thermometer and find out what Spring means, and love and so forth. But there was a spirited interchange about the relationship between science and art that I thought was useful—perhaps the point being that both principles of psychology and principles of aesthetics can be applied to the subject of increasing the quality of the stimulus and the quality of the response.

On *Challenge III,* news bias, we did not discuss the issue: is bias a good thing or a bad thing? We accepted the premise that it was undesirable, and the question then was, why is this so and what can be done about it? It was felt by some in our group that the reason we might have bias is the inability to forget that there is an axe over the head of the broadcaster. If you remove this axe, then you get a degree of security, and a degree of security would then result in less bias. Specifically, the broadcaster is uncertain that he is *really* protected by the First Amendment and, because he is uncertain of that, he cannot afford to be insensitive to the news, to the content of his news, its possible interpretation and effect by a party in power at any given time. Therefore, the solution that follows would be to have true protection under the First Amendment for the newscaster and those who make news policy and practice. There is a perceptual problem here of bias, due to the nature of the medium. For example, order of presentation effects are believed to be inherent in the nature of this medium, and that will introduce bias. There is the bias of selective retention and I think it is demonstrable that, over time, we will tend to remember that which was disagreeable. It's the phenomenon of the speck in my eye and the beam in your eye, the same principle in terms of retention here. We were aware that there is a great deal of non-verbal information being communicated in television news. This should be immediately obvious if you say, why is it that the person of the renderer is so terribly important? Why is it that we search so arduously for the right person to render the news? The identical verbal content could, of course, be rendered by any number of personages, but why is it that we look for the right one? I think that reasoning leads us to the conclusion that what we're really concerned with is the additional group of non-verbal cues that communicate along with the verbal content. And therein, in this category of non-verbal information, lies a great source of potential bias. We did not believe that sensitivity to sponsorship was a major problem, although it was thought to be impossible to forget that sponsorship interest could occasionally not be the same as professional news judgment.

As to *Challenge IV*, counter-advertising, on the base which seemed to be not an unreasonable idea—the search for truth leads us to examination of diverse viewpoints—is that one listens to many diverse voices and goes through a rational procedure to a logical conclusion. However, our discussion on counter-advertising did not really go to the issue of its ethical standing, its moral stature, whether it's right or wrong. Our discussion tended to hinge on the administrative feasibility of the concept. And on that there was unanimity that it was not an administratively feasible idea. We did not believe that an advertiser would invest in a message to say, "in five seconds this message will self-destruct." That would not attract revenue. Nor in anything did we hear that the method by which the validity of the counter-claims would be examined was not clear to us. It was felt that the counter-advertising proposition is very much the tip of the iceberg, that it has a limitless series of implications that are by no means thought through, and we could just keep generating examples that would cause problems like: do you want to go against a savings bonds advertisement? And on anything we could think of, somebody could come up with a plausible-sounding contrary position. We did think that something approaching a "Consumers' Union of the Air" might be a feasible way to handle the problem, not dealing with counter-advertising, but dealing with the problem. But we would insist that a Consumers' Union of the Air also have requirements to substantiate the validity of their claims. In general, if there is a problem in this area, if we say that the people who support counter-advertising are directing themselves to a valid problem, that may be. But counter-advertising is not the solution to it, in any case.

On *Challenge V*, politics and television, the power of the incumbent party to have access to a medium, we had an interesting session here—in more or less a systems-analysis kind of logic. This is the kind of logic in which, if the problem were how can we find a better kind of soap, the brilliant systems-analyst might say, "let's make clothes that don't get dirty." The logic says there are a variety of ways to skin a cat. Along that line, apply that kind of logic to the question of control over access. One solution was to have an absolute maximum on the amount of time that a party can stay in power. Therefore, you have defined the problem out of existence. That is, no matter how much access you have to a medium, you are out of power in this unit of time. Another suggestion along this systems-logic approach is that you can remove the perceived punitive threat from the broadcaster by reducing the regulatory power over broadcasting. This again, is the perception of the axe that's up there, whether or not it's denied officially, the sensitivity to the axe over your neck. Remove that, the argument would go, and then you will have less kowtowing by journalists to any party in power. In another stream of logic, we thought it would be helpful to institutionalize the adversary relationship. We could have it in the form, for example, of a loyal opposition type of program, or we can format into the news presentation a counter-viewpoint function. Presumably we now have a news, weather, sports kind of format—we could have news, weather, sports, editorial, counter-viewpoint format. This is really a position of structural relativity that is not geared to an absolute position that you're attacking or defending, but it is structural in the sense that it's counter. It's a commitment to the value of an alternative point of view. So, no matter what point of view is coming out here, the news function that would be filled would be to counter that with alternatives. We finally thought it would be quite feasible to develop syndicated "TV columnists of the air" who would have a broad spectrum of viewpoints, and stations could, by selection of their TV columnists of the air, present the array of opinion and counter-opinion that is now available in good newspapers.

Challenge VI, program diversity—we never grappled actually with the conceptual problem of defining diversity, except that I think we did not mean by diversity, diversity of political viewpoints or diversity of liberal-conservative outlooks. I think we meant diversity of program types. As such, we believe that diversity is a good thing. We feel that there are at least two ways that diversity can be increased. One would involve the use of re-broadcasting programs. For example, suppose that within any week's time you have 100 programs, at any one time, three or four of them being available. One could, through rebroadcasting, increase the diversity of psychological options available to any one person by rescheduling these programs in different arrangements. This could be done by a cable system. It could be done by giving an individual program more than one shot on the air. Finally, in the problem of diversity we questioned why is it that it is so rarely heard in reference to libraries where you can have millions of options available to you? We're talking here about a basic nature of the television medium as it differs from the print media. Specifically, it's in the point of control over the pacing and consumption, whether the locus of control is in the hand of the sender or in the hand of the receiver. By changing the nature of the medium, for example, to something on the order of cassettes, you change the locus of control to the point of reception, and diversity as an issue is eliminated.

Challenge VII, to which *Variety* would probably come up with a snappy headline such as "Kiddy-O Video-O." We felt very strongly that children are not to be compared with, equated with, other special audience groups. Children are special. They're special because they have no sophisticated defenses against irrational or even harmful appeals that can be

directed to them through advertising. They are special, because they themselves cannot mount an effective lobby or pressure campaign in their own
behalf. Therefore, they are not to be equated with special-interest groups
such as women, blacks, what have you. So that, if we have a policy recommendation for special audience groups, it would not necessarily mean all for
children. No matter how hard we tried to address the larger issues of the
special audience groups, we kept returning to the problem of children and
television. We felt that it was not an inherent opposition to directing commercials to children, but an inherent opposition to directing commercials to
children in the absence of knowledge of what this effect might be. We,
therefore, strongly encouraged research on the effects of television commercials on young children going through—now we're talking about young
children, seven and under—who are going through the development states
that were articulated by Ms. Roberts.

Challenge VIII, de-regulating radio, started out as almost a love-in, in
the Rho Discussion Group, inasmuch as nobody was really going against
the idea. We all said, yes, it should be de-regulated. Of course, Commissioner Wiley suggested re-regulated and we differentiated non-regulated,
and so forth. Then, in order to get any sense of drama into the session, we
said: is there no reasonable position that can be taken against this, asking
the minister, isn't there anything that can be said in favor of sin whatever?
And given that set of questions, it was felt that, with de-regulation or re-
regulation, it could be possible that the tastes would be lowered down to
whatever the market would bear. That is, right now it's conceivable that
such things as sex radio or drug-oriented music or amount of commerciali-
zation, may not be as bad as the market will bear. If you de-regulate radio,
it's conceivable that the practices would go down and seek that level. From
that point, the premise was that the self-purifying mechanisms of the open
marketplace would take care of abhorrent behavior.

In summary, I feel that there may be some major conditioned responses by broadcasters, and these will probably be of the order that we
need more advertising revenue, we need less regulation. That theme came
out repeatedly from the various broadcasters. Academes also have negative
reactions. They find it impossible to write an article without the concluding
sentence, "More research is needed on this subject." In our discussion
groups, we talked a variety of times about research needs that were generated as a result of our discussion of the problem. And many, reward-
ingly, many of these research suggestions came from our resource persons,
and not from the professors: The question, for example, how has commercial television conditioned us to have expectations from the television
set? This suggests a cross-cultural research approach. For instance, if a
Canadian sits down to a set, a Frenchman or a German sits down to a
set in his country, what expectations does he have that are a function of his

past exposure to the television product? And twenty years of commercial television, it is hypothesized, leads us to have certain expectations which may limit the options that we have psychologically beyond that which is necessary. We feel, secondly, that a study of the non-verbal aspects of television news—a la the raised eyebrow school of editorializing, a la the charges leveled by former Vice President Agnew—that this can be approached scientifically, and should be. And finally, that nothing is as important as the understanding and the protection of our nation's children in terms of what effect is indeed occurring when they are exposed to commercials that content analysis can demonstrate, a set of irrational appeals that psychology can demonstrate, as being received by a belief system that is still in developmental stages and does not have the sophistication to analyze logically, or have protective devices. And in this I think we can all agree. To be against children would be to be against mother and apple pie. And we strongly supported, in agreement with the broadcasters, research in those three areas.

COHEN: Jim Rhea of Oklahoma State University will conclude the IOTA Group summary.

RHEA: We are going to utilize a slightly different method of reporting. In keeping with the general format of this seminar, we're taking a slight deviation from the Delphi method and present to you the solutions from the Iota Group using a rank order format. This ranking was done individually by Iota Group members on a listing of solutions generated in group sessions. This was not a consensus effort. These are merely individual rankings which will give you some indication about the individual feelings within the group.

Challenge I—Public Television: Where is it, and where is it headed?

The highest ranking in Challenge I was to have the Corporation for Public Broadcasting (CPB) generate statements of its mission, scope and philosophy, so that these may serve as criteria for program selection. This was by far the most mentioned solution to Challenge I. We thought that enunciation of the goals and objectives by the CPB would clarify many of the decisions that are made. The second most frequently mentioned solution was to amend the statute to require fairness instead of objectivity and balance; to state criteria for license renewal; to permit editorials; and to cease inter-connection in favor of using those funds for local purposes. This would bring the requirements for the CPB stations generally in line with the commercial stations. The third most frequently mentioned solution was to establish a board to mediate or arbitrate between licensees and

CPB. There seemed to be a general feeling that the CPB needs to be more responsive to the needs of the public in their decision-making process.

Challenge II—Is a television aesthetic possible?

The solution mentioned most frequently was that research on visual variables such as cutting rate, camera angle and juxtaposition, be funded so that traditional rules of thumb in production need not be honored, unless they prove to be as valuable in television as they are in other media. In general, we felt that we probably didn't know enough about aesthetics in television really to use that as a basis for evaluating television. The next solutions both received an equal number of mentions and tended to cluster very close to the first solution. Our group suggested academia examine forms and techniques of television as well as the social aspects. This solution is quite similar to the idea Keith Mielke reported from the Rho group. The third solution in the cluster was that experimentation with live television should be revived and extended by the television networks, much in the tradition of *Camera 3* and programs of this genre. The feeling of the group seemed to be that we had not done enough investigation at this point to come up with a final answer.

Challenge III—Broadcast News: Is It Biased?

Here the most often mentioned solution was to establish citizen advisory groups to meditate between broadcasters and individual complaints. The feeling was that this would open the channels of communication between the listener and the newscaster. This could allow the type of problems which were mentioned to be categorized. Then, if there were consistent problem areas, this would be brought to the attention of the station and the newscaster in order to make them aware of the reactions of the audience. The second most frequently mentioned solution was to increase self-regulation by the industry. This seemed to be more of an offensive move, in order to avoid the defensive reactions to government regulation. The group felt some move should be made at the outset to avoid any additional government regulation. The third solution was to amend the First Amendment so that it extends freedom of the press to include the broadcasting industry. Our group did not deal with the *status quo*. We felt that there was going to be a change, and so we dealt with solutions that might be responsive to a change that seems to be inevitable.

Challenge IV—Is there counter-advertising in broadcasting's future?

As in the other groups, the most commonly mentioned solution was to establish consumer affairs programs on commercial stations which would rely on inputs from such sources as the Better Business Bureau, social scientists, medical and dental societies, and other responsible groups. These would actively involve listener groups, and other responsible groups, with the broadcasters. The second most mentioned solution was to promote special programs on public stations dealing with counter-advertising topics. In other words, we recommended the establishment of the same type of consumer affairs programs for public stations. Third, if we're going to have to deal with counter-advertising, then it was the feeling of the group that we should deal only with those topics that were identified through a community ascertainment study. This could eliminate reacting to anybody that might come through the doorway of a station and say "Hey, my favorite item of concern today is. . ." It was our feeling that some kind of ascertainment study, a group feeling of the community would be much more responsive to the needs of the listeners.

Challenge V—Can an incumbent party capture the airwaves?

The following two solutions seemed to have equal balance: Encourage a strong industry spokesman to advocate an industry stance regarding political pressures on broadcasters, and to extend a right of reply to the loyal opposition on any Presidential address. A solution which seemed to follow logically was that networks and stations should alternate the clearance of Presidential addresses except in very unusual circumstances. In other words, our group felt that it was not necessary or desirable for all stations to carry every speech of the President. The Iota group did not think it was necessary that time be turned over to the incumbent political party or the loyal opposition, but that they should both have an opportunity to get on the air and to get their message to the electorate. As a protection to the public, the industry should certainly be encouraged to point out any problems that might interfere with the operation of the country but that might not be obvious to the listeners and viewers.

Challenge VI—Is broadcast programming only for the mass audience? Is it mirror or telescope?

Two solutions were isolated as having the most relevance: To support research that deals with explanations and psychological values, instead of merely descriptions; and to limit the ownership of networks to those companies which are in the broadcasting business. Basically our group indicated that we really knew very little about the needs of the listeners. How necessary is it to program for special audiences? How necessary is it to go after a particular minority group? Is this good? Is it bad? Is a program that is specifically programmed for mass audience inappropriate for a minority group? We decided we really didn't know, and that research ought to be undertaken to isolate audience needs. In regard to network ownership, one of the resource persons indicated in some instances that, because of the conglomerate nature of network ownership, it seemed that innovative pro-

grams were not undertaken because of losses in other parts of the conglomerate. This was the rationale for the ownership of networks by
companies whose primary concern is broadcasting. The third solution was
to encourage networks to allot additional money to program research and
development, and to encourage additional programs that seem to serve the
needs for specific audiences.

Challenge VII—Special audiences . . . special treatment?

The most often mentioned solution was that additional research should be
funded to discover acceptable ways of advertising on television to children
who are younger than seven. Liz Roberts was the resource person in our
group, so we dealt with programming for children to quite an extent. The
second most mentioned solution was that television advertising intended
for children should be without hard sell, if directed to those under seven
years of age. Essentially what we were saying is that we really didn't know
what effect advertising had on children under seven. If we had to guess,
then we probably ought to eliminate the hard sell for children under seven.
However, we did feel that advertising with institutional appeal should be
allowed in programming for children. Our third solution was that local
public television stations and state networks of stations should provide
special programs for their own minority audiences. This was also an
attempt to indicate that we felt there was a responsibility on the part
of the public stations to serve the special audiences in their listening area.

*Challenge VIII—De-regulation for radio—is it necessary? Evil? Now?
Ever?*

The most often mentioned solution was the radio stations in large markets
should be regulated differently from those in other markets, because of the
number of signals coming to the market. In other words, it was the feeling
of the group that, because of the diversity of programming available in large
markets, radio stations ought to operate under a different set of regulations
than stations in small markets. The next more frequently mentioned
solutions were: That responsible broadcasters should be assured of license
renewal, and that the application of the Fairness Doctrine should be
simplified and clarified. It seemed to us that these two solutions are very
similar in nature and are merely asking for a definition of the rules and
regulations which now exist in order to make some sense out of the present
chaotic situation.

This gives you a brief summary of the solutions that the Iota Group
generated under the leadership of Ken Harwood. We would like to think
the solutions put forth by the Iota Group were positive suggestions to some
of the severe weather warnings forecast, not just for today, but for broadcasting in the Seventies.

Opinion Survey and Report of Findings

BACKGROUND AND PURPOSE

As part of the program of the IRTS Faculty/Industry Seminar, it was decided to poll faculty participants regarding their views on a variety of issues facing the broadcast industry, some of which were discussed by speakers addressing the group during the course of the seminar.

The purpose of the poll was to provide guidance for the future activities of IRTS as well as to inform the participants themselves of the collective views of their colleagues.

METHOD

A modification of the Delphi technique was employed in the conduct of the poll. Briefly, this technique was developed by the Rand Corporation as a means of obtaining the most reliable consensus of opinion of a group of experts for purposes of forecasting. It attempts to achieve this by a series of intensive questionnaires interspersed with controlled opinion feedback. Direct confrontation of the experts with one another is avoided, and thus reduces pressure for conformity and reluctance to change a publicly expressed opinion.

Accordingly, the IRTS poll was conducted in three separate phases, or waves. In the first wave, questionnaires were sent to prospective faculty attendees prior to their arrival. Upon arrival, completed questionnaires were tabulated and the results presented to the entire group. Participants were requested to record these responses onto a second questionnaire, identical to the first, to enable respondents to re-assess their views in light of the collective opinion of the group at large in completing the second-wave questionnaire. This questionnaire was completed and returned the next morning, prior to the beginning of the formal seminar proceedings.

Results of the second wave were again presented to the group, in the same manner as the first, immediately prior to the conclusion of the seminar, to provide input for the third-wave questionnaire, also identical to the first two. Third-wave questionnaires were returned by mail.

Of a total of 29 faculty members who attended the seminar, 25 completed both first- and second-wave questionnaires. Completed third-wave questionnaires were received from 22 participants. The high degree of cooperation indicates that the opinions reflected in this report are reasonably representative of all those in attendance (but not necessarily of all U.S. educators in the communications field, however). It might further be noted that members from colleges and universities located in all major regions of the country were represented.

The questionnaire, consisting primarily of six-point rating scales designed to detect attitude change, covered the following subjects:

> News
> Children's Programming
> Television "Clutter"
> Radio Licensing
> Television Election Coverage
> Counter-Advertising
> Program Diversity
> Television As An Art Form

SUMMARY OF FINDINGS

The results of this study have been analyzed in two ways: an assessment of the over-all *direction* of opinion in each of the areas covered, as well as an evaluation of the extent to which any *consensus* emerged resulting from the iterative process.

With respect to the latter, it must be noted that the modification of the Delphi technique employed in this study involved considerable departures from the purpose for which the technique was originally designed—that is, the forecasting of *quantitative* data based on subjective probabilities.

While this study included some aspects of forecasting (e.g., the likelihood of some form of external monitoring or control of network television news, and radio station licensing), the bulk of the questioning focused on *prevailing* attitudes. Similarly, questioning was necessarily designed to quantify intensity of opinion rather than to elicit estimates of numerical quantities as such. Accordingly, it was not known whether, if at all, any kind of consensus might emerge with respect to a particular area of inquiry.

In analyzing the differences between waves, it was found that, at most, only slight movement toward consensus occurred, due very likely to the fact that a fair degree of unanimity existed prior to the study. In a number of instances virtually no attitude shifts were observed, other than random, chance fluctuations. Question areas in which the greatest movement occurred will be noted in the highlights of findings which follow.

News (Tables A 1-8)

Overall, television news coverage received general support. A majority of respondents felt that television networks deal "fairly with all sides" in presenting the news and that fairness has increased over the past five years. Somewhat fewer, though still a majority, felt that the networks achieve sufficient diversity of viewpoints in their coverage of the news.

The possibility of increased government involvement in local station license renewals—as embodied in legislation proposed by the Nixon administration—encountered strong disapproval among educators, most of whom strongly agreed that such proposals represent "an improper attempt to intimidate TV stations and the networks and to censor the news." Opposition increased somewhat through successive waves of questioning.

While an overwhelming majority clearly felt that First Amendment guarantees of freedom of the press should extend equally to print and broadcast media, and rejected the concept of FCC monitoring of the news, a substantial minority initially expressed some dissatisfaction over leaving news judgments exclusively up to newsmen alone, feeling that station or network management or some independent body should become involved in achieving "a proper balance" in news reporting. (However, the preservation of TV newsmen's complete independence received increased support between the first and third surveys.) Moreover, there is a considerable body of opinion—a substantial majority—that some form of outside control will be placed on network news in the coming years.

In this report, however, it should be noted that this study was conducted at a time when freedom of the press was under attack both in the courts and in frequent public statements by high government officials. To the extent that these issues have more recently been overshadowed by internal problems within the current administration, it is possible that concern over threats to press freedom has since somewhat diminished. According to a recent Harris Poll, for example, a considerable majority of the public felt that the contribution of the press in exposing the facts about Watergate was an example of "a free press at its best."

Children's Programs (Tables B 1-4)

Although the greater majority of educators considered the over-all quality of network children's programs poor, they felt the quality has improved over the past several years.

These educators manifested ambivalent feelings regarding the desirability and consequences of eliminating advertising from children's programs. Most initially agreed that commercials should be eliminated, but that the quality of programming would consequently suffer.

Some shifting of opinion on these questions occurred between waves so that, by the third wave, opinion was about evenly divided on the issues of abolishing commercials. Similarly, an increasing number felt that in so doing, the quality of programming would decline.

TV "Clutter" (Tables C 1-5)

Most of the seminar participants view TV "clutter"—that is, all forms of non-program material—as an important problem, and that it has increased sharply over the last five years.

Clutter is considered less acceptable on television than in other media because of the nature of television as essentially intrusive. The source of criticism centers less around the presence of advertising messages than on the "interruption of an involving communication," as one respondent commented. Another stated: "other media are consumed at the receiver's pace . . . television provides only two alternatives—on or off."

It is therefore not surprising that a clear majority of respondents would like to see non-programming material on television reduced.

Radio (Tables D 1-5)

Reacting to a proposal that radio stations be exempt from license renewal requirements, most strongly disapproved of this proposal, and felt there was little likelihood that such requirements would in fact be lifted.

In the event radio stations become exempt from license renewal requirements, there was some feeling that this might result in an increase in the *number* of radio stations, but that the *quality* of programming and advertising effectiveness would correspondingly decline.

TV and Presidential Elections (Tables E 1-3)

Conceding, by a substantial margin, that the incumbent party has a decided advantage in its ability to utilize network television during a presidential election campaign, respondents initially were fairly evenly divided as to the extent to which they felt the Nixon Administration acted fairly or took unfair advantage of Senator McGovern in this regard during the 1972 campaign. Interestingly, however, in the second and third waves of questioning there appeared to be a sizeable shift toward the feeling that the President acted fairly in his use of television during the campaign.

By the same token, respondents increasingly felt that additional provisions are required to ensure equal opportunities for the opposing party. Some felt that this could be best accomplished by controlling campaign expenditures or setting up a special fund for this purpose. Others suggested the abolition or revision of current laws governing the allocation of time to political candidates.

Counter-Advertising (Tables F 1-4)

Seminar participants expressed strong disapproval of an FTC proposal that opponents of advertising deemed to be controversial be granted free time to express contrasting viewpoints on the air—commonly known as "counter-advertising."

Similarly, a majority agreed that this view goes beyond the original intent of the Fairness Doctrine, and that for the most part, television networks present conflicting views in their regularly scheduled news and public affairs programming.

Although seminar participants were unanimous that, should this FTC proposal be adopted, it should apply equally to all media, they were at considerable variance as to how and by whom advertising content would be deemed "controversial." Network and station management, an independent review board, FTC, FCC, and the general public were all mentioned with scattered frequency, without a clear consensus emerging. What is clear is the widespread uncertainty and doubt surrounding this issue.

Program Diversity (Tables G 1-5)

Educators were fairly evenly divided in their views about the extent to which commercial television is serving a wide variety of program interests, a view which remained fairly stable through the three waves of questioning. Most agreed, but not strongly, that little additional viewing would occur if more programs were available devoted to special interests.

In comparing public and commercial television programming, however, most felt that public television was more diverse, appealing more to different segments of the population than commercial television. Similarly, few saw commercial television moving toward greater program diversity in the near future, feeling that such efforts would likely offend the tastes and standards of "mass" audiences.

The Potential of Television as an Art Form (Table H 1)

An increasing majority felt, as the seminar progressed, that it is indeed possible for specific standards of excellence to be applied to the medium

of television. Expanding on their over-all views, some commented as
follows:

> As a medium of expression and communication it has the
> capacity to develop standards just as other media do.
>
> It has a uniquely identifiable set of creative tools; art has always
> occurred when such tools existed or were manipulated by the right
> persons.
>
> TV as a distinctive art form is a tangible reality, but commercial
> pressures hinder the medium's aesthetic potential.

Discussing the role of the TV critic in establishing standards of taste,
participants were fairly evenly divided. Those who perceived the TV critic's
role as important had this to say:

> The critic should try to protect or improve the morals of the
> public and the industry. This includes a moralistic and humanistic
> understanding of the many facets of society. Finally the critic should
> serve to purify tastes of both the public and the industry.
>
> If criticism is constructive, with suggestions for improvement, the
> critic is useful. If the critic only picks something apart with no sug-
> gestions for improvement, he is ignorant.
>
> He must continue to point out the good and the bad as he sees it.
> When a large majority of critics agree, we have begun to establish an
> aesthetic.
>
> The critic should make his readers aware of the possibilities of
> the TV medium, by citing outstanding achievements when they occur
> and by constantly prodding the medium to responsible performance.

Those who felt the TV critic's role is limited commented as follows:

> A critic comes after the fact. The establishing of criticism is
> a function of the medium. Did Van Gogh wait around for all the
> comments to come in before painting?
>
> He's an appendix. If he hurts ignore or remove him. He does no
> good or evil except to stir up an artificial, articulate, pseudo-
> intellectual minority.
>
> Most critics seem not to understand how programs are produced
> and the exigencies under which they are produced.

It is clear from these comments that the aura of authority surrounding
the TV critic is both a benefit and a bane, and that educators have not as
yet formed a consensus as to his contributions or influence in the development of standards of taste.

DETAILED TABLES

A-1

QUESTION: "There has been much discussion about whether the
television networks deal fairly in presenting the
news dealing with political and social issues. To
what extent do you feel that the TV networks deal
fairly with all sides or tend to favor one side?
Please circle the number below which comes closest
to the way you feel about this issue."

	Scale Point	WAVE I		WAVE II		WAVE III	
		#	%	#	%	#	%
"Favor One Side	1	0	0%	0	0%	1	5%
	2	4	16	4	16	2	9
	3	5	20	5	20	3	14
	4	6	24	4	16	5	22
	5	9	36	9	36	9	40
"Deal Fairly With All Sides"	6	0	0	2	8	1	5
Neutral (3.5)		1	4	1	4	1	5
(Base)		(25)	100%	(25)	100%	(22)	100%
MEAN SCALE POSITION		3.82		3.98		4.02	

A-2

QUESTION: "Would you say that, in general, there is more fairness
or less fairness in network TV news coverage today than
there was, say, five years ago?"

	Scale Point	WAVE I		WAVE II		WAVE III	
		#	%	#	%	#	%
"Less Fairness"	1	0	0%	0	0%	1	5%
	2	2	8	1	4	0	0
	3	2	8	2	8	0	0
	4	10	40	8	32	9	41
	5	7	28	12	48	9	40
"More Fairness"	6	3	12	1	4	2	9
Neutral (3.5)		1	4	1	4	1	5
(Base)		(25)	100%	(25)	100%	(22)	100%
MEAN SCALE POSITION		4.26		4.38		4.43	

A-3

QUESTION: "On the whole, taking all TV Networks and their newsmen
into consideration, to what extent do you feel sufficiently
diverse viewpoints on major issues are presented on
network TV news programs? "

	Scale Point	WAVE I		WAVE II		WAVE III	
		#	%	#	%	#	%
"Not Diverse"	1	0	0	1	4%	2	9%
	2	4	16	4	16	1	5
	3	5	20	7	28	7	31
	4	5	20	5	20	5	23
	5	8	32	7	28	6	27
"Sufficiently Diverse"	6	1	4	1	4	1	5
No Answer		2	8	0	0	0	0
(Base)		(25)	100%	(25)	100%	(22)	100%
MEAN SCALE POSITION		3.87		3.64		3.68	

A-4

QUESTION: "In your opinion, what is the best way to achieve a
proper balance in television news coverage?"

	WAVE I		WAVE II		WAVE III	
	#	%	#	%	#	%
Leave it to the best judgment of the television news staff themselves.	10	40	12	48	13	59
Network management should put more pressure on their own news staff.	4	16	4	16	3	14
Continuous monitoring and evaluation of the news by independent, non-government review committee.	5	20	2	8	1	5
Continuous monitoring and evaluation of the news by FCC.	0	0	0	0	0	0
Other	6	24	6	24	3	14
No Answer	0	0	1	4	2	9
(Base)	(25)	100%	(25)	100%	(22)	100%

A-5

QUESTION: "In proposing new legislation recently, a high
administration official stated that local TV station
license renewal would depend in part on whether
stations correct imbalance or consistent bias in
network news programs. How strongly do you agree or
disagree with this proposal?"

	Scale Point	WAVE I		WAVE II		WAVE III	
		#	%	#	%	#	%
"Strongly Disagree"	1	15	60%	14	56%	16	72%
	2	2	8	4	16	2	9
	3	1	4	2	8	1	5
	4	4	16	3	12	1	5
	5	2	8	1	4	2	9
"Strongly Agree"	6	1	4	1	4	0	0
(Base)		(25)	100%	(25)	100%	(22)	100%
MEAN SCALE POSITION		2.16		2.04		1.68	

A-6

QUESTION: "Critics of this proposal have said that it was an improper attempt by the federal government to intimidate TV stations and the networks and to censor the news. How strongly do you agree or disagree with this viewpoint?"

	Scale Point	WAVE I		WAVE II		WAVE III	
		#	%	#	%	#	%
"Strongly Disagree"	1	2	8	1	4	1	5
	2	3	12	3	12	1	5
	3	1	4	1	4	1	5
	4	4	16	2	8	2	8
	5	3	12	3	12	1	5
"Strongly Agree"	6	12	48	15	60	16	72
(Base)		(25)	100%	(25)	100%	(22)	100%
MEAN SCALE POSITION		4.56		4.92		5.23	

A-7

QUESTION: "To what extent do you feel that First Amendment
           guarantees of freedom of the press should apply
           equally to print and broadcast media?"

	Scale Point	WAVE I		WAVE II		WAVE III	
		#	%	#	%	#	%
"Guarantees For Broadcast Media Should Be Limited"	1	0	0	0	0	0	0
	2	2	8	2	8	2	9
	3	2	8	1	4	1	5
	4	3	12	2	8	0	0
	5	4	16	5	20	6	27
"Guarantees Should Apply to Both Media Equally"	6	14	56	15	60	13	59
(Base)		(25)	100%	(25)	100%	(22)	100%
MEAN SCALE POSITION		5.04		5.20		5.23	

A-8

QUESTION: "Regardless of your own personal opinion of the need, how likely do you feel that outside control, from whatever source, will be placed on network news in the next few years or so?"

	Scale Point	WAVE I		WAVE II		WAVE III	
		#	%	#	%	#	%
"Outside Control not Likely"	1	1	4	1	4	2	9
	2	5	20	5	20	2	9
	3	1	4	2	8	1	5
	4	6	24	6	24	7	32
	5	8	32	8	32	8	36
"Outside Control Very Likely"	6	4	16	3	12	2	9
(Base)		(25)	100%	(25)	100%	(22)	100%
MEAN SCALE POSITION		4.08		3.96		4.05	

B-1

QUESTION: "In general, how would you rate the quality of network
TV children's programs?"

	Scale Point	WAVE I		WAVE II		WAVE III	
		#	%	#	%	#	%
"Poor"	1	2	8	1	4	1	5
	2	10	40	9	36	6	27
	3	4	16	6	24	7	32
	4	5	20	8	32	7	32
	5	3	12	1	4	1	5
"Excellent"	6	0	0	0	0	0	0
Neutral (3.5)		1	4	0	0	0	0
(Base)		(25)	100%	(25)	100%	(22)	100%

MEAN SCALE POSITION   2.90   2.96   3.05

B-2

QUESTION: "To what extent do you feel that the overall quality of network TV children's programs have improved or declined over the past several years or so?"

	Scale Point	WAVE I		WAVE II		WAVE III	
		#	%	#	%	#	%
"Quality Has Declined"	1	0	0	0	0	0	0
	2	1	4	0	0	0	0
	3	5	20	5	20	4	18
	4	9	36	11	44	8	36
	5	7	28	9	36	9	41
"Quality Has Improved"	6	2	8	0	0	0	0
Neutral (3.5)		1	4	0	0	1	5
(Base)		(25)	100%	(25)	100%	(22)	100%

MEAN SCALE POSITION	4.14	4.16	4.20

B-3

QUESTION: "It has been suggested that, because of their undeveloped
sense of judgement, children should not be subjected to
advertising on programming aimed at them. How strongly
do you agree or disagree with this viewpoint?"

	Scale Point	WAVE I		WAVE II		WAVE III	
		#	%	#	%	#	%
"Strongly Disagree"	1	2	8	5	20	4	18
	2	5	20	3	12	4	18
	3	2	8	4	16	3	14
	4	2	8	1	4	1	5
	5	7	28	5	20	7	32
"Strongly Agree"	6	6	24	7	28	3	14
Neutral (3.5)		1	4	0	0	0	0
(Base)		(25)	100%	(25)	100%	(22)	100%
MEAN SCALE POSITION		4.02		3.76		3.54	

B-4

QUESTION: "Without advertising support, do you feel that the
quality of network TV children's programs would increase
or decrease?"

	Scale Point	WAVE I		WAVE II		WAVE III	
		#	%	#	%	#	%
"Quality Would Decrease"	1	6	24	5	20	6	27
	2	3	12	8	32	6	27
	3	2	8	3	12	3	14
	4	6	24	6	24	4	18
	5	4	16	0	0	0	0
"Quality Would Increase"	6	1	4	0	0	0	0
Neutral (3.5)		0	0	0	0	1	5
No Answer		3	12	3	12	2	9
(Base)		(25)	100%	(25)	100%	(22)	100%

MEAN SCALE POSITION	3.09	2.45	2.32

C-1

QUESTION: "Television 'clutter' has been defined as any form of
non-program material - station ID's, program announcements,
advertising messages - which interrupts program material.
How important a problem is this in your assessment of the
overall quality of commercial television?"

	Scale Point	WAVE I		WAVE II		WAVE III	
		#	%	#	%	#	%
"Not Important"	1	3	12	2	8	1	5
	2	1	4	3	12	3	14
	3	1	4	0	0	1	5
	4	6	24	5	20	6	27
	5	8	32	12	48	8	36
"Very Important"	6	5	20	3	12	3	14
Neutral (3.5)		1	4	0	0	0	0
(Base)		(25)	100%	(25)	100%	(22)	100%
MEAN SCALE POSITION		4.22		4.24		4.18	

C-2

QUESTION: "To what extent do you feel that TV "clutter" has increased or decreased over the past five years or so?"

	Scale Point	WAVE I		WAVE II		WAVE III	
		#	%	#	%	#	%
"Decreased"	1	0	0	0	0	0	0
	2	0	0	0	0	0	0
	3	1	4	2	8	2	9
	4	5	20	4	16	1	5
	5	10	40	13	52	16	72
"Increased"	6	8	32	6	24	3	14
No Answer		1	4	0	0	0	0
(Base)		(25)	100%	(25)	100%	(22)	100%
MEAN SCALE POSITION		5.04		4.92		4.90	

C-3

"How would you compare the amount of clutter on TV
in relation to the amount of clutter on radio, in
newspapers and magazines?"

	Scale Point	WAVE I		WAVE II		WAVE III	
		#	%	#	%	#	%
"Less Clutter on TV"	1	2	8	0	0	0	0
	2	5	20	3	13	6	27
	3	6	24	10	40	6	27
	4	4	16	3	12	1	5
	5	2	8	6	24	5	22
"More Clutter on TV"	6	1	4	0	0	2	9
Neutral (3.5)		1	4	0	0	1	5
No Answer		4	16	3	12	1	5
(Base)		(25)	100%	(25)	100%	(22)	100%

MEAN SCALE POSITION	3.11	3.54	3.55

C-4

QUESTION: "Do you feel that the amount of clutter on TV is more or less acceptable than in other media, such as radio, newspapers and magazines?"

	Scale Point	WAVE I		WAVE II		WAVE III	
		#	%	#	%	#	%
"Less Acceptable"	1	7	28	8	32	6	27
	2	7	28	8	32	10	46
	3	6	24	7	28	4	18
	4	1	4	0	0	0	0
	5	2	8	1	4	2	9
"More Acceptable"	6	1	4	0	0	0	0
No Answer		1	4	1	4	0	0
(Base)		(25)	100%	(25)	100%	(22)	100%
MEAN SCALE POSITION		2.45		2.08		2.18	

C-5

QUESTION: "What, if anything, do you feel should be done about
           limiting the amount of TV clutter, or non-program
           material?"

	Scale Point	WAVE I		WAVE II		WAVE III	
		#	%	#	%	#	%
"Do Not Reduce Time Allocated to Non-Program Material	1	1	4	0	0	0	0
	2	1	4	2	8	2	9
	3	1	4	2	8	1	5
	4	8	32	10	40	8	35
	5	7	28	8	32	7	32
"Sharply Reduce Amount of Time Allocated to Non-Program Material"	6	3	12	2	8	2	9
Neutral (3.5)		0	0	0	0	1	5
No Answer		4	16	1	4	1	5
(Base)		(25)	100%	(25)	100%	(22)	100%

	WAVE I	WAVE II	WAVE III
MEAN SCALE POSITION	4.33	4.25	4.26

D-1

QUESTION: "It has been suggested that radio stations be <u>exempt</u> from
broadcast license renewal requirements. How strongly do
you approve or disapprove of this proposal?"

	Scale Point	WAVE I		WAVE II		WAVE III	
		#	%	#	%	#	%
"Strongly Disapprove"	1	12	48	14	56	11	49
	2	7	28	8	32	5	22
	3	1	4	1	4	0	0
	4	3	12	0	0	1	5
	5	1	4	0	0	1	5
"Strongly Approve"	6	1	4	2	8	3	14
No Answer		0	0	0	0	1	5
(Base)		(25)	100%	(25)	100%	(22)	100%

MEAN SCALE POSITION   2.08   1.80   2.29

D-2

QUESTION: "Regardless of whether or not you approve of this proposal, how likely do you feel that radio stations will, in fact, be exempt from license renewal requirements within the next few years or so?"

	Scale Point	WAVE I		WAVE II		WAVE III	
		#	%	#	%	#	%
"Not Likely"	1	12	48	13	52	9	41
	2	7	28	8	32	10	45
	3	4	16	2	8	0	0
	4	1	4	1	4	2	9
	5	1	4	1	4	1	5
"Very Likely"	6	0	0	0	0	0	0
(Base)		(25)	100%	(25)	100%	(22)	100%
MEAN SCALE POSITION		1.88		1.76		1.91	

D-3

QUESTION: "Should it happen that radio stations are exempt from
license renewal requirements...

(a) "Would you expect that the <u>number</u> of radio stations would
increase or decrease?"

	Scale Point	WAVE I		WAVE II		WAVE III	
		#	%	#	%	#	%
"Decrease"	1	1	4	1	4	2	9
	2	2	8	2	8	3	14
	3	4	16	4	16	2	9
	4	11	44	14	56	12	54
	5	3	12	1	4	1	5
"Increase"	6	1	4	1	4	2	9
Neutral (3.5)		1	4	0	0	0	0
No Answer		2	8	2	8	0	0
(Base)		(25)	100%	(25)	100%	(22)	100%

MEAN SCALE POSITION	**3.71**		**3.65**		**3.59**	

D-4

QUESTION: (b) "Would you expect the <u>overall quality</u> of radio programming to improve or decline?"

	Scale Point	WAVE I		WAVE II		WAVE III	
		#	%	#	%	#	%
"Decline"	1	3	12	3	12	4	18
	2	10	40	13	52	9	40
	3	6	24	6	24	5	23
	4	1	4	0	0	1	5
	5	2	8	2	8	3	14
"Improve"	6	0	0	0	0	0	0
No Answer		3	12	1	4	0	0
(Base)		(25)	100%	(25)	100%	(22)	100%

MEAN SCALE POSITION	2.50	2.37	2.45

D-5

QUESTION: (c) "Would you expect radio's effectiveness as an advertising medium to increase or decline?"

	Scale Point	WAVE I		WAVE II		WAVE III	
		#	%	#	%	#	%
"Decline"	1	3	12	1	4	2	9
	2	5	20	8	32	8	36
	3	6	24	10	40	6	27
	4	4	16	2	8	3	14
	5	3	12	2	8	3	14
"Increase"	6	2	8	1	4	0	0
No Answer		2	8	1	4	0	0
(Base)		(25)	100%	(25)	100%	(22)	100%
MEAN SCALE POSITION		3.21		2.95		2.86	

E-1

QUESTION: "It has been said that in a presidential election, the
incumbent party has a greater opportunity to utilize
network television to its advantage than the opposing
party. How strongly do you agree or disagree with this
viewpoint?"

	Scale Point	WAVE I		WAVE II		WAVE III	
		#	%	#	%	#	%
"Strongly Disagree"	1	2	8	0	0	0	0
	2	2	8	3	12	1	5
	3	0	0	1	4	0	0
	4	5	20	3	12	4	18
	5	6	24	8	32	6	27
"Strongly Agree"	6	10	40	10	40	11	50
(Base)		(25)	100%	(25)	100%	(22)	100%
MEAN SCALE POSITION		4.64		4.76		5.18	

E-2

QUESTION: "During the 1972 presidential campaign, do you feel that the Nixon Administration took unfair advantage over Senator McGovern or do you feel that the Nixon Administration acted fairly in this regard?"

	Scale Point	WAVE I		WAVE II		WAVE III	
		#	%	#	%	#	%
"Nixon Adm. Took Unfair Advantage"	1	3	12	2	8	2	9
	2	5	20	5	20	4	18
	3	2	8	1	4	1	5
	4	10	40	9	36	6	27
	5	2	8	5	20	6	27
"Nixon Adm. Acted Fairly"	6	1	4	2	8	3	14
Neutral (3.5)		1	4	0	0	0	0
No Answer		1	4	1	4	0	0
(Base)		(25)	100%	(25)	100%	(22)	100%

E-3

QUESTION: "To what extent, if any, do you feel that additional provisions should be made to ensure opportunities for all major opposing parties to voice their views on television?"

	Scale Point	WAVE I		WAVE II		WAVE III	
		#	%	#	%	#	%
"Present Provisions are Satisfactory"	1	4	16	4	16	4	18
	2	5	20	3	12	3	14
	3	4	16	2	8	1	5
	4	3	12	4	16	4	18
	5	3	12	5	20	4	18
"Additional Provisions are Necessary"	6	6	24	7	28	5	23
No Answer		0	0	0	0	1	5
(Base)		(25)	100%	(25)	100%	(22)	100%

MEAN SCALE POSITION	3.56	3.96	3.76

F-1

QUESTION: "As you are probably aware, the FTC is concerned about
            television advertising for products and activities deemed
            to be controversial. They have proposed that opponents of
            such advertising be given free time to present their points
            of view, arguing that this is a proper application of the
            fairness doctrine. How strongly do you approve or disapprove
            of this proposal?"

	Scale Point	WAVE I		WAVE II		WAVE III	
		#	%	#	%	#	%
"Strongly Disapprove"	1	11	44	12	48	11	50
	2	6	24	6	24	5	23
	3	3	12	1	4	1	5
	4	1	4	3	12	2	9
	5	4	16	3	12	2	9
"Strongly Approve"	6	0	0	0	0	1	5
(Base)		(25)	100%	(25)	100%	(22)	100%

MEAN SCALE POSITION	2. 24	2.16	2.18

F-2

QUESTION: "Others have responded that this goes beyond the original intent of the fairness doctrine proposal and that for the most part, television networks do in fact present conflicting viewpoints on controversial matters in their regular news and public affairs programming. How strongly do you agree or disagree with this viewpoint?"

	Scale Point	WAVE I		WAVE II		WAVE III	
		#	%	#	%	#	%
"Strongly Disagree"	1	0	0	0	0	1	5
	2	5	20	4	16	3	14
	3	5	20	5	20	4	18
	4	3	12	5	20	6	27
	5	5	20	8	32	5	23
"Strongly Agree"	6	6	24	3	12	3	14
No Answer		1	4	0	0	0	0
(Base)		(25)	100%	(25)	100%	(22)	100%
MEAN SCALE POSITION		4.08		4.04		3.91	

F-3

QUESTION: "If the FTC's proposal is adopted with respect to advertising...

    (a) Do you feel that it should extend to all media equally or
        be limited to television?"

	WAVE I		WAVE II		WAVE III	
	#	%	#	%	#	%
"Should be extended to all media equally"	23	92	22	88	21	95
"Should be limited to television"	1	4	2	8	1	5
Don't Know	1	4	1	4	0	0
(Base)	(25)	100%	(25)	100%	(22)	100%

F-4

QUESTION: (b) "Do you feel that free time allocated to opponents both -
            amount and scheduling - should be in direct proportion
            to that used by advertisers or should such time be
            granted on a limited basis?"

	WAVE I		WAVE II		WAVE III	
	#	%	#	%	#	%
"Free time should be allocated in direct proportion to that used by advertisers"	4	16	3	12	1	5
"Free time should be limited"	13	52	17	68	18	82
"Don't know/ No opinion"	8	32	5	20	1	5
No Answer	0	0	0	0	2	9
(Base)	(25)	100%	(25)	100%	(22)	100%

G-1

QUESTION: "Some have said that there are many diverse groups in our
society with special interests who do not watch much
commercial television. They feel that their interests
are not being served by current mass-audience programming
provided by commercial TV. Together these audience
segments represent a substantial potential audience who
would watch commercial TV programming devoted to their
special interests. How strongly do you agree or disagree
with this viewpoint?"

	Scale Point	WAVE I		WAVE II		WAVE III	
		#	%	#	%	#	%
"Strongly Disagree"	1	3	12	3	12	2	9
	2	4	16	5	20	6	27
	3	3	12	2	8	2	9
	4	5	20	6	24	2	9
	5	7	28	7	28	8	36
"Strongly Agree"	6	3	12	2	8	2	9
(Base)		(25)	100%	(25)	100%	(22)	100%

MEAN SCALE POSITION   3.72   3.60   3.64

G-2

QUESTION: "Others have maintained that commercial television does a reasonably good job serving a wide variety of interests. Those who do not currently watch much commercial TV fare would probably not do much additional viewing even if special interest programming was available. How strongly do you agree or disagree with this viewpoint?"

	Scale Point	WAVE I		WAVE II		WAVE III	
		#	%	#	%	#	%
"Strongly Disagree"	1	0	0	0	0	1	5
	2	6	24	9	36	5	23
	3	3	12	2	8	1	5
	4	3	12	2	8	4	18
	5	8	32	8	32	8	36
"Strongly Agree"	6	5	20	4	16	3	14
(Base)		(25)	100%	(25)	100%	(22)	100%
MEAN SCALE POSITION		4.12		3.84		4.00	

G-3

QUESTION: "How would you compare commercial and public TV in terms of their diversity - the extent to which their programming appeals to many different segments of the population?"

	Scale Point	WAVE I		WAVE II		WAVE III	
		#	%	#	%	#	%
"Public TV More Diverse"	1	5	20	2	8	2	9
	2	6	24	8	32	7	32
	3	5	20	8	32	6	27
	4	3	12	1	4	1	5
	5	3	12	4	16	4	18
"Commercial TV More Diverse"	6	3	12	2	8	2	9
(Base)		(25)	100%	(25)	100%	(22)	100%

MEAN SCALE POSITION		3.08		3.12		3.18	

G-4

QUESTION: "In which direction do you forsee commercial TV moving --
toward greater diversity appealing to many different
groups, or toward continued concentration appealing to
large 'mass' audiences?"

	Scale Point	WAVE I		WAVE II		WAVE III	
		#	%	#	%	#	%
"Greater Diversity "	1	2	8	0	0	0	0
	2	4	16	6	24	4	18
	3	2	8	1	4	4	18
	4	4	16	2	8	0	0
	5	9	36	12	48	8	36
"Concentration on Mass Audiences"	6	4	16	4	16	6	27
(Base)		(25)	100%	(25)	100%	(22)	100%
MEAN SCALE POSITION		4.04		4.28		4.36	

G-5

QUESTION: "If commercial TV were to focus more on appealing to small, more specialized audience interests, how likely do you think such programming might offend the tastes and standards of 'mass' audiences?"

	Scale Point	WAVE I		WAVE II		WAVE III	
		#	%	#	%	#	%
"Not Likely"	1	2	8	1	4	1	5
	2	2	8	2	8	2	9
	3	5	20	3	12	1	5
	4	8	32	6	24	5	23
	5	4	16	8	32	10	45
"Very Likely"	6	4	16	4	16	2	9
No Answer		0	0	0	0	1	5
(Base)		(25)	100%	(25)	100%	(22)	100%

MEAN SCALE POSITION   <u>3.88</u>   <u>4.25</u>   <u>4.29</u>

H-1

QUESTION: "Do you feel that television programming can ever have
             specific 'standards of excellence' or an aesthetic
             established for it?"

	WAVE I		WAVE II		WAVE III	
	#	%	#	%	#	%
Yes	14	56	16	64	16	73
No	8	32	8	32	5	23
Don't Know/ No Opinion	3	12	1	4	1	5
(Base)	(25)	100%	(25)	100%	(22)	100%

Appendix A

PARTICIPANTS

IRTS Third Annual Faculty-Industry Seminar

Special Addresses by:

Walter Schwartz: President, ABC Television

Clay T. Whitehead: Director, Office of Telecommunications Policy, The White House

Richard E. Wiley: Commissioner, Federal Communications Commission

For IRTS:

Robert H. Boulware—Executive Director

Co-Chairman of Faculty/Industry Seminar:

Gene Accas	Leo Burnett USA
Aaron Cohen	National Broadcasting Company

Faculty Participants:

Chuck Baker	University of Georgia
Bertram Barer	California State University, Northridge
Richard B. Barnhill	Syracuse University
James A. Brown, S.J.	University of Southern California
K. Sue Cailteux	University of Kentucky
William H. Cianci	Rider College
Robert P. Crawford	Queens College, CUNY
Stanley T. Donner	University of Texas
Philip S. Gelb	Bronx Community College, CUNY
Richard J. Goggin, Sr.	New York University

W. Knox Hagood	University of Alabama
Kenneth Harwood	Temple University
William Hawes	University of Houston
C. A. Kellner	Marshall University
Gordon Law	Federation of Rocky Mountain States
Philip A. Macomber	Kent State University
Thomas Allison McCain	Ohio State University
Keith W. Mielke	Indiana University
Charles E. Phillips	Emerson College
Jon T. Powell	Northern Illinois University
Peter K. Pringle	University of Florida
James W. Rhea	Oklahoma State University
Roderick D. Rightmire	Ohio University
J. M. Ripley	University of Kentucky
Saul N. Scher	University of Maine
Robert Schlater	Michigan State University
Charles W. Shipley	Southern Illinois University
Robert H. Stanley	Hunter College, CUNY
G. Norman Van Tubergen	Southern Illinois University
Daniel Viamonte	University of Hartford

Industry and Special Guest Participants:

Eleanor Applewhaite	Columbia Broadcasting System
Walter E. Bartlett	Avco Broadcasting Corporation
Richard "Dick" Block	Kaiser Broadcasting
Max E. Buck	National Broadcasting Company
Giraud Chester	Goodson-Todman Productions
Bosley Crowther	Columbia Pictures; former Film Critic, The *New York Times*
James Day	Formerly President, WNET/13, 1970-73; Consultant
Keith P. Fischer	Corporation For Public Broadcasting
Nicholas Gordon	National Broadcasting Company
Neil Hickey	*TV Guide*
James C. Hirsch	Communications and Broadcasting Consulting Services
Richard W. Jencks	Columbia Broadcasting System
Robert D. Kasmire	National Broadcasting Company
Stephen B. Labunski	Chuck Blore Creative Services
Robert L. Liddel	Compton Advertising
Lee Loevinger	Hogan and Hartson; former FCC Commissioner

Dan McGrath	D'Arcy-MacManus & Masius
Howard S. Meighan	Catalyst Group Inc.
Eugene H. Methvin	*Reader's Digest*
George H. Newi	American Broadcasting Companies
John O'Connor	The *New York Times*
Alvin H. Perlmutter	Television Producer
Richard A. R. Pinkham	Ted Bates & Company
Robert Pitofsky	New York University; formerly, Director of Consumer Protection, FTC
Alfred L. Plant	Block Drug Company
A. Frank Reel	Metromedia Producers Corporation
Ms. Elizabeth Roberts	Federal Communications Commission
Lawrence H. Rogers II	Taft Broadcasting Company
Ms. Diane L. Sass	Kaiser Broadcasting
Irwin Segelstein	Columbia Broadcasting System (Columbia Records)
George Simko	Benton & Bowles
Art Topol	Ogilvy and Mather
Russell C. Tornabene	National Broadcasting Company
Charles S. Tower	Corinthian Broadcasting Corporation
Maurie Webster	Compu/Net, Inc.
Thomas H. Wolf	American Broadcasting Companies
W. Dewees ("Dewey") Yeager, Jr.	The Nestlé Company

For IRTS:

ROBERT H. BOULWARE

Mr. Boulware has been Executive Director of the International Radio and Television Society since 1968 and has a varied background in broadcast/advertising. Following his graduation from Ohio University, Athens, Ohio, with a degree in Business Administration, he joined the advertising department of Procter & Gamble in Cincinnati where he served for 10 years. Since then, he has managed radio and television stations in Cincinnati and acted as media director in major New York advertising agencies. Mr. Boulware is a naval veteran of World War II.

Co-Chairman:

Third IRTS Faculty/Industry Seminar

GENE ACCAS

Mr. Accas is Vice President, Leo Burnett USA. His communications career combines network, agency and trade association experience. He joined Burnett's Program Department in 1962, and is presently VP, Network Relations, as well as administrative head of the New York office.

His academic credentials have led to frequent involvement in broadcast seminars and forums. Mr. Accas' exhaustive study of network buying patterns, timing and pricing were presented to an industry workshop session; published as an article in a leading trade journal; and subsequently introduced as "expert testimony" in government hearings on network practices. Beyond these activities, Mr. Accas headed a committee which produced the IRTS (International Radio and Television Society) Fourth Annual Faculty-Seminar.

A native New Yorker, Mr. Accas earned a bachelor's degree, magna cum laude, plus a Phi Beta Kappa key, at Syracuse University in 1945; added a master's degree at the Fletcher School of Law and Diplomacy, Medford, Massachusetts, in 1946. In addition to vocational pursuits, Mr. Accas is a best-selling author. His *How to Protect Yourself on the Streets and in Your Home* sold some 400,000 copies.

AARON M. COHEN

Mr. Cohen was promoted to Vice President, Marketing, NBC Television Network in 1973. He is responsible for the pre-planning and media research activities of the sales function, as well as special projects, pricing and sales development.

Previously, he had been Director, Daytime Program Sales, NBC-TV, for the preceding seven months; Manager, Daytime Sales, from July, 1971, to November 1972. Prior to that, Mr. Cohen worked as Manager, Participating Program Sales, for three years.

Mr. Cohen came to NBC in 1964 as Manager, Sales Development and Merchandising, Participating Program Sales, from WCBS-TV, New York, where he had been Director of Sales Research and Development. From 1959-62, he was Manager, Research and Sales Development, for television station WPIX, New York. Before that he worked as a research analyst with the William Esty advertising agency.

A 1958 graduate of Baruch College of the City University of New York, Mr. Cohen is currently teaching a course in radio and television advertising in the college's graduate division. Mr. Cohen also received a Master's degree in Business Administration from Baruch College.

ELEANOR APPLEWHAITE

Miss Applewhaite received a B.A. in Government from Cornell University and an LL.B. from the Columbia University School of Law. After serving as a law clerk to a Federal District Court Judge in New York, she joined the CBS Law Department in 1964. Since that time, Miss Applewhaite has served in the Radio, Broadcast and Governmental Affairs Sections of the CBS Law Department. In Governmental Affairs her primary area of responsibility involves CBS policies and compliance with Congressional and FCC requirements in the areas of fairness and political broadcasting. Miss Applewhaite is on the Board of Governors, IRTS, and a member of the Association of the Bar, City of New

York, and the Federal Communications Bar Association.

CHUCK BAKER

Chuck Baker is Assistant Professor of Radio-TV-Film at the University of Georgia. His emphasis is on TV and film production, and he supervises a TV-Film Production Lab in which students produce TV programs and films for noncommercial radio and TV stations in Georgia. He is an actor and director for the Athens Town and Gown Theatre. He holds a B.A. in broadcasting and an M.A. in fine arts in theatre from the University of Georgia.

BERTRAM BARER

Professor Barer currently is Chairman and Professor of Radio-TV-Film, California State University, Northridge. Professor Barer founded the Department five years ago and its growth has reached the point where it is one of the largest on the West Coast. His areas of special interest are in programming, international broadcasting and instructional use of the media. Professor Barer's background also includes consulting in the use of mass media as a training and instructional device with government and industry. In addition, he has served in news and public affairs as a newscaster, editor and writer-reporter in major broadcasting outlets in Minneapolis, Los Angeles, as well as several smaller market areas.

RICHARD B. BARNHILL

Professor Barnhill has been Lecturer-Program Director at Syracuse University for the past eight years. In addition, he has been a consultant in Religious Communications. He has been associated, in the course of fifteen years in the broadcasting industry (both radio and TV) with WNBC-TV as Production-Operation Manager; with WVNC-TV as Educational Production Manager; with WMAL-TV and Radio as Producer-Director. He served as Executive Vice-President of Techtel Corp., industry communications. He is co-author of *Intro-*

ductory Concepts In Communications Processes.

WALTER E. BARTLETT

Mr. Bartlett is Senior Vice President-Television and a member of the Board of Directors of Avco Broadcasting Corporation. Projects undertaken during Mr. Bartlett's administration have included the current season of primetime children's program specials and Avco's annual broadcasts from the Ohio State Fair.

Before being elevated to a Senior Vice President in March, 1969, Mr. Bartlett held the position of Vice President-Television since 1964. He also served as General Manager of WLWC (TV) beginning in July, 1960, and his achievements in Columbus were noted by the Junior Chamber of Commerce which selected him as 'Outstanding Young Man of the Year" in 1961. He was elected a vice president of Avco Broadcasting in March, 1961.

Mr. Bartlett, a native of Marion, Ohio, is a 1949 Business Administration graduate of Ohio's Bowling Green University. He is a member of the Television Board of the National Association of Broadcasters and is on the Board of Directors of the Television Bureau of Advertising. He is a former Vice Chairman of the NBC Television Network Affiliates' Board of Delegates. Mr. Bartlett was appointed for two terms to the Ohio Educational Television Network Commission, and is a former president of the Ohio Association of Broadcasters.

Active in many local civic affairs, Mr. Bartlett is President of the Greater Cincinnati Chamber of Commerce.

RICHARD "DICK" BLOCK

Mr. Block was born in San Francisco. He attended Stanford University, graduating in sociology in 1949. The next year he became program director of KDFC (FM) San Francisco. From 1953 until 1957, Mr. Block worked at three San Joaquin Valley, California, TV stations as they took the air following the FCC's 1948-52 "freeze." In 1958, he became manager of KHVH-AM-TV, Honolulu.

In 1961, Mr. Block was transferred to Kaiser's home office in Oakland, California, to plan the expansion of Kaiser Broadcasting as well as work on the affiliated companies network television programming projects.

During 1963, while continuing to manage broadcast operations, Mr. Block served as vice president-general manager of Kaiser Hawaii-Kai Development Co., a 6,000-acre new town near Honolulu.

Mr. Block has taught the commercial broadcasting course at the Stanford Broadcasting & Film Institute each summer since 1967, and has lectured at many universities.

He served on the board of the National Association of Broadcasters (NAB) for the maximum two terms 1968-72. In 1971, he was elected to the board of the Television Bureau of Advertising (TVB) for a four-year term. The following year he was appointed to the board of the Association for Professional Broadcasting Education (APBE) for a two-year term. He was also appointed chairman of NAB's Research Committee.

JAMES A. BROWN, S.J.

Dr. Brown is Assistant Professor, Telecommunications Department at University of Southern California. In 1971, he was resident consultant at the CBS Television Network, New York. Dr. Brown's degrees are: A.B. (Latin) Loyola University 1955; Ph.L (Philosophy) 1957 and M.A. (English) Loyola; 1959 S.T.L. (Theology) Bellarmine School of Theology, 1967 Chicago; Ph.D. (Communications) USC, Los Angeles 1970. He was ordained a Roman Catholic priest in 1966. Dr. Brown, among other academic affiliations, served as Chairman, Radio-Television at the University of Detroit before coming to USC. He is the author of articles on communications in New Catholic Encyclopedia, and is now collaborating on the revision of the book, *Broadcast Management* with Ward Quaal (Hastings House, Publishers). He is a member of many professional associations, including APBE.

MAX E. BUCK

Mr. Buck is Vice President, National Sales, NBC Television Network, since 1968, responsible for the supervision of all NBC-TV Sales offices—Eastern, Central and Western.

Mr. Buck joined NBC in January, 1953, as Director of Merchandising for NBC Owned Stations and Director of Advertising-Merchandising-Promotion for WNBC and WNBC-TV. He was named Director of Sales and Marketing, WNBC and WNBC-TV, in March, 1957, and was appointed Station Manager, WNBC-TV in 1958.

In 1960, Mr. Buck was elected a Vice President of NBC and Eastern Sales Manager of NBC-TV, and in 1966, his responsibilities were broadened to encompass supervision of all NBC-TV Sales offices except Chicago. In addition to his duties at NBC, Mr. Buck was twice elected as President of the International Radio and Television Society.

Before joining NBC, Mr. Buck was for 11 years vice president in charge of sales and advertising for a 25-unit, $100 million supermarket chain in New Jersey. A graduate of Brooklyn College, Mr. Buck began his career in the newspaper field on the editorial staffs of the *New York Journal-American* and the *New York Times*.

K. SUE CAILTEUX

Dr. Cailteux received her Ph.D. degree at the Ohio State University in 1972. Her dissertation title is "The Political Blacklist in the Broadcast Industry: The Decade of the 1950's." She is currently an Assistant Professor in the Department of Telecommunications at the University of Kentucky and serves as Faculty Adviser to the student chapter of Women in Communications, Inc. Dr. Cailteux was program participant in the 1973 APBE convention and addressed the questions involved in the National Organization for Women's challenges. She was recently appointed to a three-year term on the Research Committee of the Mass Communications Division of the SCA.

GIRAUD CHESTER

Mr. Chester is Executive Vice President of Goodson-Todman Productions which currently produces in New York, Hollywood and Montreal 27 half-hours per week of television programs for network and syndicated telecast, including *To Tell The Truth, What's My Line?, Password, The New Price Is Right, Beat The Clock* and *I've Got A Secret*. In previous seasons Goodson-Todman Productions have produced network film series such as *Branded, The Richard Boone Theater* and *The Rebel*.

Mr. Chester has been a television executive for the past twenty years. For approximately half of this time he was associated with two of the television networks and, since 1964, he has been with the Goodson-Todman Productions. Between 1953 and 1964, Mr. Chester was a programming vice president with both NBC and ABC Television Networks where he was involved in the launching of the original NBC "Spectaculars" and *Matinee Theatre,* among other projects, and was in charge of "Operation Daybreak" which introduced ABC audiences to network daytime programming in 1958.

WILLIAM H. CIANCI

Dr. Cianci is Assistant Professor of Journalism, Rider College, Trenton, New Jersey. He received his B.A. (English) from Providence College in 1966; his M.A., from Northwestern University (Journalism-Advertising) in 1968 and his Ph.D. (Journalism-Mass Communications) from Ohio State University in 1972. Dr. Cianci has been a marketing researcher in an advertising agency, a copy editor and a reporter and feature writer for a daily newspaper in addition to his academic activities.

ROBERT P. CRAWFORD

Dr. Crawford is a member of the faculty of Queens College, City University of New York. He received his B.A. from MacAlester college in 1935; his M.A. from the University of Utah in 1947; and his Ph.D. from the University of Utah in 1951.

His academic associations, prior to Queens College, include the University of Utah and Michigan State University. Dr. Crawford's professional background includes a period as writer-announcer-producer for a commercial radio station and educational radio and TV productions for the University of Utah, Michigan State University and Queens College. He was Fulbright Scholar to Great Britain in 1963-64. Dr. Crawford is the author of a recent article on graduate programs in communications media in the *Journal of Broadcasting*.

BOSLEY CROWTHER

Mr. Crowther became critic emeritus of *The New York Times* in January, 1968, after 27 years as *The Times'* motion picture critic. Freed of the routine of reviewing some 125 motion pictures a year, in addition to writing a Sunday column, Mr. Crowther covered the great international film festivals. In effect, his reports evaluated motion pictures in America and around the world.

Mr. Crowther was born in Lutherville, Md., and was graduated from Princeton University in 1928 with honors in history. He joined *The New York Times* in the fall of that year as a general assignment reporter and rewrite man. Mr. Crowther started reviewing movies for *The Times* in 1937, when he was named assistant movie editor. From 1940, when he was appointed film critic, his audience and his reputation as a reporter and interpreter of the film grew steadily.

Mr. Crowther's books include *The Great Films: 50 Golden Years of Motion Pictures,* published by Putnam's. His previous books were *The Lion's Share: The Story of an Entertainment Empire,* and *Hollywood Rajah: The Life and Times of Louis B. Mayer.* In 1954 he was the recipient of the first award for film criticism given by the Screen Directors Guild (now the Directors Guild of America).

Upon his retirement from *The Times,* Mr. Crowther accepted a position as Consultant to Columbia Pictures, and his lifelong work—toward excellence for the medium he has covered so long—continues.

JAMES DAY

Mr. Day was President of WNET/13 from October, 1970, until January, 1973. During his tenure at WNET/13, which embraces New York's Channel 13 and is the largest national production center for the Public Broadcasting Service, programs such as these have been produced: *The Great American Dream Machine,* winner of two Emmy Awards; *Black Journal* and *Soul!,* the first American network series of, by and for Blacks; *The 51st State,* the nightly news program devoted specifically to the New York community; *Playhouse New York* (formerly *NET Playhouse*), which presents weekly dramatic productions of both classics and contemporary works. Mr. Day also was instrumental in bringing to American television such noted British series as John Galsworthy's *The Forsyte Saga* and Kenneth Clark's acclaimed *Civilisation,* which won the George Foster Peabody Award in 1971.

Prior to assuming his present post, Mr. Day served as president of NET (National Educational Television) starting in August, 1969, until that organization was merged into WNET/13. He came to NET from KQED, the network's San Francisco affiliate, which he had managed since 1953; he was its president from 1967-69. Currently, Mr. Day is a trustee of the Children's Television Workshop (producers of *The Electric Company* and *Sesame Street*), the National Reading Council, International Film Seminars and Communications Improvement, Inc.

Mr. Day is a 1941 graduate of the University of California at Berkeley. He is the winner of numerous professional awards and citations, including the first Paul Niven Award for Excellence in Electronic Journalism. In June, 1972, he received an H.L.D. (Doctor of Humane Letters) from Newark State College.

STANLEY T. DONNER

Dr. Donner was Chairman of the Department of Radio-Television-Film at the University of Texas from 1965-1971. He received the B.A. from the University of Michigan in 1932, the M.A. from North-western in 1940, and the Ph.D. from Northwestern in 1946. His academic affiliations include Northwestern where he was Director of "Reviewing Stand"; Stanford University; and the University of Texas. Dr. Donner received a Senior Fulbright Research Grant to Paris in 1955-6, and was Fulbright Lecturer to the University of London. He was U.S. representative to a 1956 Unesco Meeting on Cultural Exchange of Radio in Paris; was educational consultant to the Westinghouse Broadcasting Corporation; and is the recipient of several television awards. He is the contributing editor and author of several books, including *The Farther Vision: Educational Television Today* (University of Wisconsin Press, 1968) as well as the author of many articles in the professional journals.

KEITH P. FISCHER

Mr. Fischer joined the Corporation for Public Broadcasting January 1, 1973 as Executive Vice President. Until that time, he pursued a career in the marketing and communication fields. For the last 13 years, he had been with Grey Advertising, Inc., the nation's 7th largest advertising agency, where he had held major management posts. From 1968, until he joined the Corporation of Public Broadcasting, he was Executive Vice President of Grey.

Mr. Fischer joined CPB because of a personal conviction about the importance of public broadcasting based on the impact it has had on his family, including two small children, and because he recognized, through his communications background, the enormous impact of television and radio on our way of life. He is a graduate of Princeton University.

PHILIP S. GELB

Philip Gelb is Associate Professor in the Communication Arts and Sciences at Bronx Community College of the City University of New York. His 30-year career is about equally divided between professional work in the media and in higher education. Professor Gelb's focus is on "the American mass media as the single greatest reinforcer of shared communications assumptions and behavior in all of human history." His media credits range from CBS, Hollywood, through BBD&O, Minneapolis, to WMCA, New York. He produced many award-winning series for the National Association of Educational Broadcasters, including *Rights on Trial* and *People or Puppets*. His commercial credits range from the writing of the daily radio serial, *Joe Palooka* to the production of *The Family of Man* film.

RICHARD J. GOGGIN, SR.

Richard Goggin is Professor of Film and Television, School of the Arts, New York University. He received his B.A. (English) from Manhattan College in 1937; M.A. (Theatre and Motion Picture Studies) at UCLA in 1951; and Ph.D. (Theatre and Dramatic Literature) at Stanford in 1952-3. He also received a Certificate in Drama Studies from the University of Birmingham, England in 1947. Professor Goggin has been writer-producer-director for CBS Radio and ABC-TV; Program Director for WFIL-TV, Philadelphia. He was associated with the Educational Radio and TV Center, Ann Arbor, Michigan and served as technical advisor to Twentieth Century-Fox Film Corp. In 1969, he was Fulbright-Hays Lecturer in Communications in Belgium. He is a member of IRTS and other professional organizations.

NICHOLAS GORDON

Mr. Gordon is Vice President, Sales, NBC Radio Network. He joined NBC in 1953. He later became Manager, Rates and Program Evaluation, Owned Television Stations Division, and was head of Eastern Sales for the NBC-TV Network among other executive positions. His previous experience included Director of Research and Sales Planning for the Keystone Broadcasting System, and before that senior radio-TV analyst for the William H. Weintraub Agency in New York. He was also a consultant for research and sales planning for the Liberty Broadcasting System, assistant to the production manager of *Advertising Age* in Chicago and police reporter for Chicago's City News Bureau.

Mr. Gordon is a graduate of the University of Chicago with a Ph.B. degree (1946). Active in community affairs, Mr. Gordon is past Vice Chairman of the Riverdale Community Council, a member of the Board and of the Executive Committee and Executive Vice President of the Wave Hill Center for Environmental Studies (Riverdale/Bronx). He is also a member of the Executive Volunteer Corps of the Department of Commerce of the City of New York and a member of the American Marketing Association.

W. KNOX HAGOOD

Knox Hagood is Professor and Chairman, Department of Broadcasting and Film Communication, University of Alabama. He received his B.A. from the University of Alabama in 1947 and his M.A. from Northwestern in 1948. He served as Chairman of the Radio-TV-Film Interest Group of the SCA and the SSCA. He was Radio-TV Officer for the Public Information Office, Far East Command, 1950-52. At present Professor Hagood is Radio-TV-Film editor of *SSCA Journal*. He also served as Director of WAPI-TV, Birmingham, Alabama in 1949. His associations include SCAA, Southern SCA, APBE. He is a member of the Tuscaloosa Community Players Board and the Arts and Council Board.

KENNETH HARWOOD

Dr. Harwood is Dean of the School of Communications and Theater at Temple University, Philadelphia. He received his A.B. from the University of Southern California in 1947 and his A. M. and Ph.D. from USC in 1948 and 1950 respectively. His academic affiliations include the University of Alabama, where he served as chairman of the department of Radio and Television and the University of Southern California where he was professor and chairman of the department of Telecommunications. Dr. Harwood was also chairman, Oak Knoll Broadcasting Company, and chairman of the Broadcast Foundation. He is presently Director of the Franklin Broadcasting Company in Philadelphia. His memberships include American Sociological Association, American Psychological Association, International Communications Association, SCA, NAEB, Sigma Delta Chi.

WILLIAM HAWES

Dr. Hawes is Associate Professor of Communications (Radio-Television-Film) at the University of Houston. He did his undergraduate work at Eastern Michigan University (Speech-English-Art) and his graduate work at the University of Michigan (Speech-Broadcasting-Theatre). Dr. Hawes has served as teacher, and administrator at Eastern Michigan University, at Texas Christian University (Director of the Division of Radio-TV-Film, 1960-1964) Visiting Assistant Professor and Director of Radio, University of North Carolina, in 1965. He has also been associated with station WTOP-TV, the American Broadcasting Company, *The Houston Post*. He was manager of radio station KUHF. His articles include a contribution to the textbook, *Radio Broadcasting: Introduction To The Sound Medium* (Hastings House, Publishers). He is a member of IRTS, NAEB, RTND, SCA among others.

NEIL HICKEY

Mr. Hickey is currently New York Bureau Chief of *TV Guide*. He has held that position for nine years, during which he has written innumerable series on TV's role in the society. Mr. Hickey spent the summer of 1966 in Vietnam and produced a six-part series on TV's involvement with the war. Prior to that he was associate editor of *True* Magazine for two years; and an editor of *The American Weekly* Sunday magazine for six years before that.

Mr. Hickey is author of several books, including: *The Gentleman Was a Thief,* a biography of the famed Raffles society jewel thief of the 1920's; and *Adam Clayton Powell and the Politics of Race,* a biography of Adam Powell.

After 3½ years service as a naval officer at sea in the destroyer service he came to New York in 1956. A native of Baltimore, his journalistic career began at age 18 on Baltimore daily newspapers. He is a graduate of Loyola in Maryland.

JAMES C. HIRSCH

Mr. Hirsch heads Communications & Broadcasting Consulting Services, since 1969 when he established his own business. Mr. Hirsch has been handling planning and implementational assignments in the public affairs, advertising and marketing areas for clients from the fields of broadcasting, general business, service organizations and associations.

Prior to setting up his communications counseling service, he was with the Television Bureau of Advertising for 12 years and served as Vice President for Development and Public Affairs. Earlier Mr. Hirsch held marketing, creative services and executive management positions in the broadcasting, publishing and advertising fields in Chicago, New York and Washington, D.C.

RICHARD W. JENCKS

Mr. Jencks, CBS Vice President, Washington, has been active in the broadcast industry since 1948. After two years as assistant to the general counsel of the National Association of Broadcasters, he joined CBS in 1950 as attorney in the CBS West Coast Law Department. Three years later he became CBS West Coast resident attorney, a position he held for six years. In 1959, Mr. Jencks resigned from CBS to become president of the Alliance of Television Film Producers, Inc. When that organization merged with the Association of Motion Picture Producers in 1964, he became vice president and television administrator of the merged organization. Mr. Jencks rejoined CBS in 1965 as deputy general counsel, and became vice president, CBS Television Network, in October 1968. In February 1969 he became president, CBS/Broadcast Group. He was appointed CBS Vice President, Washington, in July 1971.

He is a director of The Advertising Council and a member of the International Radio and Television Society, the National Academy of Television Arts and Sciences, the Sierra Club, the American Bar Association and the Federal Communications Bar Association. Mr. Jencks' undergraduate education at the University of California at Berkeley was interrupted by four years of naval service in World War II, following which he was graduated from Stanford University in 1946, and from Stanford Law School in 1948. During the war he served in the Aleutians and the Caribbean and left the service as a lieutenant commander.

ROBERT D. KASMIRE

Mr. Kasmire was named Vice President, Public Relations, National Broadcasting Company in July, 1972, with executive responsibility for NBC's public relations and broadcast standards activities.

Mr. Kasmire joined NBC as Coordinator, Special Projects, Corporate Planning, in 1959. A year later he was appointed Coordinator, Corporate Information, and in 1962 was named Director, Corporate Information. Before joining the company, Mr. Kasmire was Assistant to the Secretary then Governor W. Averell Harriman of New York for two years and, before that, Director of Business Publicity for the New York State Department of Commerce for one year. He went to the state capital in June, 1953, as a reporter and editor in the Albany bureau of the Associated Press after working, in turn, as a reporter for the Meriden (Conn.) *Record* and Providence (R.I.) *Journal*, and in the news department of WJAR-TV-AM-FM in Providence, an NBC Television and Radio Network affiliate. Mr. Kasmire was graduated Phi Beta Kappa by Brown University (B.A.) in 1951. He is a director of the International Radio and Television Foundation.

C.A. KELLNER

Dr. Kellner is Associate Professor in the Speech Department at Marshall University, and area coordinator for Broadcasting. He received his B.A. (magna cum laude) from Doane College; his M.A. from the University of Cincinnati; and his Ph.D. from Ohio University (mass communications). He joined the faculty of Marshall College in 1969. His prior background in industry includes service as Vice-President, Station Services, American Research Bureau, 1964-1969; and midwest manager, ARB, Chicago from 1961-1964. His memberships include IRTS and APBE.

STEPHEN B. LABUNSKI

Mr. Labunski is a long-time broadcaster and station manager—at WDGY, Minneapolis and at WMCA, New York. He was President of the NBC Radio Division, and is now Vice-President and partner, Chuck Blore Creative Services, world's largest producers of radio commercials, as well as producers of film and television. His industry activities include IRTS, NAB and RAB, among others.

GORDON A. LAW

Dr. Law is Project Director, Satellite Technology Demonstration Federation of Rocky Mountain States, Denver, Colorado. He received his B.A. degree from the University of Denver; M.A. from Syracuse University; and Ed.D. from Washington State University. His professional background includes the following posts: Special Assignment Reporter, *The Denver Post and Rocky Mountain News;* Manager KVDU, Denver; Faculty, University of Idaho, Moscow, Idaho. Dr. Law represented the University at the annual session of the state legislature. His publications include the co-authorship of *Television Operations and Policy Handbook,* and he has written and directed film, radio shows, prepared film clips and co-produced Idaho's first statewide TV political debates. His memberships include NAEB, Phi Delta Kappa and Idaho Broadcasters Association.

ROBERT L. LIDDEL

Mr. Liddel is Senior Vice President, Media Director at Compton Advertising. He can claim first-hand knowledge of nearly every function his department performs, because during his 17 years with the agency, he has held just about every position the Media Department offers.

Starting out in media research in 1952, he went into time buying, first as an assistant and later as a timebuyer. He became assistant head timebuyer, then head timebuyer and finally associate media director. At that point Mr. Liddel left the agency in 1964 to assume the post of Vice President and Director of radio and television programming at Doyle Dane Bernbach. He returned to Compton in 1967 as Vice President and associate director of media and programming. Later that year he was elected a senior vice president of the agency. In 1969, he was named to the post of media director.

During his career with Compton, Mr. Liddel has been directly involved and influential in the handling of nearly every Compton account. He holds a B.A. degree from the University of Virginia.

LEE LOEVINGER

Judge Loevinger has been active in government and the law, as it relates to government, for more than 30 years.

Born in the city of St. Paul, Judge Loevinger is also the product of the educational system of Minnesota, from grade school through JD degree at the University of Minnesota. During World War II, he saw active duty with the Navy; attaining the rank of Lieutenant Commander. His present rank is Lt. Commander, USNR, (retired).

Judge Loevinger's list of honorary and professional memberships and awards ranges from Phi Beta Kappa through Sigma Delta Chi and the Broadcast Pioneers to the American Judicature Society. That roster of achievement is second in length only to his "catalog" of some 90 published books, articles, and monographs on law . . . economics . . . antitrust . . . communications and science.

Judge Loevinger's government service includes the NLRB; the Antitrust Division of the Department of Justice; Commissioner of the FCC; as well as a term on the bench of the Minnesota Supreme Court. Currently, Judge Loevinger is a partner with the Washington law firm of Hogan and Hartson.

PHILIP ALAN MACOMBER

Dr. Macomber has the B.A. degree from Otterbein College in 1950; M.A. from Ohio State University 1952; Ph.D., Ohio State University 1959. His teaching experience includes Otterbein College; Mississippi Southern University; Ohio State University; Kent State University. Dr. Macomber was facilities director, producer, director, art director at Ohio State University, WOSU-TV, from its inception 1956 to 1960 and Professor of Speech, in charge of television, Kent State University, 1960 to date. He is Chairman of the Executive Committee of Northeastern Educational Television of Ohio, Inc., which operated Channel 45 at Salem, Ohio.

Dr. Macomber has been involved in the production of over 1,000 instructional television programs for all grade levels from kindergarten in the public school system to graduate work at the State University. He has been instrumental in developing a campus-wide CCTV-CATV system on the campus of Kent State University. One of the three production studios of Channel 45, a PBS station serving 2½ million Ohioans, is located at Kent State University.

THOMAS ALLISON McCAIN

Dr. McCain is Assistant Professor of Communications at Ohio State University. He received his B.S. from Wisconsin State University in 1965, his M.S. from Marquette University in 1967 and his Ph.D. from the University of Wisconsin in 1972. Dr. McCain's areas of specialization include mass communication research, TV research, mass communications law, media structure and organization. His publications include several monographs and papers presented at the Speech Communication Association. A book in progress is to be titled *Mass Communication: A Social Science Perspective*. Dr. McCain's professional associations include, National Association for Professional Broadcasting Education, Association for Education in Journalism, among others.

DANIEL J. McGRATH

Mr. McGrath is currently Vice President, Corporate Broadcast Group, for the D'Arcy-MacManus & Masius Advertising agency. He earned his B.A. Degree in Philosophy at St. Mary Of The Lake College, Mundelein, Illinois. He subsequently attended the University of Chicago Graduate Business School. Mr. McGrath was previously affiliated with numerous advertising agencies, including J. Walter Thompson Co., Doyle, Dane Bernbach, and Wells, Rich, Greene as a broadcasting executive.

HOWARD S. MEIGHAN

Mr. Meighan is a pioneer in broadcasting. He was a member of the first advertising agency radio department, J. Walter Thompson Company, 1929. He joined CBS in 1934 as spot salesman, became manager Radio Sales; V. P. Station Administration; first President CBS Radio; Vice President and General Executive CBS, Inc. In Hollywood, he devised the concept and general design of Television City, and the idea of video tape. Mr. Meighan retired from CBS in 1958 to found Videotape Productions and develop introduction and use of video tape in association with Ampex and Minnesota Mining. He sold the Videotape interests to 3M in 1962 and established The Catalyst Group Inc. of which he is President. Catalyst is a broad gauged entity which brings together men, money and ideas. Aside from several non-broadcasting activities of Catalyst, it does have certain interests in special application of cable telecommunications.

In the field of broadcasting Mr. Meighan is a member of Broadcast Pioneers; the American Academy of Television Arts and Sciences; Director of the International Radio and Television Society; Chairman of the Board of International Radio and Television Foundation.

EUGENE H. METHVIN

Mr. Methvin was born in Vienna, Georgia, where his father was a country weekly editor and publisher of *The Vienna News*. Mr. Methvin studied journalism at the University of Georgia School of Journalism. On campus he lettered in football and debate and belonged to Sigma Nu fraternity and Sigma Delta Chi, professional journalism society, which named him the most outstanding male graduate of 1955. He was also a member of Phi Beta Kappa and worked briefly as a reporter on *The Atlanta Constitution*. He graduated with a Bachelor of Arts in Journalism degree, cum laude, with a supplementary major and postgraduate study in law and international affairs.

After graduation he spent three years in the U.S. Air Force as a jet fighter pilot, flying the F-86 and F-102 all-weather interceptors. In 1958 he joined the *Washington Daily News* as a general assignment reporter, and in 1960 he joined the *Reader's Digest* Washington bureau. He is at present an associate editor of the magazine. An article by Mr. Methvin in the January '65 *Reader's Digest*, "How the Reds Make a Riot," won for the magazine the coveted award for public service in magazine journalism given annually by Sigma Delta Chi.

KEITH W. MIELKE

Dr. Mielke is Associate Professor and Chairman of the Department of Radio-TV, Indiana University. He received the B.M.E. degree from Philipps University, Oklahoma in 1956; M.S. (Television-Radio) Syracuse University (1961) and Ph.D. (Communications) from Michigan State University, 1965. During the academic year 1973-74, Dr. Mielke was at the Center for Research in Children's Television, Harvard University. He also has served as Research Consultant with the Children's Television Workshop. He is Vice-Chairman, Mass Communication Division, SCA; Associate Editor, *Educational Broadcasting Review*; Editorial Consultant, *Journal of Broadcasting* and of *Audio-Visual Communication Review*. His recent publications include a chapter on "Evaluation of Learning from Televised Instruction" in *Instructional Television: Bold New Venture* (I.U. Press, 1971). He will be represented in a Ford Foundation publication entitled *Educational Television in Developing Countries.* His memberships include SCA, NAEB and APBC.

GEORGE H. NEWI

Mr. Newi is Vice President in Charge of Daytime Sales for the ABC Television Network. He was an Account Executive, Eastern Division, for ABC-TV since July, 1964. He came to the ABC Television Network in February, 1963, as Assistant Daytime Sales Manager, and served as Director of Sports Sales from October, 1963, until July, 1964. Earlier, he had been with McCann-Erickson, Inc., which he joined in December, 1959, as Assistant Director of New Program Development. He also served as Director of Daytime Programming for the agency. Before that, he had been with Compton Advertising, Inc., where he was in media research and was a broadcast time buyer. A graduate of Syracuse University, Mr. Newi was a radio-television and English major. He served as a First Lieutenant with the Army Signal Corps in Korea.

JOHN O'CONNOR

Mr. O'Connor is the television critic of the *New York Times.* He comes by the post naturally, since he is that rare breed (almost extinct, certainly endangered)— the native-born New Yorker. He attended The City College and did graduate study in drama at the Yale Graduate School.

His first permanent, full-time employment was as an instructor at The City College of the City of New York. Following this, he quietly entered the Fourth Estate. Starting in a production capacity at the *Wall Street Journal,* Mr. O'Connor rose through copy and re-write to reviewing. The *Journal* created the post of Arts Editor for him, and his coverage and writings embraced not only film, but opera, the dance, theater, and the youngest art—television. After 10 years with the Dow-Jones daily, Mr. O'Connor joined the *New York Times* in 1971, where he has maintained the high standard of television criticism established by that paper.

ALVIN H. PERLMUTTER

Mr. Perlmutter has been executive producer of NET's Emmy Award-winning *The Great American Dream Machine* since its inception in January 1971. He was named an executive producer of public-affairs programs at NET in 1963. Mr. Perlmutter came to NET from the National Broadcasting Company, where he had served as director of public-affairs programming and subsequently as program manager of WNBC-TV, New York.

Among the more than 100 major NET programs for which he has been responsible during the past seven years have been the *At Issue* series, including documentaries about *Death on the Highways* and *The Great Label Mystery;* and such NET Journal programs as *The Poor Pay More, Homefront '67, The Smoking Spiral, What Harvest for the Reaper, The Drinking American,* and *Speak Out on Drugs.* Mr. Perlmutter launched NET's monthly *Black Journal* series in the summer of 1968 and served as executive producer for the first four programs.

His film and television production organization, Spectrum Associates, Inc., has, over the past years, produced a number of institutional and industrial films for various organizations. He is a former national trustee of the National Academy of Television Arts and Sciences and a former governor of the Academy's New York chapter. He was graduated from Syracuse University in 1949.

CHARLES E. PHILLIPS

Professor Phillips is Chairman of the Mass Communication Department at Emerson College, Boston, Mass. Professor Phillips received his B.S. from the University of Illinois and his M.S. from the same institution. He has been associated professionally with WCBS in Springfield, Illinois and also with WTAX in Springfield.

RICHARD A. R. PINKHAM

Mr. Pinkham, Senior Vice President in charge of Media and Programs and a Director of Ted Bates & Company, Inc., has been in virtually every facet of the media universe: magazines, newspapers, television, and outdoor advertising.

He attended the Buckley School in New York and later went to The Choate School, Wallingford, Connecticut. He was graduated from Yale University in 1936. He began his business career with Time, Inc. In 1941, Mr. Pinkham became an Account Executive with the Lord & Thomas advertising agency, New York, but left the company before Pearl Harbor to join the U. S. Navy. He served for four years, emerging as a Lieutenant Commander. Following his discharge, Mr. Pinkham joined the *New York Herald Tribune* where he became a member of the Board of Directors. In 1951, Mr. Pinkham went to the National Broadcasting Company as Manager of Network Planning. He was the Executive Producer of the *Today* show in 1952 and was also responsible for launching NBC's *Home* show. He was subsequently named Vice President in charge of Network Television Programs.

Mr. Pinkham is past President of the International Radio & Television Society, and a former Chairman of the Broadcast Policy Committee of the American Association of Advertising Agencies. He is a Trustee of Emerson College, and a Director of Channel 13, in New York City.

ROBERT PITOFSKY

Mr. Pitofsky has already left his mark— a searching for the "rights of man"—in our decade. He is best known—to marketing and communications people, at least—as the aggressive Director of The FTC's Bureau of Consumer Protection, a post he held for three busy years, 1970-73. His other government service included a stint with Justice, in Washington.

Mr. Pitofsky was in private practice in New York after his first Washington assignment, serving six years with one of the city's leading law firms. This was followed by an additional six years teaching law at New York University, a campus to which he returned in January, 1973.

Mr. Pitofsky's education was at NYU; his Ll.B. is from Columbia. His principal fields of law include antitrust, regulated industries, the Federal courts, and Constitutional law. He is a prolific author of books, articles and book reviews.

ALFRED L. PLANT

Mr. Plant joined the Block Drug Company in 1955 as Advertising Manager. In 1960, he was appointed Vice President-Advertising for the Company.

Previous to joining Block, Mr. Plant had been with Warwick & Legler in charge of the drug division. His previous agency affiliations were Grey Advertising Agency and the Federal Advertising Agency until that agency went out of business in 1952. Mr. Plant served in World War II as Information and Education Officer on the staff of General Wedemeyer in the China Theatre. He was a Major.

Mr. Plant has also been active in the Association of National Advertisers for many years. He was Chairman of the A.N.A.'s Television Committee and, in 1965, was elected a Director of the A.N.A. for three years and appointed a member of the Executive Committee of that organization. He now serves as Co-Chairman of the A.N.A./4 A's Television Joint Policy Committee. Mr. Plant is Vice President of the International Radio & Television Society and serves on its Board of Directors.

JON T. POWELL

Dr. Powell is Associate Professor and Coordinator of Radio-Film-Television, Department of Speech Communication, Northern Illinois University, DeKalb, Illinois. Dr. Powell received his B.A. (Magna Cum Laude) from St. Martin's College, Olympia, Washington in 1954, his M.S. from the University of Oregon in 1956, and his Ph.D. from the University of Oregon in 1963. He has served on the faculty of Ohio University and Southern Oregon College where he was Director of Radio-Television. He has produced and hosted educational television programs for commercial stations and has produced and recorded radio programs. His many publications include articles in *Federal Communication Bar Journal*, a contribution on broadcasting in Rhodesia and Zambia in *Broadcasting in Africa: A Continental Survey of Radio & Television,* and a study for the *Central States Speech Journal.*

PETER K. PRINGLE

Dr. Pringle is Assistant Professor of Journalism and Communication at the University of Florida and host-producer with WUFT-TV, Gainesville, Florida. He received the B.A. (Honors) degree from London University in 1963, the M.A. (Journalism and Communication) from the University of Florida in 1966 and the Ph.D. (Mass Communication) from Ohio University, 1969. He was the recipient of a Rotary Foundation Fellowship for International Understanding in 1964-65. Dr. Pringle's professional background includes work as a newspaper reporter in England, broadcast news writer and editor with the Associated Press in New York and Senior sub-editor and scriptwriter for the BBC Television News, 1970-71.

A. FRANK REEL

Mr. Reel is President of Metromedia Producers Corporation. He comes to broadcast programming via the law. His early education was in Milwaukee public and private schools. Then, to Harvard, for undergraduate and law degrees.

Mr. Reel practiced law in Boston for over 15 years. At the end of the War, he was Defense Counsel for General Yomyuki Yamashita at the War Crimes Trial in Manila in 1945, and before the U.S. Supreme Court the following year. Out of that experience came his well known, and widely respected book, *The Case of General Yamashita,* first published in 1949; republished in 1971.

Mr. Reel was National Executive Secretary of AFRA until 1953; his production company experience began with Ziv, later with United Artists. Since 1968, he has been with MPC, first as Vice President of Business Affairs, and then as President.

RODERICK D. RIGHTMIRE

Dr. Rightmire is Professor and Director of the School of Radio-Television, Ohio University, Athens, Ohio. His academic background includes Bachelor's and Master's degrees from Boston University and the Ph.D. from Michigan State University. Dr. Rightmire has been an instructor and faculty program director of WBUR at Boston University; manager of KUT-FM, assistant professor and radio production supervisor at the University of Texas; assistant manager of WRVR in New York City; and assistant professor and administrative assistant to the chairman of the Department of Television and Radio at Michigan State University. He is a member of the Board of Directors of the Broadcast Education Association and is active in many other professional organizations.

J. M. RIPLEY

Dr. Ripley is Professor, and former Chairman, Department of Telecommunications at the University of Kentucky, Lexington, Ky. He received the B.A., M.A. and Ph.D. degrees from Ohio State University and also taught at Ohio State in 1960-61. Dr. Ripley was Associate Director of the Broadcasting Service, Southern Illinois U. from 1955-1960 and was Associate Professor at the University of Wisconsin, 1961-7. He was associated with WBNS-TV, Columbus, Ohio. He is the author of numerous articles and co-author of *American Broadcasting* (College Printing, Madison, Wis.). Dr. Ripley is a member of the Board of Directors of APBE and was President of the RTF Interest Group of SCA. His memberships include APBE, NAEB among others.

MS. ELIZABETH J. ROBERTS

Ms. Roberts is Director of a Special Task Force on Children's Television at the Federal Communications Commission.

A native of St. Louis, Missouri, Ms. Roberts holds B.A. and M.A. degrees from Marquette University and has completed courses toward a Ph.D. She was a member of the Faculty of Marquette, teaching classes in values, ethics and social philosophy until 1969. She served as Coordinator and Research Specialist at the White House Conference on Children and Youth. She worked particularly in the areas of creativity and value development for the Children's Conference and aided in organizing the Youth Conference.

In March, 1971, she joined the staff of National Public Radio as Executive Assistant to the Program Director. In September, 1971, she was appointed to the Federal Communications Commission Task Force. The Commission has pending an "Inquiry" into children's television. The Inquiry is designed to collect the widest possible range of information on all aspects of the medium. Ms. Roberts has been responsible for evaluating the comments filed, advising the Commission and keeping it informed on new developments, and coordinating with other Federal agencies and private groups.

LAWRENCE H. ROGERS II

Mr. Rogers is President of Taft Broadcasting Company, Cincinnati-based broadcasting, motion picture and entertainment group. One of the nation's largest licensees of broadcasting stations, Taft is also owner of Hanna-Barbera Productions, Hollywood's biggest animation production company. Mr. Rogers joined Taft in 1960 as Vice President in charge of Operations, was made Executive Vice President in 1961, and was elected President of the company in 1963.

Mr. Rogers pioneered the use of editorials on television and radio beginning in 1956. Earlier he had built the nation's first long distance microwave relay system for local TV. He introduced daily editorials to all Taft's radio and television markets. He is widely known as a public spokesman, not only for Taft but for the broadcasting industry as a whole.

Mr. Rogers has served on the Television Code Review Board, the Television Information Committee, and the Editorial Committee. He is one of the founders and a former Board Chairman and Treasurer of the Television Bureau of Advertising. He is former Vice Chairman of the NBC Television Affiliates Board and served on the Board of Governors of the ABC-TV Affiliates. He is Vice President and a member of the Board of Directors of the Association of Maximum Service Telecasters in Washington, D.C. He has served as a consultant to the United States Information Agency and traveled abroad in its behalf. A native of New Jersey, he was graduated from Lawrenceville School in 1939, and with honors from Princeton University where he has served as a representative on the Graduate Council.

DIANE L. SASS

Ms. Sass is Vice President, research and marketing, of Kaiser Broadcasting Corporation and was formerly vice president for research and program development for Avco Radio and TV Sales.

Diane Sass began her broadcasting career as a research director with A. C. Nielsen Co. in 1956 and became the first woman accountant executive. She joined Avco in 1965 as research director and was elected vice president in 1968. Ms. Sass is a member of Phi Beta Kappa and received her Bachelor's Degree summa cum laude from Hunter College. She was awarded the M.A. from New York University in 1956.

SAUL N. SCHER

Dr. Scher is Associate Professor, Radio-TV-Film, Department of Speech, University of Maine at Orono. He has held simliar posts at the University of Maryland and University of Massachusetts. Dr. Sher received his B.A. (English) from Queens College, City University of New York, 1954, his M.F.A. (Drama) from Columbia University in 1960 and his Ph.D. (Mass Communications) from New York University in 1965. His research includes many articles and reviews in *Television Quarterly, Educational Broadcasting Review, Journal of Broadcasting,* and others. He is at present completing the manuscript of an anthology of television criticism, *The Critics Look at Television* (Wadsworth Publishing Company).

ROBERT SCHLATER

Dr. Schlater is Professor and Chairman of the Department, TV-Radio, Michigan

State University. He received his B.A. (History) from the University of Nebraska, 1943, his M.S. (Journalism) from Columbia University, 1948, and his Ph.D. (Communications) Michigan State University, 1966. Dr. Schlater's professional background includes teaching English at the University of Nebraska and Journalism at the same institution. He was Radio News writer for the Providence *Journal;* Promotion and Advertising Assistant, Armour & Co.; Producer-Director and Program Manager KUON-TV. His military service includes both Europe and Korea and he is a member of the consulting faculty, U.S. Army Command and General Staff College, Fort Leavenworth, Kansas. He is the author of numerous articles in *Journal of Broadcasting* and *Educational Broadcasting Review.*

WALTER A. SCHWARTZ

Mr. Schwartz was named President of ABC Television on July 17, 1972. Previously he had been President of the ABC Radio Network since August, 1967, after serving four years as Vice President and General Manager of WABC, the ABC Owned Radio Station in New York.

An active broadcast industry leader, Mr. Schwartz is a member of the Board of Directors of the National Association of Broadcasters; past President of the New York State Broadcasters Association and a member of its Board of Directors; past chairman of the New York State Broadcasters Executive Conference; a member of the Board of Advisors of the Bedside Network; a member of the International Radio & Television Society; and the New York Advertising Club. In 1964, he was the recipient of the National Headliner's Award for excellence in broadcast editorials, and the Mayor's Special Commendation from the City of New York. He received the de Villiers Humanitarian Award of the National Leukemia Society in 1965. In May, 1968, he was the recipient of the Wayne State University Alumni Award Citation for his contributions ot the broadcast industry. A native of Detroit, Mr. Schwartz was graduated with a B.A. degree from Wayne University in 1951.

IRWIN SEGELSTEIN

Mr. Segelstein was Vice President, Program Administration, CBS Television Network. He is now President of Columbia Records Division of CBS.

Mr. Segelstein joined the Network in June 1965 as Vice President, Programs, New York, coming from Benton & Bowles, Inc., advertising agency, where he had been Vice President in Charge of Programming. He had joined Benton & Bowles, Inc., in 1947 as a member of the radio department. With the advent of television, he became Director of Film Programming, Director of Television Programs, Director of Programming and then Vice President. He was born in New York City and attended the College of the City of New York.

CHARLES W. SHIPLEY

Dr. Shipley is Chairman, Department of Radio-Television, Southern Illinois University in Carbondale, Illinois and also Director of SIU-C Broadcasting Service. He was graduated with the B.F.A. degree from University of Kansas in 1940, received the M.A. from Northwestern University in 1949 and the Ph.D. from Florida State University in 1971. He has also had a 25-year career as radio news editor and television spokesman for numerous advertisers in the United States. His research includes "Entertaining Information: A Study of the Quiz Format in U. S. Network Radio Programming, 1930-1950," done in 1971.

GEORGE J. SIMKO

Mr. Simko began his career in advertising with Kenyon & Eckhardt in February, 1953. In 1960 he left Kenyon & Eckhardt to join Benton & Bowles as a Media Buyer. In succeeding years he became Assistant Media Director, Associate Media Director, and in May of 1968 was appointed Vice President and Manager of the Media Department. In July of 1970 he was named to the position of Senior Vice President, Director of Media Management and elected a member of the Agency's Board of Directors. He is also a member of the Agency's Strategy Review Board.

Mr. Simko is on the Board of Directors of the International Radio and Television Foundation and is Vice President of the Media Directors' Council. He is also a member of the Media Policy Committee of the 4A's.

DR. ROBERT H. STANLEY

Dr. Stanley has taught at several colleges and universities including Mount Holyoke College and Ohio University. Professor Stanley is presently Department Representative at Hunter College of the City of New York where he teaches courses in the character, structure and impact of America's communication media. Dr. Stanley is currently doing research in the area of broadcast regulation.

Professor Stanley received his B.A. from the State University of New York at New Paltz, his M.A. from Queens College and his Ph.D. from Ohio University.

ART TOPOL

Mr. Topol joined Ogilvy & Mather in 1959 as a Media Buyer. He advanced to Media Director in 1964. He became Vice-President in 1965 and Manager of Media and Broadcasting in 1968. He was named Associate Director of Broadcasting in 1970. Currently, his primary responsibility is network broadcast for all accounts.

Before joining Ogilvy & Mather, he was Media Buyer at Donahue & Coe; Dowd, Redfield & Johnstone; and the William Esty Company. Prior to entering the agency field, he was affiliated with The Screen Gems division of Columbia Pictures as Sales Representative and Sales Service Director in New York and with NBC in the network controllers office, station relations and sales services. He started with NBC as a tour guide in 1951.

RUSSELL C. TORNABENE

Mr. Tornabene is Vice President and General Manager of the NBC Radio Network. Mr. Tornabene was previously General Manager, NBC News, Radio Division. He joined NBC in Washington in October, 1951, as News Editor on the local desk of the NBC-owned stations WRC and WRC-TV.

Mr. Tornabene was NBC News' radio and television coordinator on President Eisenhower's trip to Asia and Europe in 1959, and to South America in 1960; President Kennedy's meeting with Latin American leaders in Costa Rica in March, 1963, and his four-nation tour of Europe in the summer of 1963. In May of 1972, Mr. Tornabene traveled to Russia, Poland and Iran to produce the NBC Radio coverage of President Nixon's visits with the leaders of those countries.

Mr. Tornabene is a graduate of Indiana University with a Master's degree. He is first Vice President (President elect) of the Deadline Club, Sigma Delta Chi, New York City; a member of the Board of Governors of the Overseas Press Club of America Foundation; and a member of the International Radio and Television Society and Radio/Television News Directors Association.

G. NORMAN VAN TUBERGEN

Dr. Van Tubergen is Assistant Professor of Journalism and Research Associate at Southern Illinois University, Carbondale, Ill. He received his B.A. from the University of New Mexico in 1963, M.A. from the University of Iowa, 1965 and Ph.D. from the University of Iowa, 1968. His teaching background includes both New York University and the University of Iowa. Dr. Van Tubergen has done educational television production, radio newscasting, film production and agency market research. His research papers include "Audience Perception of Newscaster Personality," among others. He was the recipient of a NAB Research Grant.

CHARLES S. TOWER

Mr. Tower is Vice President of Corinthian Broadcasting Corporation. Since May 1960, Mr. Tower has been Vice President for Television of the National

Association of Broadcasters. He joined NAB in February, 1949, was named assistant to the vice president of the Employer-Employee Relations Department in February, 1953, and became manager of the department in June, 1955. The name of the department was changed to Broadcast Personnel and Economics in June, 1958.

Mr. Tower formerly worked for the Radio Corporation of America at its RCA Victor Division home office in Camden, New Jersey. His work there included manufacturing cost control and personnel relations. He also worked for two years as a field examiner with the National Labor Relations Board, working out of the Pittsburgh and Boston offices.

Mr. Tower is a graduate of Williams College, Harvard Business School and Boston University School of Law. While attending law school, he served as lecturer on personnel and labor relations at Boston University College of Business Administration. He is a member of the Massachusetts bar and the Federal Communications Commission Bar Association.

DANIEL VIAMONTE

Dr. Viamonte is Chairman of the Department of Communication and Theatre at the University of Hartford in Connecticut. Dr. Viamonte has been active in education, theatre and mass media including professional experience in acting and directing in theatre, radio and television. He is currently the President of the Speech Association of Connecticut. He was the recipient of the "outstanding graduate award" in Mass Communications at Wayne State University where he earned his doctorate degree in 1969. He received his Master's in Radio and Television from Syracuse University; the Bachelor's in Speech and Theatre from Hofstra University; and, the Associate of Arts from Orange County Community College. Professor Viamonte has been instrumental in the development of programs in Speech, Theatre and Mass Communications at Boston College, Greenfield Community College and the University of Hartford.

MAURIE WEBSTER

Mr. Webster was appointed to the newly-created position of Executive Vice President of Compu/Net, Inc. effective November 1, 1973. Since 1969 Mr. Webster has been Vice President, Division Services, for CBS Radio. As Division Services Vice President for CBS Radio, Mr. Webster has supervised computer development for the CBS Radio Network and the CBS Owned AM and FM stations.

Mr. Webster's broadcasting career began at KVI, Tacoma, Washington. Four years later he joined CBS at KNX, Los Angeles, as an announcer-director. He subsequently became a program Supervisor and later Operations Manager for KNX, and in 1958 became Vice President and General Manager of KCBS, San Francisco.

Mr. Webster is President of the International Radio and Television Society (IRTS), New York, and a member of the board of the IRTS Foundation, of which he is past president. He is a member of the Board of Managers of the Broadcasting and Film Commission of the National Council of Churches and Chairman of the Communications Commission of the Fifth Avenue Presbyterian Church, New York.

Mr. Webster attended the University of Puget Sound in Tacoma, Washington, and UCLA in Los Angeles.

CLAY THOMAS WHITEHEAD

Dr. Whitehead became the first director of the Office of Telecommunications Policy in September 1970, after being nominated by the President and confirmed by the Senate.

He received his BS degree in electrical engineering from Massachusetts Institute of Technology in 1960, and later earned his Ph.D. in management, also from M.I.T., with concentration on policy analysis and economics. Mr. Whitehead has taught courses in electronics and political science at M.I.T. He served for two years in the U.S. Army where he attained the rank of Captain, working on problems of biological and chemical warfare. As a consultant to the Rand Corporation in the early 1960's, he worked on studies of arms control, air defense and the space program. After completing his Ph.D. Mr. Whitehead joined Rand full time to help plan and organize a policy studies program for health services and other domestic policy areas.

Following the election in 1968, Mr. Whitehead was a member of the President-elect's task force on budget policies and assisted on transition matters. He joined the White House staff in January 1969. As Special Assistant to the President, his responsibilities included the space program, atomic energy, maritime affairs, communications, liaison with regulatory agencies, and several specific economic and organizational matters.

RICHARD E. WILEY

Commissioner Wiley was appointed to the Federal Communications Commission by President Nixon on January 4, 1972. He became Chairman in 1974.

A native of Illinois, Mr. Wiley graduated with distinction from Northwestern University and holds law degrees from both Northwestern (J.D.) and Georgetown University (Ll.M.) Law Schools. His professional career has included service as a Captain in the Army Judge Advocate General's Office at the Pentagon; as Assistant General Counsel of Bell & Howell Company; as a partner in the Chicago law firm of Burditt, Calkins and Wiley and; beginning in September of 1970, as General Counsel of the Federal Communications Commission. Additionally, he taught law school for 7 years and was a Commissioner of the State of Illinois Court of Claims.

Mr. Wiley has also been active in professional association activities, having served as Chairman of the 50,000-member Young Lawyers Section of the American Bar Association, a member of the ABA's House of Delegates and on the Council of its Administrative Law Section. He is currently a National Officer of the Federal Bar Association and immediate past Chairman of its General Counsel's Committee. In addition, Mr. Wiley was founding editor-in-chief of *Law Notes*, the largest legal quarterly publication in

the United States, and is the author of numerous articles in legal journals.

THOMAS H. WOLF

Mr. Wolf was appointed to the newly-created post of Vice President and Director of Television Documentary Programs for ABC News in November, 1966. Under his guidance, ABC News has enlarged its documentary programming schedules and broadened the scope of its coverage in news specials.

ABC News specials under Mr. Wolf's supervision have won nearly 40 awards for excellence including five coveted George Foster Peabody awards. One program alone, *Africa*, accounted for 11 major awards including a Peabody and an Emmy Award. Recent ABC News specials produced under Mr. Wolf's supervision include: *Heroes and Heroin*, a study of drug addiction among U.S. servicemen in Vietnam and returning servicemen in the U.S.; *Terror in Northern Ireland*, an examination of the civil war in Northern Ireland that received an Overseas Press Club award in 1972 and *Oceans: The Silent Crisis*, an ABC News "Inquiry" special dealing with the pollution of the world's oceans through industrial waste disposal in fresh water rivers that drain into the oceans.

The highly-popular ABC News young people's program, *Make A Wish*, is also produced under the direct supervision of Mr. Wolf. *Make A Wish* has received critical acclaim from educators and television reviewers alike. In 1972, the program won the George Foster Peabody Award for its outstanding contribution to children's television.

A graduate, magna cum laude, of Princeton University and diplomate of Woodrow Wilson School of Public and International Affairs in 1937, Wolf began his career with *Time* and *Life* magazines that same year. From 1940 to 1946 he was with NEA Service, Inc., first as national editor specializing in politics, and then as European Manager of NEA and Acme Photos. He also served as radio correspondent in London and Paris for NBC. Mr. Wolf has written articles for *This Week, Reader's Digest, Collier's, Holiday,* and *New Republic.*

W. DEWEES ("DEWEY") YEAGER, JR.

Mr. Yeager, has been Advertising Manager of The Nestlé Company since 1966. His prior marketing experience includes lengthy "tours of duty" at two of the country's largest, and most respected advertising agencies—J. Walter Thompson and Young & Rubicam. Mr. Yeager's educational ladder includes The Haverford School and Trinity College.

During World War II, he served as Lieutenant in the Air Force. He is active in trade associations, and serves on the Radio Committee of the Association of National Advertisers.

Appendix B

THE TELEVISION CODE *

National Association of Broadcasters

Seventeenth Edition, April 1973

PREAMBLE

Television is seen and heard in nearly every American home. These homes include children and adults of all ages, embrace all races and all varieties of philosophic or religious conviction and reach those of every educational background. Television broadcasters must take this pluralistic audience into account in programming their stations. They are obligated to bring their positive responsibility for professionalism and reasoned judgment to bear upon all those involved in the development, production and selection of programs.

The free, competitive American system of broadcasting which offers programs of entertainment, news, general information, education and culture is supported and made possible by revenues from advertising. While television broadcasters are responsible for the programming and adver-tising on their stations, the advertisers who use television to convey their commercial messages also have a responsibility to the viewing audience. Their advertising messages should be presented in an honest, responsible and tasteful manner. Advertisers should also support the endeavors of broadcasters to offer a diversity of programs that meet the needs and expectations of the total viewing audience.

The viewer also has a responsibility to help broadcasters serve the public. All viewers should make their criticisms and positive suggestions about programming and advertising known to the broadcast licensee. Parents particularly should oversee the viewing habits of their children, encouraging them to watch programs that will enrich their experience and broaden their intellectual horizons.

PROGRAM STANDARDS

I. Principles Governing Program Content

It is in the interest of television as a vital medium to encourage programs that are innovative, reflect a high degree of creative skill, deal with significant moral and social issues and present challenging concepts and other subject matter that relate to the world in which the viewer lives.

Television programs should not only reflect the influence of the established institutions that shape our values and culture, but also expose the dynamics of social change which bear upon our lives.

To achieve these goals, television broadcasters should be conversant with the general and specific needs, interests and aspirations of all the segments of the communities they serve. They should affirmatively seek out responsible representatives of all parts of their communities so that they may structure a broad range of programs that will inform, enlighten *and entertain* the total audience."

Broadcasters should also develop programs directed toward advancing the cultural and educational aspects of their communities.

To assure that broadcasters have the freedom to program fully and responsibly, none of the provisions of this Code should be construed as preventing or impeding broadcast of the broad range of material necessary to help broadcasters fulfill their obligations to operate in the public interest.

The challenge to the broadcaster is to determine how suitably to present the complexities of human behavior. For television, this requires exceptional awareness of considerations peculiar to the medium.

Accordingly, in selecting program subjects and themes, great care must be exercised to be sure that treatment and presentation are made in good faith and not for the purpose of sensationalism or to shock or exploit the audience or appeal to prurient interests or morbid curiosity.

II. Responsibility Toward Children

Broadcasters have a special responsibility to children. Programs designed primarily for children should take into account the range of interests and needs of children, and should contribute to the sound, balanced development of children.

In the course of a child's development, numerous social factors and forces, including tele-

vision, affect the ability of the child to make the transition to adult society.

The child's training and experience during the formative years should include positive sets of values which will allow the child to become a responsible adult, capable of coping with the challenges of maturity.

Children should also be exposed, at the appropriate times, to a reasonable range of the realities which exist in the world sufficient to help them make the transition to adulthood.

Because children are allowed to watch programs designed primarily for adults, broadcasters should take this practice into account in the presentation of material in such programs when children may constitute a substantial segment of the audience.

All the standards set forth in this section apply to both program and commercial material designed and intended for viewing by children.

III. Community Responsibility

1. Television broadcasters and their staffs occupy positions of unique responsibility in their communities and should conscientiously endeavor to be acquainted fully with the community's needs and characteristics in order better to serve the welfare of its citizens.

2. Requests for time for the placement of public service announcements or programs should be carefully reviewed with respect to the character and reputation of the group, campaign or organization involved, the public interest content of the message, and the manner of its presentation.

IV. Special Program Standards

1. Violence, physical or psychological, may only be projected in responsibly handled contexts, not used exploitatively. Programs involving violence should present the consequences of it to its victims and perpetrators.

Presentation of the details of violence should avoid the excessive, the gratuitous and the instructional.

The use of violence for its own sake and the detailed dwelling upon brutality or physical agony, by sight or by sound, are not permissible.

2. The treatment of criminal activities should always convey their social and human effects.

The presentation of techniques of crime in such detail as to be instructional or invite imitation shall be avoided.

3. Narcotic addiction shall not be presented except as a destructive habit. The use of illegal drugs or the abuse of legal drugs shall not be encouraged or shown as socially acceptable.

4. The use of gambling devices or scenes necessary to the development of plot or as appropriate background is acceptable only when presented with discretion and in moderation, and in a manner which would not excite interest in, or foster, betting nor be instructional in nature.

5. Telecasts of actual sports programs at which on-the-scene betting is permitted by law shall be presented in a manner in keeping with Federal, state and local laws, and should concentrate on the subject as a public sporting event.

6. Special precautions must be taken to avoid demeaning or ridiculing members of the audience who suffer from physical or mental afflictions or deformities.

7. Special sensitivity is necessary in the use of material relating to sex, race, color, creed, religious functionaries or rites, or national or ethnic derivation.

8. Obscene, indecent or profane matter, as proscribed by law, is unacceptable.

9. The presentation of marriage, the family and similarly important human relationships, and material with sexual connotations, shall not be treated exploitatively or irresponsibly, but with sensitivity. Costuming and movements of all performers shall be handled in a similar fashion.

10. The use of liquor and the depiction of smoking in program content shall be de-emphasized. When shown, they should be consistent with plot and character development.

11. The creation of a state of hypnosis by act or detailed demonstration on camera is prohibited and hypnosis as a form of "parlor game" antics to create humorous situations within a comedy setting is forbidden.

12. Program material pertaining to fortune-telling, occultism, astrology, phrenology, palm-reading, numerology, mind-reading, character-reading, and the like is unacceptable if it encourages people to regard such fields as providing commonly accepted appraisals of life.

13. Professional advice, diagnosis and treatment will be presented in conformity with law and recognized professional standards.

14. Any technique whereby an attempt is made to convey information to the viewer by transmitting messages below the threshold of normal awareness is not permitted.

15. The use of animals, consistent with plot and character delineation, shall be in conformity with accepted standards of humane treatment.

16. Quiz and similar programs that are presented as contests of knowledge, information, skill or luck must, in fact, be genuine contests and the results must not be controlled by collusion with or between contestants, or by any other action which will favor one contestant against any other.

17. The broadcaster shall be constantly alert to prevent inclusion of elements within a program dictated by factors other than the requirements of the program itself. The acceptance of cash payments or other considerations in return for including scenic properties, the choice and identification of prizes, the selection of music and other creative program elements and inclusion of any identification of commercial products or services, their trade names or advertising slogan within the program are prohibited except in accordance with Sections 317 and 508 of the Communications Act.

18. Contests may not constitute a lottery.

19. No program shall be presented in a manner which through artifice or simulation would mislead the audience as to any material fact. Each broadcaster must exercise reasonable judgment to determine whether a particular method of presentation would constitute a material deception, or would be accepted by the audience as normal theatrical illusion.

20. A television broadcaster should not present fictional events or other non-news material as authentic news telecasts or announcements, nor should he permit dramatizations in any program which would give the false impression that the dramatized material constitutes news.

21. The standards of this Code covering program content are also understood to include, wherever applicable, the standards contained in the advertising section of the Code.

V. Treatment of News and Public Events

General

Television Code standards relating to the treatment of news and public events are, because of constitutional considerations, intended to be exhortatory. The standards set forth hereunder encourage high standards of professionalism in broadcast journalism. They are not to be interpreted as turning over to others the broadcaster's responsibility as to judgments necessary in news and public events programming.

News

1. A television station's news schedule should be adequate and well-balanced.

2. News reporting should be factual, fair and without bias.

3. A television broadcaster should exercise particular discrimination in the acceptance, placement and presentation of advertising in news programs so that such advertising should be clearly distinguishable from the news content.

4. At all times, pictorial and verbal material for both news and comment should conform to other sections of these standards, wherever such sections are reasonably applicable.

5. Good taste should prevail in the selection and handling of news:

Morbid, sensational or alarming details not essential to the factual report, especially in connection with stories of crime or sex, should be avoided. News should be telecast in such a manner as to avoid panic and unnecessary alarm.

6. Commentary and analysis should be clearly identified as such.

7. Pictorial material should be chosen with care and not presented in a misleading manner.

8. All news interview programs should be governed by accepted standards of ethical journalism, under which the interviewer selects the questions to be asked. Where there is advance agreement materially restricting an important or newsworthy area of questioning, the interviewer will state on the program that such limitation has been agreed upon. Such disclosure should be made if the person being interviewed requires that questions be submitted in advance or if he participates in editing a recording of the interview prior to its use on the air.

9. A television broadcaster should exercise due care in his supervision of content, format, and presentation of newscasts originated by his station, and in his selection of newscasters, commentators, and analysts.

Public Events

1. A television broadcaster has an affirmative responsibility at all times to be informed of public events, and to provide coverage consonant with the ends of an informed and enlightened citizenry.

2. The treatment of such events by a television broadcaster should provide adequate and informed coverage.

VI. Controversial Public Issues

1. Television provides a valuable forum for the expression of responsible views on public issues of a controversial nature. The television broadcaster should seek out and develop with accountable individuals, groups and organizations, programs relating to controversial public issues of import to his fellow citizens; and to give fair representation to opposing sides of issues which materially affect the life or welfare of a substantial segment of the public.

2. Requests by individuals, groups or organizations for time to discuss their views on controversial public issues, should be considered on the basis of their individual merits, and in the light of the contribution which the use requested would make to the public interest, and to a well-balanced program structure.

3. Programs devoted to the discussion of controversial public issues should be identified as such. They should not be presented in a manner which would mislead listeners or viewers to believe that the program is purely of an entertainment, news, or other character.

4. Broadcasts in which stations express their own opinions about issues of general public interest should be clearly identified as editorials. They should be unmistakably identified as statements of station opinion and should be appropriately distinguished from news and other program material.

VII. Political Telecasts

1. Political Telecasts should be clearly identified as such. They should not be presented by a television broadcaster in a manner which would mislead listeners or viewers to believe that the program is of any other character.

(Ref.: Communications Act of 1934, as amended, Secs. 315 and 317, and FCC Rules and Regulations, Secs. 3.654, 3.657, 3.663, as discussed in NAB's "Political Broadcast Catechism & The Fairness Doctrine.")

VIII. Religious Programs

1. It is the responsibility of a television broadcaster to make available to the community appropriate opportunity for religious presentations.

2. Programs reach audiences of all creeds simultaneously. Therefore, both the advocates of broad or ecumenical religious precepts, and the exponents of specific doctrines, are urged to present their positions in a manner conducive to viewer enlightenment on the role of religion in society.

3. In the allocation of time for telecasts of religious programs the television station should use its best efforts to apportion such time fairly among responsible individuals, groups and organizations.

IX. General Advertising Standards

1. This Code establishes basic standards for all television broadcasting. The principles of acceptability and good taste within the Program Standards section govern the presentation of advertising where applicable. In addition, the Code establishes in this section special standards which apply to television advertising.

2. A commercial television broadcaster makes his facilities available for the advertising of products and services and accepts commercial presentations for such advertising. However, a television broadcaster should, in recognition of his responsibility to the public, refuse the facilities of his station to an advertiser where he has good reason to doubt the integrity of the advertiser, the truth of the advertising representations, or the compliance of the advertiser with the spirit and purpose of all applicable legal requirements.

3. Identification of sponsorship must be made in all sponsored programs in accordance with the requirements of the Communications Act of 1934, as amended, and the Rules and Regulations of the Federal Communications Commission.

4. Representations which disregard normal safety precautions shall be avoided.

Children shall not be represented, except under proper adult supervision, as being in contact with,

or demonstrating a product recognized as potentially dangerous to them.

5. In consideration of the customs and attitudes of the communities served, each television broadcaster should refuse his facilities to the advertisement of products and services, or the use of advertising scripts, which the station has good reason to believe would be objectionable to a substantial and responsible segment of the community. These standards should be applied with judgment and flexibility, taking into consideration the characteristics of the medium, its home and family audience, and the form and content of the particular presentation.

6. The advertising of hard liquor (distilled spirits) is not acceptable.

7. The advertising of beer and wines is acceptable only when presented in the best of good taste and discretion, and is acceptable only subject to Federal and local laws *(See Television Code Interpretation No. 4)*

8. Advertising by institutions or enterprises which in their offers of instruction imply promises of employment or make exaggerated claims for the opportunities awaiting those who enroll for courses is generally unacceptable.

9. The advertising of firearms/ammunition is acceptable provided it promotes the product only as sporting equipment and conforms to recognized standards of safety as well as all applicable laws and regulations. Advertisements of firearms/ammunition by mail order are unacceptable. The advertising of fireworks is acceptable subject to all applicable laws.

10. The advertising of fortune-telling, occultism, astrology, phrenology, palm-reading, numerology, mind-reading, character-reading or subjects of a like nature is not permitted.

11. Because all products of a personal nature create special problems, acceptability of such products should be determined with especial emphasis on ethics and the canons of good taste. Such advertising of personal products as is accepted must be presented in a restrained and obviously inoffensive manner.

12. The advertising of tip sheets, race track publications, or organizations seeking to advertise for the purpose of giving odds or promoting betting or lotteries is unacceptable.

13. An advertiser who markets more than one product should not be permitted to use advertising copy devoted to an acceptable product for purposes of publicizing the brand name or other identification of a product which is not acceptable.

14. "Bait–switch" advertising, whereby goods or services which the advertiser has no intention of selling are offered merely to lure the customer into purchasing higher-priced substitutes, is not acceptable.

15. Personal endorsements (testimonials) shall be genuine and reflect personal experience. They shall contain no statement that cannot be supported if presented in the advertiser's own words.

X. Presentation of Advertising

1. Advertising messages should be presented with courtesy and good taste; disturbing or annoying material should be avoided; every effort should be made to keep the advertising message in harmony with the content and general tone of the program in which it appears.

2. The role and capability of television to market sponsors' products are well recognized. In turn, this fact dictates that great care be exercised by the broadcaster to prevent the presentation of false, misleading or deceptive advertising. While it is entirely appropriate to present a product in a favorable light and atmosphere, the presentation must not, by copy or demonstration, involve a material deception as to the characteristics, performance or appearance of the product.

Broadcast advertisers are responsible for making available, at the request of the Code Authority, documentation adequate to support the validity and truthfulness of claims, demonstrations and testimonials contained in their commercial messages.

3. The broadcaster and the advertiser should exercise special caution with the content and presentation of television commercials placed in or near programs designed for children. Exploitation of children should be avoided. Commercials directed to children should in no way mislead as to the product's performance and usefulness.

Appeals involving matters of health which should be determined by physicians should not be directed primarily to children.

4. Children's program hosts or primary cartoon characters shall not be utilized to deliver commercial messages within or adjacent to the programs which feature such hosts or cartoon characters. This provision shall also apply to lead-ins to commercials when such lead-ins contain sell copy or imply endorsement of the product by program host or primary cartoon character.

5. Appeals to help fictitious characters in television programs by purchasing the advertiser's product or service or sending for a premium should not be permitted, and such fictitious characters should not be introduced into the advertising message for such purposes.

6. Commercials for services or over-the-counter products involving health considerations are of intimate and far-reaching importance to the consumer. The following principles should apply to such advertising:

a. Physicians, dentists or nurses *or actors representing physicians, dentists or nurses* shall not be employed directly or by implication. These restrictions also apply to persons professionally engaged in medical services (e.g., physical therapists, pharmacists, dental assistants, nurses' aides).

b. Visual representations of laboratory settings may be employed, provided they bear a direct relationship to bona fide research which has been conducted for the product or service. *(See Television Code, X, 11)* In such cases, laboratory technicians shall be identified as such and shall not be employed as spokesmen or in any other way speak on behalf of the product.

c. Institutional announcements not intended to sell a specific product or service to the consumer and public service announcements by non-profit organizations may be presented by accredited physicians, dentists or nurses, subject to approval by the broadcaster. An accredited professional is one who has met required qualifications and has been licensed in his resident state.

7. Advertising should offer a product or service on its positive merits and refrain from discrediting, disparaging or unfairly attacking competitors, competing products, other industries, professions or institutions.

8. A sponsor's advertising messages should be confined within the framework of the sponsor's program structure. A television broadcaster should avoid the use of commercial announcements which are divorced from the program either by preceding the introduction of the program (as in the case of so-called "cow-catcher" announcements) or by following the apparent sign-off of the program (as in the case of so-called trailer or "hitch-hike" announcements). To this end, the program itself should be announced and clearly identified, both audio and video, before the sponsor's advertising material is first used, and should be signed off, both audio and video, after the sponsor's advertising material is last used.

9. Since advertising by television is a dynamic technique, a television broadcaster should keep under surveillance new advertising devices so that the spirit and purpose of these standards are fulfilled.

10. A charge for television time to churches and religious bodies in not recommended.

11. Reference to the results of bona fide research, surveys or tests relating to the product to be advertised shall not be presented in a manner so as to create an impression of fact beyond that established by the work that has been conducted.

ADVERTISING STANDARDS

XI. Advertising of Medical Products

1. The advertising of medical products presents considerations of intimate and far-reaching importance to the consumer because of the direct bearing on his health.

2. Becuase of the personal nature of the advertising of medical products, claims that a product will effect a cure and the indiscriminate use of such words as "safe," "without risk," "harmless," or terms of similar meaning should not be accepted in the advertising of medical products on television stations.

3. A television broadcaster should not accept advertising material which in his opinion offensively describes or dramatizes distress or morbid situations involving ailments, by spoken word, sound or visual effects.

XII. Contests

1. Contests shall be conducted with fairness to all entrants, and shall comply with all pertinent laws and regulations. Care should be taken to avoid the concurrent use of the three elements which together constitute a lottery — prize, chance and consideration.

2. All contests details, including rules, eligibility requirements, opening and termination dates should be clearly and completely announced and/or shown, or easily accessible to the viewing public, and the winners' names should be released and prizes awarded as soon as possible after the close of the contest.

3. When advertising is accepted which requests contestants to submit items of product identification or other evidence of purchase of products, reasonable facsimiles thereof should be made acceptable unless the award is based upon skill and not upon chance.

4. All copy pertaining to any contest (except that which is required by law) associated with the exploitation or sale of the sponsor's product or service, and all references to prizes or gifts offered in such connection should be considered a part of and included in the total time allowances as herein provided. *(See Television Code, XIV)*

XIII. Premiums and Offers

1. Full details of proposed offers should be required by the television broadcaster for investi-

gation and approved before the first announcement of the offer is made to the public.

2. A final date for the termination of an offer should be announced as far in advance as possible.

3. Before accepting for telecast offers involving a monetary consideration, a television broadcaster should satisfy himself as to the integrity of the advertiser and the advertiser's willingness to honor complaints indicating dissatisfaction with the premium by returning the monetary consideration.

4. There should be no misleading descriptions or visual representations of any premiums or gifts which would distort or enlarge their value in the minds of the viewers.

5. Assurances should be obtained from the advertiser that premiums offered are not harmful to person or property.

6. Premiums should not be approved which appeal to superstition on the basis of "luckbearing" powers or otherwise.

XIV. Time Standards for Non-Program Material.

In order that the time for non-program material and its placement shall best serve the viewer, the following standards are set forth in accordance with sound television practice:

1. Non-Program Material Definition:

Non-program material, in both prime time and all other time, includes billboards, commercials, promotional announcements and all credits in excess of 30 seconds per program, except in feature films. In no event should credits exceed 40 seconds per program. The 40-second limitation on credits shall not apply, however, in any situation governed by a contract entered into before October 1, 1971. Public service announcements and promotional announcements for the same program are excluded from this definition.

2. Allowable Time for Non-Program Material.

a. In prime time on network affiliated stations, non-program material shall not exceed nine minutes 30 seconds in any 60-minute period.

In prime time on independent stations, non-program material shall not exceed 12 minutes in any 60-minute period.

In the event that news programming is included within the three and one-half hour prime time period, not more than one 30-minute segment of news programming may be governed by time standards applicable to all other time.

Prime time is a continuous period of not less than three and one-half consecutive hours per broadcast day as designated by the station between the hours of 6:00 PM and Midnight.

b. In all other time, non-program material shall not exceed 16 minutes in any 60-minute period.

c. Children's Weekend Programming Time — Defined as that contiguous period of time between the hours of 7:00 AM and 2:00 PM on Saturday and Sunday. In programming designed primarily for children within this time period, non-program material shall not exceed 12 minutes in any 60-minute period.

3. Program Interruptions.

a. Definition: A program interruption is any occurrence of non-program material within the main body of the program.

b. In prime time, the number of program interruptions shall not exceed two within any 30-minute program, or four within any 60-minute program.

Programs longer than 60 minutes shall be pro-rated at two interruptions per half-hour.

The number of interruptions in 60-minute variety shows shall not exceed five.

c. In all other time, the number of interruptions shall not exceed four within any 30-minute program period.

d. In children's weekend time, as above defined in 2c, the number of program interruptions shall not exceed two within any 30-minute program or four within any 60-minute program.

e. In both prime time and all other time, the following interruption standard shall apply within programs of 15 minutes or less in length:

    5-minute program — 1 interruption;
    10-minute program — 2 interruptions;
    15-minute program — 2 interruptions.

f. News, weather, sports and special events programs are exempt from the interruption standard because of the nature of such programs.

4. No more than four non-program material announcements shall be scheduled consecutively within programs, and no more than three non-

program material announcements shall be scheduled consecutively during station breaks. The consecutive non-program material limitation shall not apply to a single sponsor who wished to further reduce the number of interruptions in the program.

5. A multiple product announcement is one in which two or more products or services are presented within the framework of a single announcement. A multiple product announcement shall not be scheduled in a unit of time less than 60 seconds, except where integrated so as to appear to the viewer as a single message. A multiple product announcement shall be considered integrated and counted as a single announcement if:

a. the products or services are related and interwoven within the framework of the announcement (related products or services shall be defined as those having a common character, purpose and use); and

b. the voice(s), setting, background and continuity are used consistently throughout so as to appear to the viewer as a single message.

Multiple product announcements of 60 seconds in length or longer not meeting this definition of integration shall be counted as two or more announcements under this section of the Code. This provision shall not apply to retail or service establishments. (Effective September 1, 1973)

6. The use of billboards, in prime time and all other time, shall be confined to programs sponsored by a single or alternate week advertiser and shall be limited to the products advertised in the program.

7. Reasonable and limited indentification of prizes and donors' names where the presentation of contest awards or prizes in a necessary part of program content shall not be included as non-program material as defined above.

8. Programs presenting women's service features, shopping guides, fashion shows, demonstrations and similar material provide a special service to the public in which certain material normally classified as non-program is an informative and necessary part of the program content. Because of this, the time standards may be waived by the Code Authority to a reasonable extent on a case-by-case basis.

9. Gratuitous references in a program to a non-sponsor's product or service should be avoided except for normal guest identification.

10. Stationary backdrops or properties in television presentations showing the sponsor's name or product, the name of his product, his trade-mark or slogan should be used only incidentally and should not obtrude on program interest or entertainment.

INTERPRETATIONS

Interpretation No. 1

June 7, 1956, Revised June 9, 1958
"Pitch" Programs

The "pitchman" technique of advertising on television is inconsistent with good broadcast practice and generally damages the reputation of the industry and the advertising profession.

Sponsored program-length segments consisting substantially of continuous demonstrations or sales presentation, violate not only the time standards established in the Code but the broad philosophy of improvement implicit in the voluntary Code operation and are not acceptable.

Interpretation No. 2

June 7, 1956
Hollywood Film Promotion

The presentation of commentary or film excerpts from current theatrical releases in some instances may constitute commercial material under the Time Standards for Non-Program Material. Specifically, for example, when such presentation, directly or by inference, urges viewers to attend, it shall be counted against the commercial allowance for the program of which it is a part.

Interpretation No. 3

January 23, 1959

Prize Identification

Aural and/or visual prize identification of up to ten seconds duration may be deemed "reasonable and limited" under the language of Paragraph 7 of the Time Standards for Non-Program Material. Where such identification is longer than ten seconds, the entire announcement or visual presentation will be charged against the total commercial time for the program period.

Interpretation No. 4

March 4, 1965

Drinking on Camera

Paragraph 7, Section IX, General Advertising Standards, states that the "advertising of beer and wine is acceptable only when presented in the best of good taste and discretion." This requires that commercials involving beer and wine avoid any representation of on-camera drinking.

REGULATIONS AND PROCEDURES

The following Regulations and Procedures shall obtain as an integral part of the Television Code of the National Association of Broadcasters:

I. Name

The name of this Code shall be *The Television Code of the National Association of Broadcasters.* *

II. Purpose of the Code

The purpose of this Code is cooperatively to maintain a level of television programming which gives full consideration to the educational, informational, cultural, economic, moral and entertainment needs of the American public to the end that more and more people will be better served.

---

*By-Laws of the National Association Broadcasters, Article VI, section 8, C: "Television Board. The Television Board is hereby authorized: — (4) to enact, amend and promulgate standards of practice or codes for its Television members, and to establish such methods to secure observance thereof as it may deem advisable: —."

III. Subscribers

Section 1. Eligibility

Any individual, firm or corporation which is engaged in the operation of a television broadcast station or network, or which holds a construction permit for a television broadcast station within the United States or its dependencies, shall, subject to the approval of the Television Board of Directors as hereinafter provided, be eligible to subscribe to the Television Code of the NAB to the extent of one subscription for each such station and/or network which it operates or for which it holds a construction permit; provided, that a non-television member of NAB shall not become eligible via Code subscription to receive any of the member services or to exercise any of the voting privileges of a member.

Section 2. Certification of Subscription

Upon subscribing to the Code, subject to the approval of the Television Board of Directors, there shall be granted forthwith to each such subscribing station authority to use the "NAB

Television Seal of Good Practice," a copyrighted and registered seal to be provided in the form of a certificate, a slide and/or a film, signifying that the recipient thereof is a subscriber in good standing to the Television Code of the NAB. The seal and its significance shall be appropriately publicized by the NAB.

Section 3. Duration of Subscription

Subscription shall continue in full force and effect until thirty days after the first of the month following receipt of notice of written resignation. Subscription to the Code shall be effective from the date of application subject to the approval of the Television Board of Directors; provided, that the subscription of a television station going on the air for the first time shall, for the first six months of such subscription, be probationary, during which time its subscription can be summarily revoked by an affirmative two-thirds vote of the Television Board of Directors without the usual processes specified below.

Section 4. Suspension of Subscription

Any subscription, and/or the authority to utilize and show the above-noted seal, may be voided, revoked or temporarily suspended for television programming, including commercial copy, which, by theme, treatment or incident, in the judgment of the Television Board constitutes a continuing, willful or gross violation of any of the provisions of the Television Code, by an affirmative two-thirds vote of the Television Board of Directors at a regular or special meeting; provided, however, that the following conditions and procedures shall apply:

A. *Preferring of Charges – Conditions Presedent:*

Prior to the preferring of charges to the Television Board of Directors concerning violation of the Code by a subscriber, the Television Code Review Board (hereinafter provided for) (1) Shall have appropriately, and in good time, informed and advised such subscriber of any and all complaints and information coming to the attention of the Television Code Review Board and relating to the programming of said subscriber, (2) Shall have reported to, and advised, said subscriber by analysis, interpretation, recommendation or otherwise, of the possibility of a violation or breach of the Television Code by the subscriber, and (3) Shall have served upon the subscriber, by Registered Mail a Notice of Intent to prefer charges, at least twenty days prior to the filing of any such charges with the Television Board of Directors. During this period the Television Code Review Board may, within its sole discretion, reconsider its proposed action based upon such written reply as the subscriber may care to make, or upon such action as the subscriber may care to take program-wise, in conformance with the analysis, interpretation, or recommendation of the Television Code Review Board.

(i) Notice of Intent

The Notice of Intent shall include a statement of the grounds and reasons for the proposed charges, including appropriate references to the Television Code.

(ii) Time

In the event that the nature of the program in question is such that time is of the essence, the Television Code Review Board may prefer charges within less than the twenty days above specified, provided that a time certain in which reply may be made is included in its Notice of Intent, and provided that its reasons therefor must be specified in its statement of charges preferred.

B. *The Charges:*

The subscriber shall be advised in writing by Registered Mail of the charges preferred. The charges preferred by the Television Code Review Board to the Television Board of Directors shall include the grounds and reasons therefor, together with specific references to the Television Code. The charges shall contain a statement that the conditions precedent, herein before described, have been met.

C. *Hearing:*

The subscriber shall have the right to a hearing and may exercise same by filing an answer within 10 days of the date of such notification.

D. *Waiver:*

Failure to request a hearing shall be deemed a waiver of the subscriber's right thereto.

E. *Designation:*

If hearing is requested by the subscriber, it shall be designated as promptly as possible and at such time and place as the Television Board may specify.

F. *Confidential Status:*

Hearings shall be closed; and all correspondence between a subscriber and the Television Code Review Board and/or the Television Board of Directors concerning specific programming shall be confidential; provided, however, that the confidential status of these procedures may be waived by a subscriber.

G. *Presentation; Representation:*

A subscriber against whom charges have been preferred, and who has exercised his right to a hearing, shall be entitled to effect presentation of his case personally, by agent, by attorney, or by deposition and interrogatory.

H. *Intervention:*

Upon request by the subscriber-respondent or the Television Code Review Board, the Television Board of Directors, in its discretion, may permit the intervention of one or more other subscribers as parties-in-interest.

I. *Transcript:*

A stenographic transcript record shall be taken and ·shall be certified by the Chairman of the Television Board of Directors to the office of the Secretary of the National Association of Broadcasters, where it shall be maintained. The transcript shall not be open to inspection unless other-wise provided by the party respondent in the proceeding.

J. *Television Code Review Board; Counsel:*

The Television Code Review Board may, at its discretion, utilize the services of an attorney from the staff of the NAB for the purpose of effecting its presentation in a hearing matter.

K. *Order of Procedure:*

At hearings the Television Code Review Board shall open and close.

L. *Cross-Examination:*

The right of cross-examination shall specifically obtain. Where procedure has been by deposition or interrogatory, the use of cross-interrogatories shall satisfy this right.

M. *Presentation:*

Oral and written evidence may be introduced by the subscriber and by the Television Code Review Board. Oral argument may be had at the hearing and written memoranda or briefs may be submitted by the subscriber and by the Television Code Review Board. The Television Board of Directors may admit such evidence as it deems relevant, material and competent, and may determine the nature and length of the oral argument and the written argument or briefs.

N. *Authority of Presiding Officer; of Television Board of Directors:*

The Presiding Officer shall rule upon all interlocutory matters, such as, but not limited to, the admissibility of evidence, the qualifications of witnesses, etc. On all other matters, authority to act shall be vested in a majority of the Television Board unless otherwise provided.

O. *Films, Transcriptions, etc.:*

Films, kinescopes, records, transcriptions, or other mechanical reproductions of television programs, properly identified, shall be accepted into evidence when relevant.

P. *Continuances and Extensions:*

Continuance and extension of any proceeding or for the time of filing or performing any act required or allowed to be done within a specific time may be granted upon request, for a good cause shown. The Board or the Presiding Officer may recess or adjourn a hearing for such time as may be deemed necessary, and may change the place thereof.

Q. *Findings and Conclusions:*

The Television Board of Directors shall decide the case as expeditiously as possible and shall notify the subscriber and the Television Code Review Board, in writing, of the decision. The decision of the Television Board of Directors shall contain findings of fact with conclusions, as well as the reasons or bases therefor. Findings of fact shall set out in detail and with particularity all basic evidentiary facts developed on the record (with appropriate citations to the transcript of record or exhibit relied on for each evidentiary fact) supporting the conclusion reached.

R. *Reconsideration or Rehearing:*

A request for reconsideration or rehearing may be filed by parties to the hearing. Requests for reconsideration or rehearing shall state with particularity in what respect the decision or any matter determined therein is claimed to be unjust, unwarranted, or erroneous, and with respect to any finding of fact shall specify the pages of record relied on. If the existence of any newly-discovered evidence is claimed, the request shall be accompanied by a verified statement of the facts together with the facts relied on to show that the party, with due diligence, could not have known or discovered such facts at the time of the hearing. The request for rehearing may seek:

a. Reconsideration
b. Additional oral argument
c. Reopening of the proceedings
d. Amendment of any findings, or
e. Other relief.

S. *Time for Filing:*

Requests for reconsideration or rehearing shall be filed within ten (10) days after receipt by the resonndent of the decision. Opposition thereto may be filed within five (5) days after the filing of the request.

T. *Penalty, Suspension of:*

At the discretion of the Television Board, application of any penalty provided for in the decision may be suspended until the Board makes final disposition of the request for reconsideration or rehearing.

U. *Disqualification:*

Any member of the Television Board may disqualify himself, or upon good cause shown by any interested party, may be disqualified by a majority vote of the Television Board.

Section 5. Additional Procedures

When necessary to the proper administration of the Code, additional rules of procedure will be established from time to time as authorized by the By-Laws of the NAB; in keeping therewith, special consideration shall be given to the procedures for receipt and processing of complaints and to necessary rules to be adopted from time to time, taking into account the source and nature of such complaints; such rules to include precautionary measures such as the posting of bonds to cover costs and expenses of processing same; and further provided that special consideration will be given to procedures insuring the confidential status of proceedings relating to Code observance.

Section 6. Amendment and Review

Because of the new and dynamic aspects inherent in television broadcast, the Television Code, as a living, flexible and continuing docu-ment, may be amended from time to time by the Television Board of Directors; provided that said Board is specifically charged with review and reconsideration of the entire Code, its appendices and procedures, at least once each year.

Section 7. Termination of Contracts

All subscribers on the air at the time of subscription to the Code shall be permitted that period prior to and including the earliest legal cancellation date to terminate any contracts, then outstanding, calling for program presentations which would not be in conformity with the Television Code, provided, however, that in no event shall such period be longer than fifty-two weeks.

IV. Affiliate Subscribers

Section 1. Eligibility

Any individual, firm or corporation, which is engaged in the production or distribution, lease, or sale of recorded programs for television presentation, subject to the approval of the Television Code Review Board as hereinafter provided, shall be eligible to become an affiliate subscriber to the Television Code of the NAB.

Section 2. Certification of Subscription

Upon becoming an affiliate subscriber to the Code, subject to the approval of the Television Code Review Board, there shall be granted forthwith to each such affiliate subscriber authority to use a copyrighted and registered seal and declaration, in a manner approved by the Television Code Review Board, identifying the individual firm or corporation as an affiliate subscriber to the Television Code of the NAB. Such authority shall not constitute formal clearance or approval by the Television Code Review Board of specific film programs or other recorded material.

Section 3. Duration of Affiliate Subscription

The affiliate subscription shall continue in full force and effect until thirty days after the first of the month following receipt of a written notice of resignation. The affiliate subscription to the Code shall be effective from the date of application subject to the approval of the Television Code Review Board.

Section 4. Suspension of Affiliate Subscription

Any affiliate subscription and the authority to

utilize and show the above-noted seal may be voided, revoked, or temporarily suspended for the sale or distribution for television presentation of any film or other recorded material which by theme, treatment, or incident, in the judgment of the Television Code Review Board, constitutes a continuing, willful or gross violation of any of the provisions of the Television Code, by a majority vote of the Television Code Review Board at any regular or special meeting. The conditions and procedures applicable to subscribers shall not apply to affiliate subscribers.

Section 5. Representation of Affiliate Subscribers

Any affiliate subscriber or group of affiliate subscribers may authorize an individual or association to act for them in connection with their relations with the Television Code Review Board by filing a written notice of such representation with the Board. Such representation, however, in no way will limit the right of the Television Code Review Board to suspend individual affiliate subscribers in accordance with the provisions of Section 4.

V. Rates

Each subscriber and affiliate subscriber shall pay "administrative" rates in accordance with such schedule, at such time, and under such conditions as may be determined from time to time by the Television Board (see Article VI, section 8, C. Television Board (3) and (4), By-Laws of the NAB); provided, that appropriate credit shall be afforded to a television member of the NAB against the regular dues which he or it pays to NAB.

VI. The Television Code Review Board

Section 1. Composition

There shall be a continuing committee entitled the Television Code Review Board to be composed of not more than nine members, all of whom shall be from subscribers to the Television Code. They shall be appointed by the President of NAB, subject to confirmation by the Television Board, and may include one member from each of the subscribing nationwide television networks. Members of the Television Board shall not be eligible to serve on the Review Board. Due consideration shall be given, in making the appointments, to factors of diversidication of geographical location, market size, company representation and network affiliation.

No person shall continue as a member of the Television Code Review Board if the station or entity he represents ceases to subscribe to the Television Code. In such case a vacancy occurs in the office immediately, and a successor may be appointed to serve out the unexpired term.

All terms shall be for two years, commencing at the close of the annual meeting of the membership following appointment.

A. *Limitation of Service:*

No person shall serve for more than two terms of two years each, consecutively, as a member of the Television Code Review Board; provided, however, this limitation shall not apply to network representatives.

Serving out the unexpired term of a former member shall not constitute a term within the meaning of this section.

B. *Meetings:*

The Television Code Review Board shall meet at least twice in each calendar year on a date to be determined by the Chairman. The Chairman, or the Code Authority Director, may, at any time, on at least five days written notice, call a special meeting of the Board.

C. *Quorum:*

For all purposes, a majority of the members of the Television Code Review Board shall constitute a quorum.

Section 2. Authority and Responsibilities

The Television Code Review Board is authorized and directed:

(1) To recommend to the Television Board of Directors amendments to the Television Code; (2) to consider, in its discretion, any appeal from any decision made by the Code Authority Director with respect to any matter which has arisen under the Code, and to suspend, reverse, or modify any such decision; (3) to prefer formal charges, looking toward the suspension or revocation of the authority to show the Code seal, to the Television Board of Directors concerning violations and breaches of the Television Code by a subscriber; (4) to be available to the Code Authority Director for consultation on any and all matters affecting the Television Code.

VII. Code Authority Director

Section 1. Director

There shall be a position designated as the Code Authority Director. This position shall be filled by appointment of the President of NAB, subject to the approval of the Board of Directors.

Section 2. Authority and Responsibilities

The Code Authority Director is authorized and directed: (1) To maintain a continuing review of all programming and advertising material presented over television, especially that of subscribers to the Television Code of NAB; (2) to receive, screen and clear complaints concerning television programming; (3) to define and interpret words and phrases in the Television Code; (4) to develop and maintain appropriate liaison with governmental agencies and with responsible and accountable organizations and institutions; (5) to inform, expeditiously and properly, a subscriber to the Television Code of complaints or commendations, as well as to advise all subscribers concerning the attitudes and desires program-wise of accountable organizations and institutions, and of the American public in general; (6) to review and monitor, if necessary, any certain series of programs, daily programming, or any other program presentations of a subscriber, as well as to request recorded material, or script and copy, with regard to any certain program presented by a subscriber; (7) to reach conclusions and make recommendations or prefer charges to the Television Code Review Board concerning violations and breaches of the Television Code by a subscriber; (8) to recommend to the Code Review Board amendments to the Television Code.

A. *Delegation of Powers and Responsibilities:*

The Code Authority Director shall appoint such executive staff as is needed, consistent with resources, to carry out the above described functions, and may delegate to this staff such responsibilities as he may deem necessary.

A Selected Bibliography

(This bibliography represents a brief selected list of books which may be useful as supplementary and background reading to the IRTS Seminars)

Agnew, C. M. & N. O'Brien, *Television Advertising*. New York: McGraw-Hill, 1958

Agee, W. V., Ed. *Mass Media In a Free Society*. Lawrence, Kansas: University of Kansas Press, 1969

Barnouw, Eric *A Tower of Babel: A History of Broadcasting in The United States to 1933*. New York: Oxford University Press, 1966

Barnouw, Eric *The Golden Web: A History of Broadcasting in The United States 1933-1953*. New York: Oxford University Press, 1968

Barnouw, Eric *The Image Empire*. New York: Oxford University Press, 1970

Bettinghaus, E. P. *Persuasive Communication*. New York: Holt, Rinehart and Winston, 1968

Blanchard, R. O., Ed. *Congress and the News Media*. New York: Hastings House, 1974

Bluem, A. W. *Documentary in American Television*. New York: Hastings House, 1965

Carnegie Commission on Educational Television *Public Television: A Program for Action*. New York: Bantam Books, 1967

Chester, Edward *Radio Television and American Politics*. New York: Sheed & Ward, 1969

Coons, John E. *Freedom and Responsibility in Broadcasting*. Evanston, Illinois: Northwestern University Press, 1961

De Fleur, Melvin *Theories of Mass Communication*. New York: David McKay, 1970 (rev. ed.)

Devol, K. S., Ed. *Mass Media and The Supreme Court.* New York: Hastings House, 1971

Diamant, L., Ed. *The Broadcast Communications Dictionary.* New York: Hastings House, 1974

Donner, S. T., Ed. *The Meaning of Commercial Television.* Austin, Texas: University of Texas Press, 1966

Educational Television. The Center for Applied Research in Education, 1965

Emery, Walter P. *Broadcasting and Government.* East Lansing, Michigan: Michigan State University Press, 1961

Fang, Irving E. *Television News.* New York: Hastings House, 1972 (rev. & enl. ed.)

Galbraith, J. K. *The Affluent Society.* Boston, Massachusetts: Houghton Mifflin, 1958

Gillmor, D. M. & J. A. Barron *Mass Communication Law: Cases and Comment.* St. Paul, Minnesota: West Publishing, 1969

Head, Sydney *Broadcasting in America.* Boston, Massachusetts: Houghton Mifflin, 1972 (rev. ed.)

Herman Land Associates *Television and the Wired City.* Washington, D.C.: National Association of Broadcasters, 1968

Hilliard, R. L., Ed. *Radio Broadcasting: An Introduction to The Sound Medium.* New York: Hastings House, 1974 (rev. ed.)

Himmelweit, Hilde, et al *Television and the Child.* London, England: Oxford University Press, 1958

Kahn, Frank J., Ed. *Documents of American Broadcasting.* New York: Appleton-Century Crofts, 1968

Kittross, J. M. & K. Harwood *Free and Fair: Courtroom Access and The Fairness Doctrine.* Philadelphia, Pennsylvania: Temple University Press, 1970

Koenig, A. E. & R. B. Hill *The Farther Vision: Educational Television Today.* Madison, Wisconsin: University of Wisconsin Press, 1967

Lang, K. & G. Lane *Politics and Television.* Chicago, Illinois: Quadrangle Books, 1968

Larsen, Otto W., Ed. *Violence and The Mass Media.* New York: Harper & Row, 1968

Levin, Harvey J. *Broadcast Regulation and Joint Ownership of Media.* New York: New York University Press, 1960

Lichty, L. & J. Ripley II *American Broadcasting: Introduction and Analysis, Readings.* Madison, Wisconsin: College, 1970 (2nd ed.)

Lichty, L. W. & M. C. Topping *American Broadcasting: A Source Book on the History of Radio and Television*. New York: Hastings House, 1974

Macneil, Robert *The People Machine*. New York: Harper & Row, 1968

Mayer, Martin *Madison Avenue, U.S.A.* New York: Harper & Row, 1958

McGinnis, Joe *The Selling of the President, 1968*. New York: Trident, 1968

Peterson, Theodore, et al *The Mass Media and Modern Society*. New York: Holt, Rinehart and Winston, 1965

President's Task Force on Communications Policy. Final Report. Washington, D.C.: Government Printing Office, 1969

Quaal, W. L. & L. A. Martin *Broadcast Management*. New York: Hastings House, 1968

Roe, Yale *The Television Dilemma*. New York: Hastings House, 1962

Rucker, Bryce W. *The First Freedom*. Carbondale, Illinois: Southern Illinois Press, 1967

Schiller, H. I. *Mass Communications and American Empire*. New York: August M. Kellsey, 1969

Schramm, Wilbur, et al *The People Look at Educational Television*. Stanford, California: The Stanford University Press, 1963

Shayon, Robert L., Ed. *The Eighth Art*. New York: Holt, Rinehart and Winston, 1962

Small, William *To Kill A Messenger: Television News and The Real World*. New York: Hastings House, 1970

Smead, Elmer E. *Freedom of Speech by Radio and Television*. Washington, D.C.: Public Affairs Press, 1959

Smith, Alfred G., Ed. *Communication and Culture*. New York: Holt, Rinehart and Winston, 1966

Steinberg, Charles S., Ed. *Mass Media and Communication*. New York: Hastings House, 1972 (rev. & enl. ed.)

Steiner, Gary A. *The People Look at Television*. New York: Knopf, 1963

Summers, H. B. & R. E. Summers *Broadcasting and The Public*. Belmont, California: Wadsworth, 1966

Wainwright, C. A. *Television Commercials*. New York: Hastings House, 1970 (rev. ed.)

White, D. M. & R. Averson, Eds. *Sight Sound and Society*. Boston, Massachusetts: Beacon Press, 1968

Yu, Frederick T. C. *Behavioral Sciences and The Mass Media*. Russell Sage Foundation, 1968

Index